DEAD TIME

Cultural Memory

in

the

Present

Mieke Bal and Hent de Vries, Editors

DEAD TIME

Temporal Disorders
in the Wake of Modernity
(Baudelaire and Flaubert)

Elissa Marder

STANFORD UNIVERSITY PRESS

STANFORD, CALIFORNIA

Stanford University Press
Stanford, California
© 2001 by the Board of Trustees of the
Leland Stanford Junior University

Printed in the United States of America
On acid-free, archival-quality paper

Library of Congress Cataloging-in-Publication Data
Marder, Elissa.
  Dead time ; temporal disorders in the wake of modernity
  (Baudelaire and Flaubert) / Elissa Marder
       p.   cm.—(Cultural memory in the present)
  Includes bibliographical references and index.
    ISBN 0-8047-4071-2 (alk. paper)—ISBN 0-8047-4072-0
  (pbk. : alk. paper)
    1. Baudelaire, Charles, 1821–1867. Fleurs du mal.
    2. Flaubert, Gustave, 1821–1880. Madame Bovary.
    3. Time in literature.   I. Title.   II. Series.
  PQ2191.F63 M27   2002
  841'8—dc21   2001042611

Typeset by BookMatters in 11/13.5 Adobe Garamond

Original printing 2001

For Claire

Contents

Acknowledgments

This book is the result of years of listening to others and learning from them. I hope that the many people who have spoken to me about this work throughout the years will hear and recognize their own voices in it. I am indebted first to my teachers at Cornell, in Paris, and at Yale who taught me how to read. Special thanks to Richard Klein, Marie Depussé, Barbara Johnson, Fredric Jameson, Peter Brooks, Denis Hollier, and most especially to Shoshana Felman. I have also enjoyed the privilege of having been taught by some of the greatest readers and thinkers of our time. This book would have been impossible and unthinkable without the enduring teaching and writings of Jacques Derrida, Paul de Man, and Jean-François Lyotard.

I have also learned from the intellectual generosity of my friends and colleagues. In particular, I extend warm thanks to: April Alliston, Kathy Aschheim, Tom Cohen, Lalitha Gopalan, Rindala El-Khoury, Emma Henderson, Tom Keenan, John Michael, Kelly Oliver, José Quiroga, Walid Ra'ad, Amanda Walker, and Gail Weiss.

My friend Mary Quaintance inspired me to write on Baudelaire. Her own tragically unfinished writings on Baudelaire haunt these pages.

Very special thanks to a number of friends and colleagues who read and commented on portions of the manuscript: Ian Balfour, Eduardo Cadava, Elisabeth Ladenson, Kevin Newmark, Marc Redfield, Avital Ronell, Naomi Schor, and Charlie Shepherdson. Other friends provided me with much needed emotional support. Heartfelt thanks to Arnold Barkus, Gabrielle Hamill, Laura Kurgan, Ivan Miller, Micah Rafferty, Vivian Selbo, and Judith Shulevitz. Sean Miller believed in me and helped to will this book into existence. Along the way, Frank Lachmann learned more about French literature than he ever thought he would.

My family has given me their love and support throughout. Thanks to Dorothy Marder, Eric Marder, Eve Marder, Efrem Marder, and Barbara Marder.

This book was almost entirely written while I was teaching at Emory University. There, I was blessed to have encountered a number of wonderful colleagues. I have benefited especially from conversations with Yvan Bamps, Candace Lang, Bobby Paul, and John Johnston. A number of Emory students have become close friends and colleagues. I have been fortunate to have worked with and learned from Stefanie Harris and Monica Kelley. Bruno Chaouat has read most of the book, helped translate parts of it into French, and made invaluable suggestions. Angela Hunter helped prepare the final version of the manuscript. I would like to thank the students who attended my graduate seminars at Emory. Donald Stein, former Dean of the Graduate School at Emory University, supported the project and provided funds in order to ensure its publication. I would also like to thank Elizabeth Berg and Helen Tartar at Stanford University Press. I am deeply grateful for their ongoing support of this book.

My colleague Philippe Bonnefis read the entire manuscript, helped me publish portions of it in French, made impeccable corrections and elegant suggestions. Most especially, my department chair, Dalia Judovitz, gave me faith in the project and in myself. I cannot thank her enough for her remarkable, steadfast generosity.

I cannot imagine having written this book without the friendship of Sharon Willis, whose intelligence, wit, and humor have been a source of inspiration for over twenty years. Cathy Caruth inspired me by her own example, and offered encouragement and guidance at every turn. She read the manuscript and helped me to understand what I was trying to say. Zrinka Stahuljak gave me love, support, and companionship while I was writing this book. I could not have done it without her. Claire Nouvet listened to every word and heard more than I was capable of saying. Her work and her voice are on every page. This book is dedicated to her, with deepest thanks and deepest love. Finally, special thanks to Geoff Bennington, who helped me finish this book and made me want to write more in the future.

Versions of Chapters 2 and 4 have been previously published in *Diacritics*. I thank the editors for permission to reprint them here.

E.M.

Development imposes the saving of time. To go fast is to forget fast, to retain only the information that is useful afterwards, as in "rapid reading." But writing and reading which advance backwards in the direction of the unknown thing "within" are slow. One loses one's time seeking time lost. Anamnesis is the other pole—not even that, there is no common access—the *other* of acceleration and abbreviation.
—Jean-François Lyotard

Introduction
"Our Contemporaries," Baudelaire and Flaubert

> The duration of a literary work's influence stands in inverse relation
> to the conspicuousness of its subject matter.
> —Walter Benjamin

We no longer live in a time that seeks to define its own experience
primarily through the work of literature. Although literature still exists, certainly, it has lost the job it once had. Other more immediate—and less mediated—means of communication have displaced it from its former function as a medium of collective experience. There are very few contemporary
literary works—as opposed to memoirs, photography, movies, TV, popular
music, internet sites, and the like—that might still have the power to solicit
the sustained interest of the reading public and incite a collective response.
We only occasionally talk to each other through literary works. We do not
hold our common conversations in "literary" language.

Recalcitrant Readers

More than half a century ago, Walter Benjamin, one of the first "cultural critics" of the twentieth century, turned his attention to this phenomenon and its implications. In his essay "Some Motifs in Baudelaire,"
Benjamin locates the first clear signs of this transformation of the language
of culture in the decline of lyric poetry.

If conditions for a positive reception of lyric poetry have become less favorable, it is reasonable to assume that only in rare instances is lyric poetry in rapport with the experience of its readers. This may be due to a change in the structure of their experience. Even though one may approve of this development, one may be all the more hard put to it to say precisely in what respect there may have been a change.[1]

In the "Motifs" essay, Benjamin makes it his mission to describe this "change in the structure of experience." But he is confronted with the following challenge: through what modality of language could one possibly convey the changing form and function of language itself? Curiously, and this is quite significant, he chooses to devote his attention to the language of a poet, Baudelaire, in order to derive a vocabulary for speaking about the very change in experience that had already rendered the experience of poetry "obsolete" for most readers.

Benjamin decides to mediate his presentation of the experience of modernity through the language of Baudelaire's poetry for several reasons. First, he calls attention to the seemingly contradictory fact that Baudelaire's poems became widely read during the very historical period that saw a definitive decline in the popular reception of poetic works. He points out that "there has been no success on a mass scale in lyric poetry since Baudelaire." Furthermore, the appearance of Baudelaire's poetry coincided with the historical moment during which the "change in the structure of experience" first manifested itself: "The period in question dates back roughly to the middle of the last century." Benjamin then suggests that Baudelaire's poetry managed to reach even recalcitrant readers because through his poems, Baudelaire had found a way of speaking to readers both about their own experiences and about their inability to express those experiences.

And this brings us to one of the central points of Benjamin's essay. He argues that the change in the structure of the "experience" in modernity derives, in part, from an overwhelming increase in external stimuli that prevents the impact of particular experiences from becoming assimilated, processed, and remembered. The increase in external stimuli extends to the realm of modes of communication. Technologies develop that are specifically designed to grasp particular experiences in their immediacy. However, Benjamin argues, the more particular experiences are recorded as *unmediated* impressions, the less they contribute to an enduring sense of experience. He writes:

Historically, the various modes of communication have competed with one another. The replacement of the older narration by information, of information by sensation, reflects the increasing atrophy of experience. (113)

Therefore, if "unmediated" communication cannot transmit the meaning of an experience, it makes sense that Benjamin turns to a highly "mediated" form of experience—poetry—in order to articulate the specific ways in which this change in experience makes itself felt. Through a series of close readings of Baudelaire's poems, Benjamin ultimately ascribes this "atrophy of experience" to what he calls the "shock experience" of modern life.

In the time that has elapsed since Benjamin first presented his prescient description of the "shock experience" in the "Motifs" essay, the changing experience of modern life has continued to produce new and varied forms of "temporal disorders." Following Benjamin's lead, this book aims to read the temporal disorders of the present day through close readings of the temporal inscriptions of modernity that are found in the literary texts of Baudelaire and Flaubert. By reading the descriptions of time and memory that are embedded in these nineteenth-century works, we discover that—after all this time—these authors may have become our contemporaries. Many of the temporal structures associated with the so-called postmodern moment are already imprinted in their works. By returning to their texts, we can examine some of the ongoing temporal effects of modernity's unassimilated legacy.

Modernity and Its Historical Fictions

> Baudelaire's fame, as opposed to that of Rimbaud which is more
> recent, has not yet known any écheance. The common difficulty
> in approaching the core of Baudelaire's poetry is, to speak in a
> formula, this: There is about this poetry still nothing out of date.
> —Walter Benjamin, "Central Park"

The works of Baudelaire and Flaubert have consistently assumed a peculiar place in literary and cultural history. From the time of their first publication through the present day, *Les Fleurs du mal* and *Madame Bovary* continue to shock and fascinate their readers. In 1857, both works were prosecuted by Second Empire legal authorities. In 1999, both works are still read by a relatively large segment of the reading public. They are widely translated and are even treated as major works by literary traditions other than French.

Although both authors expressed contempt for the culture of their day, rejected the notion of historical progress and overtly turned their backs on the future, their writings have continued to play an ongoing, active role in describing the very epoch they wanted no part of.[2] They are, one could say, the two authors from the nineteenth century that the twentieth century can't live without. *Les Fleurs du mal* and *Madame Bovary* remain two of the defining—and most durable—works of contemporary modernity.

But before examining what our ongoing fascination with these works might tell us about the experience of modernity, we must pause for a moment to say more about the way in which this term has been invoked in recent years. Although "modernity" is often used to designate the specific historical period that was inaugurated in the mid–nineteenth century, it is better understood as a way of experiencing time rather than as a period in time. As Jean-François Lyotard observes in "Rewriting Modernity":

We can see that historical periodization belongs to an obsession that is characteristic of modernity. Periodization is a way of placing events in a diachrony, and diachrony is ruled by the principle of revolution. In the same way that modernity contains the promise of its overcoming, it is obliged to mark, to date, the end of one period and the beginning of the next. Since one is inaugurating an age dedicated to the entirely new, it is right to set the clock to the new time, to start it from zero again.[3]

Although modernity produces the notion of historical periodization as one of its defining symptoms, it cannot be confined to that historical period (the nineteenth century) from which it presumably arose. Fredric Jameson has called modernity a "catastrophe" that

dashes traditional structures and lifeways to pieces, sweeps away the sacred, undermines immemorial habits and inherited languages, and leaves the world as a set of raw materials to be reconstructed rationally and in the service of profit and commerce, and to be manipulated and exploited in the form of industrial capitalism.[4]

At the risk of doing violence to the thinking of both Lyotard and Jameson, it might be possible to read these two divergent descriptions of "modernity" in relation to one another. One could say that modernity seeks to "reset the clock" and invent new temporal technologies precisely because it has lost touch with other ways of keeping time. Lyotard suggests that "sequential" time disrupts, rather than guarantees, rhythms of temporal continuity. Thus, the new "clock" of modernity can be seen as a catastrophe that misrecognizes itself as linear "progress."

For both Lyotard and Jameson, one of the temporal symptoms of modernity is the development of complex technologies for measuring time. They argue that the ability to measure time, however, increases in inverse proportion to the human ability to express it and to create meaning through it. The temporal experience of modernity resists definition. Because it can no longer be contained in older, more traditional narrative forms and because it actively produces new systems for categorizing time that exclude any way of taking account of how it transforms lived experience, the temporality of modernity challenges us to look away from lived life and toward literature in order to describe its mechanisms and to record its effects.

The Pathologies of Modern Literature

By consciously retreating from the reality of the world around them into the supposedly "fictive" temporality of literature, both Baudelaire and Flaubert began to redefine the very activity and function of literature. They both refer to the act of writing as a druglike experience; time spent writing is an antidote to the corrosive temporality of lived life. And, for the first time, in their works, literature—and literary "style"—is given a specific new mission. Now the writing of literature is expected not only to compensate for the failures of lived experience; it is seen as a way of counteracting the failure of life to provide an experience of temporal continuity. From this point on, a new definition of literature begins to emerge: it is conceived as a preferable alternative to lived life as well as a continuation of it by other means. To be fair, this was more an explicit project for Flaubert than it was for Baudelaire. Although Baudelaire, as Jean-Paul Sartre points out rather viciously, certainly "failed" to live his life, he himself did not rigorously attempt to redeem this failure through an active decision "to live" uniquely through "the life" of his poetry. Much later, however, in their responses to Sartre's attacks against Baudelaire's "failed life," both Maurice Blanchot and Georges Bataille will make this case for him.[5] Flaubert, on the other hand, actively removed himself from life in the name of literature. In so doing, he carved out the path that would be closely followed by his two "modernist" successors: Proust and Kafka.

Given the considerable difficulties these two authors experienced in relating to the cultural institutions of their day—in addition to the difficulties they experienced with being able to accord meaning to the temporality of lived life—it is not surprising to discover that both Baudelaire and Flaubert have become renowned, in part, on account of the novel temporal structures and unusual representations of time that we find in their works. As part of their unrelenting struggle to ward off the effects of historical and technological "progress," they devoted their attention to matters of literary style. However, in their very attempt to resist the onslaught of progress through literary language, they develop new stylistic techniques— in both poetry and prose—that paradoxically describe, in mediated and distorted form, the impact of the very historical effects they were trying to avoid. Through the rhetoric of their style, Baudelaire and Flaubert articulate some of the most elusive (hence insidious) consequences of the industrial age. More specifically, we find that these rhetorical formulations of "temporal disorders" provide us with new ways of thinking about how the psychic structures that organize memory, perception, language, and the sexed body are reconfigured through the temporal experience of modernity.

Temporal Disorders and Sexual Perversions

But much of this, it might seem, has become common knowledge. Why is there any need to retell this particular story? And why retell it now? One way of beginning to answer this question is to observe that Benjamin's description of the "shock" experience of modernity has come to occupy a position in recent intellectual history that is somewhat analogous to the historical position occupied by Baudelaire's poetry. Benjamin's writings on Baudelaire have made a profound impact on contemporary debates about modernity (and postmodernity) and are cited by large numbers of readers who have little or only passing interest in Baudelaire. The level of interest generated by the cultural insights that Benjamin derives from Baudelaire's poetry arguably outstrips general interest in Baudelaire's poems. Consequently, many of Benjamin's readers (who are clearly drawn to the essay's "urgent" and "timely" concerns regarding how the shock experience allows us to think about cultural phenomena like technology, urban experience, photography, factory labor, etc.) remain unmoved by Benjamin's own claim that his cultural critiques were, by necessity, first formulated in poetic language. This is, after all, one of the main points of his essay.

In the last two decades, Benjamin scholarship has become something of a critical industry. However, one finds that there is a general (but by no means universal) tendency in this work to divide up Benjamin's works along disciplinary lines. Simply put, this means that cultural critics tend to read his works as descriptions of social realities, whereas literary critics focus more on his complex theories of language and his innovative style of reading. One cannot read the "Motifs" essay, however, without paying close attention to the ways in which these two dimensions of his work are articulated through each other. It is no accident that the "Motifs" essay begins with a discussion of Baudelaire's peculiar relationship to his readers. By approaching Baudelaire's poetry through his address to his readers, Benjamin implicitly asks us to read his reading of modernity as woven into his practice of close reading. Throughout the essay, Benjamin insists upon the importance of "hidden figures" in Baudelaire. Benjamin, like Baudelaire, always relies on such "hidden figures." Thus, some of Benjamin's most suggestive formulations never quite enter the language of his argument; they remain embedded in his literary readings and can only be uncovered through close reading.

One of the premises of this book is that Benjamin's "Motifs" essay— in its "hidden figures" and in its rigorous method for uncovering those hidden figures through close reading—can provide us with new ways of rethinking the ramifications of the changing but ongoing effects of modern temporality. By preserving Benjamin's reading methods but by shifting the focus of our analysis to a different (but by no means exhaustive) set of "contemporary" "motifs"—culled from Flaubert's prose as well as from Baudelaire's poetry—we find that the literature of modernity still speaks to us about how we live in time today. As we have already seen, Benjamin investigates how the "shock experience" of urban life—in a public sphere dominated by men and determined by mass communication and communication with the masses—creates disturbances in the formation of what he calls, via Proust and Freud, "voluntary" and "involuntary" forms of memory. Benjamin, however, never explicitly addresses how the "shock experience" might produce analogous effects in a "private sphere" now redefined through modernity. In other words, although Benjamin alludes obliquely to this issue, he never overtly examines how the shock experience must inevitably make an impact on the psychic structures that determine the assimilation of sexual difference as well as on the cultural expressions of sexual life.

Here we can observe that in the "Motifs" essay Benjamin never explicitly wonders why, in most of Baudelaire's poems, almost all expressions of temporality (and history) are systematically grafted onto unusual representations of the female body. In Baudelaire's poetry, feminine figures regulate most expressions of temporality and when they appear, these feminine figures assume the function of "shock absorbers." Although Baudelaire's poetic figuration of female figures cannot tell us very much about the status of "real women" in either public or private sphere (and hence cannot form the basis for the kind of "feminist sociology" of modernity recently invoked by several feminist cultural critics[6]), these feminine "shock absorbers" provide us with a different way of understanding how Baudelaire's poetry responds to the temporality of modernity. On the body of his feminine figures, Baudelaire inscribes a poetic description of the temporal function of addiction: through them, the poet attempts to deny loss, escape reality, and stop time.

When, moreover, we turn to Flaubert, we discover no clear traces of the "shock experience" of modernity in *Madame Bovary*. Nor do we find any powerful evocations of "voluntary and involuntary" memory. Curiously, we find the inverse. Although "memory"—in all forms—is strikingly absent from Flaubert's novel, the book is permeated with bizarre forms of forgetting. And when, like Benjamin, we turn to Freud and the language of psychoanalysis to help us find a psychic structure that might correspond to Flaubert's literary figures of "forgetting," we discover that we have entered into a discussion of the temporal dimension of fetishism. From a structural perspective, fetishism—the ultimate perversion—is as much (or more) about temporal anxiety as it is about sexual gratification per se. More precisely, fetishism is a way of denying temporal loss as well as being a denial of sexual difference.[7] Like addiction—which it resembles in its temporal structure—fetishism not only disavows loss, but it preempts the very formation of memory. The psychic purpose of fetishism is to insure that even potential losses are "erased" before they are even perceived.

Anamnesis and the Language of Literature

All of which brings us back, in a roundabout sort of way, to the methodological practice of "close reading" and the status of "literature" today. Over the last ten years or so, the literary function of language has become, as Naomi Schor recently put it, something of a "bad object." She defines what she means by "bad objects" as follows:

At any given time, within the carefully policed precincts of the academy, some critical objects are promoted to the status of good objects (say, not so long ago, dead authors) while others are tabooed (say, in the old days, experience). I am drawn to what I perceive rightly or wrongly as the bad objects. What I am invoking, then, is something on the order of the female fetishism I once promoted, a sort of critical perversion. To deliberately make an object choice branded as bad is risky business at worst and at best a means to go beyond certain impasses, to read at an angle, to be an intellectual bad girl.[8]

Schor's declaration of her predilection for "bad objects" follows a mournful admission of the fact that, in recent years, feminist critics have seemingly lost all interest in the study of literary forms. She wonders about what feminism loses when it abandons its investment in literary objects and forgets all about the formal concerns of "literariness." She writes,

I remain a feminist, and I feel myself going back to literature as a feminist, but differently so. This may be my contrarian side speaking. The question for me is: will a *new* feminist literary criticism arise that will take literariness seriously while maintaining its vital ideological edge? (xiv)

By fixating on a "bad object," Schor suggests, one risks falling out of step with one's own time and losing one's "ideological edge." But by the same token, Schor implies that the "bad object" can serve as a kind of memory trace of a mode of inquiry that does not simply obey the dubious temporality of "progress."

Even more recently, in a book wittily entitled *Loiterature*, Ross Chambers proposes that, in the wake of modernity, "literature" and "culture studies" can intersect in their shared propensity for "dawdling," "digressing," and just generally "hanging out."[9] Chambers suggests that when literature and cultural studies meet up in this historical juncture we know as the "present," they sometimes join together and indulge in a pleasurable form of contemplative idling he calls "loiterature." He writes, loiterature "has its beginnings in the Enlightenment and can be understood as one historical response among many to the emergence of a new, bourgeois world of work" (38). Because it comes into being as a response to the imperatives of the linear temporality of both positivism and capitalist efficiency, loiterature becomes cultural critique when it resists the lure of positive forms of knowledge and refuses to "get to the point."

Chambers's book certainly provides welcome relief from some of the more strident (and less historically sensitive) tendencies in recent criticism that insist upon pitting "literary" and "cultural studies" against each other along rigid (and shortsighted) "ideological" grounds. Thus, it would be a good thing if his book could (simultaneously): (1) convince (orthodox) literary critics to consider the possibility that the ostensibly "trivial" subjects of certain forms of cultural studies need not necessarily be seen as "bad objects"; and (2) seduce (dogmatic) cultural critics to slow down and become more suspicious of reading methods that leave little room for doubt, uncertainty, or, in Chambers's own words, "irony."

Although he points out that modernity can just as easily produce negative preoccupations as well as the joyful play of "loiterature," in this book (as opposed to his earlier book, *The Writing of Melancholy: Modes of Opposition in Early French Modernism*), Chambers clearly decides to focus on the affirmative "resistance" of loiterature rather than on the negative power of melancholy. His point is that in "loiterature," modernity produces an ironic form of resistance to some of its own most paralyzing effects. Thus, pleasure and "digression" are "methodological" components of loiterature's critical practice: loiterature discovers hidden reservoirs of seriousness in trivialities and interrogates the authority of received ideas about truth and meaning in contemporary politics and culture.

But the defining limit of loiterature is, precisely, time. Loiterature requires "time" in order to do its own thing. Chambers suggests that when loiterature comes into being, it makes this time for itself. As a *response* to the increasing velocity of modernity, loiterature sets itself up as a "shock absorber" that slows time down to a leisurely idle. It is here, however, that Chambers is forced to reckon with the force of speed itself. Not surprisingly, we find that when he explicitly addresses the question of "speed" in a chapter devoted to Baudelaire, a note of anxious melancholy creeps into his argument.

Speed, I know, first began to affect the practice of reading with the emergence of print technology and the invention of the book, so it's a bit late to be complaining about it now. But folks who tell us we shouldn't mourn the probable passing of that self-same book in the information age (because it too was once new technology resisted by belated people) are ignoring a couple of points. For one thing, what's disturbing these days isn't so much the probable disappearance of books, which can be faced with some equanimity, as the possible loss of certain modes of reading—I'll call them "critical" reading—that require time and are incompatible with haste. The speed reader doesn't have time for reflection and is inclined to take things at face value.[10]

Speed, concedes Chambers, not only limits the amount of actual time available for reading, but also changes the very methods and practice of reading itself. Speed readers not only read different textual objects from slow readers; they tend to read those objects in a different way. They are inclined, as Chambers remarks, "to take things at face value." At this point it becomes clear why speed readers would have no time for either literature or literariness. The very definition of literature, after all, is that it never takes things at face value. Literariness happens when words fly off in different directions, refuse to get to the point, and always say something other than what they mean as well as what they mean.

A few pages later, however, Chambers reasserts the power of loiterature over his melancholic insight concerning speedy readers. He suggests, cheerfully, that "rapid change can make a reader out of anyone, flâneur or no" (217). Because rapid change is disorienting, he implies, it requires one to read. But it is not at all certain that speed produces reflective readings. It seems more likely that readings produced by speed and in haste would tend to be *reactive* rather than reflective. The speed reader must cut to the chase and eliminate anything that doesn't immediately relieve anxiety and restore a sense of comfort.

But there is more. Speedy readings not only privilege certain kinds of objects over others—its "good objects" are timely and user-friendly—but they also tend to rely on mechanical methods of analysis. Speedy readings almost always feel "mass-produced." Therefore, it comes as no surprise that one is rarely surprised by them. On some level, they are "tired" from the get-go. But since, by definition, they are in step with their time, they announce—like the eleven o'clock news—actualities that appear under the sign of an "urgent" but strangely static newness. Furthermore, since, like the news, speedy readings always say exactly what they mean and little else, once they communicate their message, they become very quickly outdated. They eliminate any tedious or laborious forms of "technique"; they produce knowledge efficiently and pay scant attention to uncodifiable "hidden figures" or other forms of random negativity.

In his essay "Rewriting Modernity," Jean-François Lyotard provides a critical analysis of the speed of modernity and proposes a way to respond to it. He invokes the psychoanalytic techniques of "free floating attention," "free association," and "working through" as possible methods for resisting the prescriptions of modernity's temporal disorders. Both "free association" and "working through" are time-consuming processes that use time in order to counteract the effects of the shock experience.

A rule of this sort ["freely floating attention"] obliges the mind to be "patient", in a new sense: no longer that of passively and repetitively enduring the same ancient and actual passion, but of applying its own passibility, a same respondent or "re-spons," to everything that comes to the mind, to give itself as a passage to the events which come to it from a "something" that it does not know. . . . By proceeding in this way, one slowly approaches a scene, the scene of something. One describes it. One does not know what it is. One is sure only that it refers to some past, both furthest and nearest past, both one's own past and others' past. This lost time is not represented like in a picture, it is not even presented. It is what presents the elements of a picture, an impossible picture. Rewriting means registering these elements.

It is clear that this rewriting provides no knowledge of the past. This is what Freud thinks too. Analysis is not subject to knowledge, but to "technique", art. The result is not the definition of a past element. On the contrary, it presupposes that the past itself is the actor or agent that gives to the mind the elements with which the scene will be constructed.[11]

"Rewriting," Lyotard suggests, is a temporal technique that enables us to counter the temporal disorders of modernity. But this method of "working through" the shock experience of modernity requires a special form of very active passivity. This passivity (a form of listening to scenes without words) unblocks hidden passages and allows the past to pass through us and meet us in the present. By suspending knowledge or judgment about what we think we know, in the "hiatus" of not-knowing, the past—history—reinscribes its traces on us. This technique, Lyotard asserts, is an "art" and is accessible through art, rather than through other more "positive" forms of knowledge production. It is, one might add, the form of work that is performed by literature and that "passes" through "literariness."

This book is based on the premise that through its literature modernity passes on some of its most vital legacies to us. Literature remains one of our links to the experience of our most recent remote past, the time we like to call "history." As we blithely watch literature pass away, we close a passage to our collective relationship to the past. Thus, paradoxically, we need to read literature today precisely because we are quickly forgetting how to read literature today. Furthermore, in "giving up" literature (as "reactionary" or as "boring" or as "apolitical") are we sure that we know exactly what gets lost with it? Or have we even begun to forget to ask that question because we think that we already know the answer?

The argument of this book emerges slowly through a series of close readings of literary texts that unfold over time. It might appear to some readers that there is nothing "new" in it. But that would not necessarily mean that we've heard it all before. By "rewriting" the modernist literary works of Baudelaire and Flaubert, we can, perhaps, listen differently to what we tell ourselves about our experience of time today. The close readings in this book are intended to serve as untimely meditations on our present moment. As "our contemporaries," Baudelaire and Flaubert are still speaking to us today. When read closely, we find that their literary texts prove to be remarkably articulate about aspects of our experience that we ourselves have trouble describing. Because they still had access to a means of expression (literature) that allowed them to "present the elements of an impossible picture," their works endure as paintings of (post)modern life. By reading those scenes, we might discover that remembering how to read literature could turn out to be, perversely, one of the most urgent tasks of our time.

1

Women Tell Time: Traumatic and Addictive Temporality in *Les Fleurs du mal*

> The true subjects of the *Fleurs du mal* are to be found at inconspicuous points. They are, to remain in images, the as yet untouched strings of the unheard (of) instruments upon which Baudelaire fantasied.
> —Walter Benjamin, "Central Park"

Feminine Indiscretions: "Always the Same Thing"

> J'ai toujours été étonné qu'on laissât les femmes entrer dans les églises. Quelles conversations peuvent-elles tenir avec Dieu?
> —Baudelaire

Listen to the opening notes of one of Baudelaire's least read and, more tellingly, least *heard* poems: "Une fois, une seule, aimable et douce femme . . ." [One time, only once, lovable and sweet woman . . .].[1] The poem is called "Confession" and in it the poet recalls how, "one time, only once" in the dead of night, under a full moon, against the backdrop of the sleeping city of Paris, the beloved woman suddenly plunges into speech! The very fact that a woman—a human woman—might and could speak is enough, in the Baudelairean world, to register that act as singular event and transgression. Hence, even before we have heard what she says or how she says it, this discrete indiscretion is already marked as a "Confession." But whose? Does the poem's title refer to the unspeakable thoughts that emanate from that woman like a piercing wake-up call, or does it refer to the poet's own "confession" concerning his own fascinated horror of the sound of the female voice?

If, for the time being, we work with the latter hypothesis, we discover that this particular aspect of Baudelaire's "confession" has fallen, for the most part, on deaf ears. Although the poet's horror at the sound of the female voice runs through *Les Fleurs du mal* like an operatic leitmotif, and although Baudelaire's contempt for women is one of the dominant themes in his projected book of "confessions" (*Mon Coeur mis à nu*), it has rarely been the subject for a sustained critical (in the philosophical sense) or literary interpretation. In the *Passagen-Werk*, Walter Benjamin observes that Baudelaire's readers are men.[2] Many of those (male) readers seem to treat his misogyny as if it were somehow unrelated to his poetic merit. Among the courageous (and/or outrageous) examples of self-consciously male readers who *do* integrate some reflection on Baudelaire's misogyny into their understanding of his poetic enterprise, we generally find analyses of female figures that do not include any discussion of their alarming ability to speak. These readings do enable us to appreciate the complexity of the mission that Baudelaire delegates to his feminine figures. Sartre, for example, accuses Baudelaire of depicting his women as cold and unfeeling because he needs to project his own narcissistic sterility onto them.[3] Giorgio Agamben (following Benjamin) daringly claims that "it is a stroke of luck that the founder of modern poetry should have been a fetishist."[4] Leo Bersani brashly asserts that "in a sense Baudelaire does ignore the woman; . . . his turning away from her is the sign of his intense desire for her."[5] And, of course, there is Walter Benjamin, whose attention to marginal feminine figures in Baudelaire leads him to establish the prostitute and the lesbian as two of the crucial cornerstones of his reflections on modern allegory. But of the speaking woman in Baudelaire, even Benjamin does not have much to say. He alludes to the question throughout "Central Park" and comes close to it when he notes that "Baudelaire never once wrote a whore-poem from the perspective of the whore."[6] Although Benjamin does not address this issue directly, it is, I would argue, a necessary component of and corollary to all of his (better known) work on the way in which Baudelaire treats the relationship between time and the experience of modernity in his poems.

Ironically, and perhaps fittingly, it is Baudelaire himself who has the most to say about the place and function of the woman's voice in his poems.[7] If one pays strict attention to what he says to and about the female voice, one discovers that there is a rigorous poetic method to his flaunted misogyny.[8] At stake is nothing less than an explicit exposition of the temporal foundations on which his poems are built. As a general rule, as most readers agree, most of the women in *Les Fleurs du mal* are mute and/or inhuman. They appear as angels, demons, worms, corpses, nixes, chimera, sphinxes, cats, beasts, disembodied hair, vampires, giants, statues, paintings, and so on. This systematic muteness renders those rare moments in which women suddenly start speaking all the more striking. For when the woman does speak, it produces a shock. And, even more important, the "shock" produced by the woman's voice becomes the very subject of the poem. Although we will return to "Confession" much later, this is, as already stated, certainly what happens there. But this shock is not limited to "Confession," nor does it occur, as that poem would have it (perhaps wishfully), "only once." Instead, as we shall see, the shock of the woman's voice is also associated with a particular kind of empty repetition—the repetition of the always-the-same.

"Semper eadem" (Always the same thing) is the Latin title of a poem that deals explicitly with the question of the speaking woman. In fact, "Semper eadem" begins with a question by a speaking woman who is promptly told, in shockingly prosaic terms, to "shut up":

"D'où vous vient, disiez-vous, cette tristesse étrange,
Montant comme la mer sur le roc noir et nu?"
—Quand notre coeur a fait une fois sa vendange,
Vivre est un mal. C'est un secret de tous connu,

Une douleur très simple et non mystérieuse,
Et, comme votre joie, éclatante pour tous.
Cessez donc de chercher, ô belle curieuse!
Et, bien que votre voix soit douce, taisez-vous!

Taisez-vous, ignorante! âme toujours ravie!
Bouche au rire enfantin! Plus encor que la Vie,
La Mort nous tient souvent par des liens subtils.

Laissez, laissez mon coeur s'enivrer d'un *mensonge*,
Plonger dans vos beaux yeux comme dans un beau songe,
Et sommeiller longtemps à l'ombre de vos cils. (*OC* 1:41)

[You said, from where within you stirs this strange grief,
Rising like the sea on bare and barren rock?
—When our heart has even once reaped its harvest
To live is evil pain. It's a secret known by all,

A very simple pain, not mysterious,
And, like your joy, bursting forth for all.
Cease, then, to understand, O curious beauty!
And, though your voice be sweet, shut up!

Shut up, idiot! Soul in constant rapture!
Mouth of childish laughter! More, still, than Life,
Death often holds us in subtle bondage.

Let go, and let my heart become drunken by a lie,
As in a beautiful dream, let it plunge into your beautiful eyes,
And sleep for a long time under the shade of your lashes!]

If read prosaically, that is to say, according to its manifest content, this poem provides a lucid (but provisional) explanation for why Baudelaire requires that his women be all eyes and no voice. At its most literal level, the poem presents the problem as follows: the woman's question about the narrator's grief exposes and reawakens his ancient and unrelenting awareness of the pain of life. So he tells her to shut up. But if her voice reminds him of the unbearable pain of life in time, her eyes, by contrast, provide him with the means to escape that reality. Her voice makes him conscious of his exile from life, but her eyes replace that (lost) life by allowing him to become drunk with illusion and fall asleep. In Baudelaire's world, we will find that the woman's mouth almost always opens up a temporal abyss, whereas her eyes (which must remain open but devoid of sight) hold the world in place, outside of time.

By opening her mouth (before the opening of the poem) the woman exposes the "open secret" that "to live is (to be) in pain." The pain is linked to the poet's experience of time. In the line "Quand notre coeur a fait une fois sa vendange" we understand that he has, in some sense, outlived his own life. His heart, having been once "harvested," cannot reflower. As Benjamin puts it in "Some Motifs in Baudelaire": "For someone who is past experiencing, there is no consolation. Yet it is this very inability to experience that lies at the heart of rage. An angry man 'won't listen.'"[9] But if the man inhabits an autumnal world, the woman, by contrast, is all spring. Her childish laughter ("bouche au rire enfantin") places her, in Baudelaire's world, at the level of plant life. As he notes in his essay "L'Essence du rire": "Le rire des enfants est comme un épanouissement de fleur. C'est la joie de recevoir, la joie de s'ouvrir, la joie de contempler, de vivre, de grandir. C'est une joie de plante" [For the laughter of children is like the blossoming of a flower. It is the joy of receiving, the joy of breath-

ing, the joy of contemplating, of living, of growing. It is vegetable joy]
(original, *OC* 2:534; translation from *The Painter of Modern Life*, 156). But
"plant life" is life that does not know death. Her joy blooms into his "fleur
du mal"—flower of pain. By silencing the woman's joy, he turns it into
wine. In the final lines, the narrator's "heart," which appeared as a depleted
vineyard in the first stanza, becomes capable of becoming drunk in her
eyes. That drunkenness restores the very thing that the woman's voice had
put into question: time. The irrevocable "une fois" from the first stanza has
given way to a drunken illusion of time that can be experienced (if only in
sleep) as duration ("longtemps").

At the very core of this poem lies the repeated command "Taisez-
vous!" "Taisez-vous ignorante!" This highly unpoetic exclamation is situated at the structural hinge of the sonnet: it terminates the opening quatrains and opens the concluding tercets. Thus, although the source of the
poem is the woman's flowery voice, at the heart of the poem we hear the
poet's prosaic scream. The harsh refrain "Shut up! Shut up, idiot!" introduces strains of a voice rarely heard in the lyric prior to Baudelaire—its
abrupt rudeness betrays the frustrated irritation of a tired and angry man.
But it is through this tired and angry voice that we find one of the most resonant incarnations of the poetic voice in *Les Fleurs du mal*. The notion that
a poet only speaks in order to say "shut up" is, after all, a strange one. The
entire poem is staged as an unwanted conversation that interferes with the
poet's stated desire—which is to go to sleep. The woman's question "Where
does this sadness come from?" is doubly unbearable. First, it is unbearable
because it actually produces the very sadness it inquires about by forcing
the poet to become painfully conscious of the dissipation of his own life.
But the question is also unbearable quite simply because it is spoken at all.
This fact introduces a potent axiom that runs through *Les Fleurs du mal*:
wherever there is conversational speech (as opposed to soliloquy or apostrophe) there is consciousness of time, and wherever there is consciousness
of time, there is pain.

"Semper eadem" is not the only poem in which the poet commands
the woman to shut up. In "Sonnet d'Automne" ("Autumn Sonnet") we find
that something similar occurs. "Sonnet d'Automne" begins with the lines:

Ils me disent, tes yeux, clairs comme le cristal:
"Pour toi, bizarre amant, quel est donc ma mérite?"
—Sois charmante et tais-toi! Mon coeur, que tout irrite,
Excepté la candeur de l'antique animal . . .

[They say to me, your clear crystal eyes:
"For you, strange lover, what then is my merit?"
—Be charming and shut up! My heart, irritated by everything
Except the candor of the ancient animal . . .]

Here, however, the woman does not speak with her mouth, but her eyes. The woman's eyes want to know what the poet sees in her. These eyes, like the question they ask, are quite different from most of the feminine eyes in Baudelaire because they see. More precisely, we understand that these eyes see because they are endowed with speech. By speaking, they see him, they read "the infernal secret" in his heart; in their clear lucidity they show the poet (and the reader) that they know that he knows that he only permits these woman's eyes to speak at all so that he can tell them to shut up.

In both "Semper eadem" and "Sonnet d'Automne," the women who "speak" are defined uniquely through their eyes and mouth (they have no other body parts), while the poet has nothing other than his unhappy "heart." In "Semper eadem," this heart longs to get "drunk," whereas in "Sonnet d'Automne" his heart is "irritated."[10] By speaking, the women "open up" the pain in the poet's heart. By telling them to "shut up," the poet closes the woman's mouth from laughing and her eyes from speaking in order to seal himself off from the painful knowledge that is communicated through those feminine apertures. In his essay "L'Essence du rire," Baudelaire explains that the eyes and the mouth are the organs through which one relives the "accident" of the primal Fall. He writes:

Il est certain, si l'on veut se mettre au point de vue de l'esprit orthodoxe, que le rire humain est intimement lié à l'accident d'une chute ancienne, d'une dégradation physique et morale. Le rire et la douleur s'expriment par les organes où résident le commandement et la science du bien ou du mal: les yeux et la bouche. (*OC* 2:527–28)

[It is certain, if one wishes to place oneself in the point of view of orthodox thinking, that human laughter is intimately linked to the accident of an ancient fall, a physical and moral degradation. Laughter and pain are expressed through the organs in which reside the command and the science of good or evil: the eyes and the mouth.]

"Sonnet d'Automne" explicitly links the woman's speaking eyes to the figure of this "ancient fall." There, the poet specifies that his heart is irritated by everything *except*—as he puts it—"la candeur de l'antique animal." The "candor" of that ancient animal is the candor of the human animal (most likely the prelapsarian woman) before the Fall into sin. For Baudelaire, the Fall is always a fall into consciousness of the self and of time. Depictions of this fall into self-consciousness traverse *Les Fleurs du mal*. It most famously appears in "L'Irrémediable" and its effects can be heard in the infernal conversation that the unhappy heart has with itself in its final strophes:

> Tête-à-tête sombre et limpide
> Qu'un coeur devenu son miroir!
> . . .
> —La conscience dans le Mal!
>
> [Sombre and limpid face-to-face
> Is a heart become its own mirror!
> . . .
> —Consciousness in Evil!]

It is critical to understand that theological themes, in Baudelaire, always have temporal functions and historical ramifications. As we shall see, for Baudelaire, the "science of good and evil" is first and foremost determined as a relationship to temporality. In some sense, "good" and "evil" are terms that only acquire significance to the extent that they determine temporal possibilities or failures. This is the explicit project of the final strophe of "Hymne à la Beauté": "De Satan ou de Dieu, qu'importe? Ange ou Sirène /Qu'importe, si tu rends, . . . /L'univers moins hideux et les instants moins lourds?" [From Satan or from God, what matter? Angel or Siren/What matter, if you make . . . /The universe less hideous and instants less heavy?]. And again, once we see that Baudelaire assesses "good" and "evil" in temporal terms, we are able to understand why demonic deities figure prominently in the two poems that treat time explicitly in *Les Fleurs du mal*: "L'Ennemi" and "L'Horloge." The unnamed "enemy" in "L'Ennemi" is both Satan and Time. The poem restages the Fall by depicting the poet's life as an autumn garden which may yield no spring flowers. Similarly, the personified talking clock who condemns the poet to death in "L'Horloge" is called a "sinister god."

The "ancient fall" is conceived as a fall both *into* time and *out* of it. One falls into time by becoming conscious of it, but the moment one becomes conscious of time, one falls out of it because consciousness of time prevents one from being able to live in it. As Baudelaire explains in "Hygiène":

À chaque minute nous sommes écrasés par l'idée et la sensation du temps. Et il n'y a que deux moyens pour échapper à ce cauchemar,—pour l'oublier: le Plaisir et le

Travail. Le Plaisir nous use. Le Travail nous fortifie. Choississons. Plus nous nous servons d'un de ces moyens, plus l'autre nous inspire de répugnance. On ne peut oublier le temps qu'en s'en servant. (*OC* 1:669)

[At every minute we are crushed by the idea and sensation of time. And there are only two means of escaping this nightmare,—to forget it: Pleasure and Work. Pleasure wears us down. Work fortifies us. Let us choose. The more we employ one of these means, the more the other inspires repugnance in us. On can forget time only by using it.]

Although I am getting ahead of myself here, I hasten to remark that throughout most of *Les Fleurs du mal,* and certainly in the cityscapes of the "Tableaux parisiens," the ability to forget time through either pleasure or work is rendered dubious. And, as Benjamin points out, this is nowhere more evident than in the figure of the prostitute who has been forced to transform pleasure into work.[11] This collapse of pleasure into work motivates these lines from "Crépuscule du matin": "Les débauchés rentraient, brisés par leurs travaux" [The debauchees were returning home, broken by their labours]. More often, as we saw in "Semper eadem," sleep takes the place of "pleasure," and even sleep must be procured through artificial means: the woman's eyes are desirable because they provide the promise of a drunken slumber. In *Les Fleurs du mal,* the male speaker almost never wants to sleep with the woman—he wants the woman to put him to sleep.

But, most importantly, this "Fall"—although irrevocable—is not something that happened "once" and "only once," but something that keeps happening in every lived moment. Thus, one meaning of the "Fall" in Baudelaire is the fall into the present moment. Whenever one falls into the present moment, however, one falls into the same moment over and over again. This is what is meant by the Latin title of the poem "Semper eadem." It is no accident that Baudelaire reanimates a dead language—Latin—in order to express this fall into the present. We can assume that whenever Baudelaire alludes to a fallen world (be it Christian or pagan), he is quite likely also speaking about the present day. What "Semper eadem" means is: to live is to relive the Fall. No time is more horrifying—and more insidious—than the "instants lourds" of the present. Its horror is so great that Baudelaire often chooses to mediate its impact by veiling it under the allegorical sign of an "ancient fall." Furthermore, as our discussions of "Semper eadem" and "Sonnet d'Automne" have indicated, all conversational speech is potentially sinister. Speaking brings one into the present, and Death (like Satan) always speaks in the present tense. In "Semper eadem," although the poet invokes the irrevocable fall of his heart through a passé composé, "Quand notre coeur a fait une fois sa vendange," he slips into the present tense to express his chilling observation that "Vivre est un mal." He then attempts to get out of the abyss of this sinister present tense throughout the remaining verses of the poem by launching into a relentless, urgent, and increasingly hysterical series of imperatives: "Cessez . . . Taisez-vous . . . Taisez-vous . . . Laissez, laissez." These imperatives are nothing less than a plea to escape the tyranny of the consciousness of the present that the woman's question has awakened in him. The final imperatives "Laissez, laissez" provide the verbal support for the complementary infinitives through which he expresses his wish for a future drunken sleep. But "Semper eadem" does not grant that wish; it remains nothing more than a frozen promise expressed through the final series of unconjugated verbs: "s'enivrer," "plonger," and "sommeiller." Although it is possible to imagine that the form of oblivion that the poet seeks could only be expressed by verbs without tense or person, it is equally true that the poem cannot assure that the poet ever manages to attain that timeless state.

As we have seen, both "Semper eadem" and "Sonnet d'Automne" have numerous common elements. In both poems, the poet begins to speak by telling a woman to "shut up," but then attempts to justify his action by explaining that he needs to silence her because he suffers from a particular form of fatigue brought on by the recollection of an irrevocable fall out of (and into) time. The affective experience of this fatigue is depicted seasonally; its poetic emblem is the autumn. In "Central Park," Benjamin observes that "the home of the creative endowment is, in Baudelaire's experience, the Autumn. The great poet is, as it were, the creature of Autumn" (48). In addition to "Semper eadem" and "Sonnet d'Automne" the poems that are most clearly marked as autumn poems are "L'Ennemi," "Causerie," and "Chant d'Automne." Both "Causerie" and "Chant d'Automne" stage conversations addressed to female figures who are presumably present (but who remain silent), and in both poems the poet equates these women with the autumn sky. Thus, "Causerie" begins with the line "Vous êtes un beau ciel d'automne, clair et rose" [You are a beautiful autumn sky, clear and pink], and in "Chant d'Automne" the poet says: "Amante ou soeur, soyez la douceur éphémère/D'un glorieux automne ou d'un soleil couchant" [Lover or sister, be the ephemeral tenderness/Of a glorious autumn or a setting sun]. As we proceed, we will see why the "ideal" place for a woman—in Baudelaire's cosmos—is either as a replacement for the entire firmament or set within in it as one of its illuminating "heavenly" bodies: the sun, the moon, or the stars.

Although we will leave the figure of the woman suspended in the autumn sky for now—in order to return to it later—we must observe here that the poet does not simply metaphorically compare the woman *to* the sky but asserts that she actually *is* that autumn sky. In "Causerie" he declares, using the present tense of the verb "to be," that she *is* a clear, pink autumn sky (italics mine). In "Chant d'Automne," using the imperative, he entreats the woman to be either an autumn sky or a setting sun. In both cases, Baudelaire uses the verb "to be" to create a metaphor that refuses to accept its own metaphorical status. Furthermore, we would suggest that the reason he does so results from a certain crisis in "being" rather than from the inaccessibility of more "metaphorical" language. Or rather, more precisely, we would say that it is this very crisis in being that blocks his access to metaphorical language. Thus, when he asks the woman to "be" a sky, in effect he is asking her to fill the abyss between language and being that he experiences. Here we encounter another powerful axiom of *Les Fleurs du mal*: whenever the verb "to be" (être) appears in the present tense (or as an imperative), it refers to a temporal condition rather than to an objective state of being. We are even tempted to reduce this thought to its purest form: in Baudelaire, Being is Time. Moreover, whenever the verb "to be" occurs in the first person present (i.e., any occurrence of "je suis . . ."), it always denotes a *pathological* temporal state rather than a psychological condition or an ontological description. Thus, when the allegorical figure of Beauty says "Je suis belle," she refers to her privileged position of existing as an atemporal entity outside of time (in eternity). Conversely, when the speaker in "Spleen (II)" says "Je suis un cimetière abhorré de la lune" [I am a cemetery abhorred by the moon] and "Je suis un vieux boudoir plein de roses fanées" [I am an old boudoir full of withered roses]), he refers to the state of existing in a state of temporal exile, having been dropped from the calendar just as the "old sphinx" in that poem drops off the map. But the most blatant (and most bleak) example of this phenomenon occurs in "L'Horloge." In that poem, an allegorical personification of the present moment ("Maintenant") says: "Je suis Autrefois,/Et j'ai pompé ta vie avec ma trompe immonde!" [I am Past,/And I have sucked out your life with my foul prong!].

The Temporal Firmament

But before we are ready to examine why Baudelaire asks his women to replace the autumn sky, we must first look more closely at the figure of the firmament itself. In its "ideal" state, the firmament defines what Baudelaire means by the term "Idéal" in the cycle of poems that are collected under the title "Spleen et Idéal." The "ideal" firmament is the name for what was lost in the "ancient fall." This ideal firmament gathers together the dimensions of time and space and creates an accord between them. The vault of the sky holds the world together and establishes its limits in the horizon. It holds space in place by making a frame for it. In giving space, it allows all of the objects in the world to be seen by creating spatial relations between them. Without space, true perception is not possible. Similarly, the firmament allows one to "keep time" (as opposed to the more sinister options of "losing" it or "telling" it) through the rhythmic, measured movements of its seasonal, diurnal, and nocturnal heavenly lights. Paradoxically, the sky "grounds" the world. By making time and place possible, the firmament shapes the world and gives it dimension; thus it provides a home for those who live under its shelter.

As guardian of time and space, the firmament does not partake of "nature." One might go so far as to say that the sky—in Baudelaire—is made of language and it is this celestial language that gives time, memory, and perception to man. As that which gives time to man through language, the sky is divine. But since Baudelaire's poems presuppose the loss of God (I suppose we must wait for Nietzsche to record His actual demise) and hence take place in the postlapsarian "semper eadem" of the present day—the "ideal" firmament can only appear when it is recreated, reconstituted, and reconstructed through poetic labor. This is why, in "La Beauté," for example, the allegorical figure of Beauty fills the void in the firmament created by the departure of God and the absent sun: "Je trône dans l'azur comme un sphinx incompris" [I reign in the blue like a sphinx misunderstood]. But in the perpetually present time of the present day—always marked by the present tense of the "Spleen" poems—the gods have departed from the heavens, the sun never even appears, and the sky crashes down onto the world instead of propping it up. This is literally what happens in the opening lines of "Spleen (IV)": "Quand le ciel bas et lourd pèse comme un couvercle/ . . . Il nous verse un jour noir plus triste que les nuits" [When the low heavy sky weighs down like a lid/ . . . It pours us a black day sadder than the night]. Or, again, in "Le Couvercle," we find that sky clamps down on the world like a lid of a vat that suffocates all humanity:

> En haut, Le Ciel! Ce mur de caveau qui l'étouffe,
> Plafond illuminé pour un opéra bouffe . . .
> Le Ciel! Couvercle noir de la grande marmite
> Où bout l'imperceptible et vaste Humanité.

> [On high, the Sky! This cellar wall that stifles him,
> Ceiling lit for an *opéra bouffe* . . .
> The Sky! Black lid of the great pot
> Where vast imperceptible Humanity boils.]

Through these depictions of the firmament in "Spleen et Idéal," we can begin to appreciate why Baudelaire accords such a privileged status to the "upturned gaze" in the "Tableaux parisiens" poems. There, futile appeals to an empty sky reflect the alienating experience of modern life in the city. Most famously, in "Le Cygne" Baudelaire invokes Ovid's description of the creation of the world to show how radically the experience of life in the modern city differs from that of life in the ancient world. For Ovid, in *The Metamorphoses*, human time begins when humans are set apart from the animals because they are endowed with the ability—and the responsibility—to converse with the Gods by reading the stars. By reading the stars, one assumes a place in the world (in time and space) because one sees oneself reflected in the language of God. But whenever this "upturned gaze" appears in the "Tableaux parisiens," it bears the stigmata of failed communication, rage, and exile. In "Le Cygne" the poet describes how the swan—who is exiled in time and place—looks up at a starless and empty blue sky to accuse God for having abandoned him in the arid ruins of the modern city of Paris:

> Vers le ciel quelquefois, comme l'homme d'Ovide,
> Vers le ciel ironique et cruellement bleu,
> Sur son cou convulsif tendant sa tête avide,
> Comme s'il adressait des reproches à Dieu!

> [Toward the sky sometimes, like Ovid's man,
> Toward the sky, ironic and cruelly blue,
> On his convulsive neck stretching his avid head,
> As though addressing reproaches to God!]

One need not be able to see to need to look up at the sky. In "Les Aveugles," the poet describes his horror of the sightless eyes of the blind men ("from whose eyes the eternal light has departed") who raise their heads to the sky but find neither conversation nor consolation there:

> Leurs yeux, d'où la divine étincelle est partie,
> Comme s'ils regardaient au loin, restent levés
> Au ciel; on ne les voit jamais vers les pavés
> Pencher rêveusement leur tête appesantie.

> [Their eyes, from which the divine spark has departed,
> As though looking far, stay raised
> To the sky; you never see them dreamily leaning
> Their heavy head toward the street.]

"Les Aveugles" explicitly links the blind men's vacant gaze at the silent sky to the jarring sounds of daily life in the city:

> Ils traversent ainsi le noir illimité,
> Ce frère du silence éternel. O cité!
> Pendant qu'autour de nous tu chantes, ris et beugles . . .

> [Thus they traverse the unlimited black,
> This brother of eternal silence. O city!
> While around us you sing, laugh and roar . . .]

The eternal silence of the sky is echoed in the deafening sounds of the city. This correspondence allows one to understand that the firmament not only "grounds" the world, but reflects it as its mirror image. The firmament paints a picture of the world because in it Baudelaire renders the experiences of time in visual terms, although this notion of "vision" is not simply reducible to the empirical act of "seeing." In this sense, the firmament is the canvas that allows all of his poems—not merely the Parisian scenes—to be read as "paintings of modern life."

The Firmament and the Decline of the Aura

We can better understand the temporal (and historical) dimension of the firmament and the role that perception plays in Baudelaire's poetry by turning to Walter Benjamin's discussion of the "aura" in the penultimate section (XI) of his essay "Some Motifs in Baudelaire." For Benjamin, the experience of the "aura" refers to a mode of perception that both requires and sustains temporal continuity. Each act of perception governed by the aura communicates unconscious information about the past.

Experience of the aura thus rests on the transposition of a response common in human relationships to the relationship between the inanimate or natural object and man. The person we look at, or who feels he is being looked at, looks at us in turn. To perceive the aura of an object we look at means to invest it with the ability to look at us in return. This experience corresponds to the data of the *mémoire involontaire*. (These data, incidentally, are unique; they are lost to the memory that seeks to retain them. Thus they lend support to a concept of the aura that comprises the "unique manifestation of a distance.") . . . This endowment is a wellspring of poetry. Whenever a human being, an animal, or an inanimate object thus endowed by the poet lifts up his eyes, it draws him into the distance. (148)

Critical to this passage is the notion that the perception of any relationship, either in the world or with the world, requires an act of memory. Furthermore, only "involuntary memory"—that is, memory stored as unconscious data—can endow a perception with *Erfahrung*—experience in its fullest sense.[12] Thus, when one receives the returned gaze of the world, one is "remembered" by the world through those very parts of the self—the unconscious memory traces—that one has forgotten. The unconscious memory traces that are sent back from the world give meaning and structure to one's gaze.

But as readers of the "Motifs" essay know well, Benjamin only invokes the concept of the "aura" in order to demonstrate how the "shock" of modern life becomes implicated in its decline. In the idea that "perception" requires the ability "to forget" certain impressions and to store those impressions "unconsciously," Benjamin refers implicitly to Nietzsche and explicitly to Freud. It is Nietzsche who encourages Benjamin to think about this "crisis in perception" as a specifically historical phenomenon. In "On the Uses and Disadvantages of History for Life," Nietzsche writes:

Imagine the extremest possible example of a man who did not possess the power of forgetting at all and who was thus condemned to see everywhere a state of becoming: such a man would no longer believe in his own being, would no longer believe in himself, would see everything flowing asunder in moving points and would lose himself in this stream of becoming. . . . It is altogether impossible *to live* at all without forgetting. . . . To determine . . . the boundary at which the past has to be forgotten if it is not to become the gravedigger of the present, one would have to know exactly how great the *plastic power* of a man, a people, a culture is: I mean by plastic power the capacity to develop out of oneself in one's own way, to transform and incorporate into oneself what is past and foreign, to heal wounds, to replace that which has been lost, to recreate broken moulds.[13]

As Benjamin points out in his discussion of "shock" earlier in the "Motifs" essay, the barrage of stimuli of modern life produces a state that under-mines this essential "ability to forget." He turns to Freud, however, in order to understand why the effect of this barrage of stimuli does not simply re-sult in the fragmentation of being described by Nietzsche. Borrowing from Freud, Benjamin argues that the psyche is forced to defend itself from ex-ternal stimuli through defensive acts of conscious perception. Furthermore, these defensive acts of conscious perception actively interfere with the for-mation of unconscious memory traces. Citing Freud's discussion of trauma in *Beyond the Pleasure Principle*, he writes:

The basic formula of this hypothesis is that "becoming conscious and leaving be-hind a memory trace are processes incompatible with one another within one and the same system." Rather, memory fragments are "often most powerful and most enduring when the incident which left them behind was one that never entered consciousness." Put in Proustian terms, this means that only that which has never been experienced explicitly and consciously, what has not happened to the subject of experience, can become a component of the *mémoire involontaire*. (114)

Throughout the essay, Benjamin associates the "decline of the aura" to what he calls a "crisis of perception." Again, he relies on the notion that perception involves more than the mere capacity to see: it both depends upon and supports a temporal organization of the world. He argues that the rise of technologies of mechanical reproduction—and photography in particular—extends the range and purview of voluntary memory at the ex-pense of the unconscious memory traces carried by involuntary memory. He describes how photography participates in the "decline of the aura" in one of the essay's most famous passages:

If the distinctive feature of the images that rise from the *mémoire involontaire* is seen in their aura, then photography is decisively implicated in the phenomenon of the "decline of the aura." What was inevitably felt to be inhuman, one might even say deadly, in daguerreotypy was the (prolonged) looking in the camera since the camera records our likeness without returning our gaze. Where this expecta-tion is met (which, in the case of thought processes, can apply equally to the look of the eye of the mind and to a glance pure and simple), there is an experience of the aura to the fullest extent. (147)

Here it is important to recall that even though photography provides him with the clearest example of the "decline of the aura," it is not the main focus of the essay. Instead, Benjamin argues that it is in Baudelaire's lyric poetry that one finds the most eloquent exposition of the mechanism (and implications) of that decline. For Benjamin, it is precisely because Baudelaire struggled to transform the lyric into the repository for every aspect of modern life that was most at odds with the lyric tradition that his poetry becomes a vivid description of the experience of modern life.[14] In the famous concluding lines of the essay, Benjamin invokes the figure of the firmament—Baudelaire's firmament—in order to express why Baudelaire's poetry makes possible the perception of the decline of the aura:

> This is the nature of something lived through (*Erlebnis*) to which Baudelaire has given the weight of an experience (*Erfahrung*). He indicated the price for which the sensation of the modern age may be had: the disintegration of the aura in the experience of shock. He paid dearly for consenting to this disintegration—but it is the law of his poetry, which shines in the sky of the Second Empire as a "star without atmosphere." (154)

In his final sentence of the "Motifs" essay, Benjamin describes Baudelaire's poetry as a "star" inscribed in a world (the sky of the Second Empire) that has lost its own capacity to constitute itself as a "firmament." Significantly, throughout his writings on Baudelaire, Benjamin repeatedly insists upon the fact that Baudelaire banishes all stars from the heavens in his poetry. As Eduardo Cadava points out, "Benjamin more than once notes that stars never appear in the writings of Baudelaire—or if they do, that they are always in the process of fading or disappearing. . . . We could even say that such a reading is organized around an understanding of the role the stars play in the poet's various allegories of history."[15] Cadava argues that Benjamin reads the figure of the fallen star as the quintessential emblem of the "decline of the aura." Like the figures in the "Tableaux parisiens" who "look up at the sky" in order to discover that the gods have departed from the heavens, Benjamin "looks up at the sky" in order to show how Baudelaire's poetry illuminates his historical moment. By reading the fallen star in Baudelaire's poetry, Benjamin shows how that poetry becomes the reflected light of what has passed away—the unconscious memory traces carried by involuntary memory. Through this gesture, Benjamin very precisely translates the figures of Baudelaire's theologically articulated "temporal fall" into the historically motivated notion of the "decline of the aura."[16]

Stellar Shock Absorbers

But the stars do not simply fall, fade, or disappear in Baudelaire's poetry. The place left vacant by their absence is almost always (with the significant exception of the poem "Obsession") inscribed on the female body. In a poem that Benjamin does not mention, "Le Flambeau vivant," the woman's eyes are compared first to the light cast by candles that, burning in broad daylight, must compete with the light of the sun. But then the poem goes on to say that while the light of the candles burns under the sign of Death, the light of the woman's eyes also shines like stars singing the promise of a new morning ("Réveil"), and cannot be extinguished by the light of the sun:

> Charmants Yeux, vous brillez de la clarté mystique
> Qu'ont les cierges brûlant en plein jour; le soleil
> Rougit, mais n'éteint pas leur flamme fantastique
>
> Ils célèbrent la Mort, vous chantez le Réveil;
> Vous marchez en chantant le réveil de mon âme,
> Astres dont nul soleil ne peut flétrir la flamme!

> [Charming Eyes, you shine with the mystic light
> Of candles burning in daylight; the sun
> Glows, but does not extinguish their fantastic flame
>
> They celebrate Death, you sing Awakening;
> You march singing the awakening of my soul,
> Stars whose flame no sun can fade!]

Although the stars are explicitly named in the poem, they are not to be found in the heavenly vault. They have fallen from the sky and taken up residence in the eyes of a woman. The poem stages a competition between two kinds of celestial illumination: the light of the sun and the light of the woman's eyes. These two kinds of lights correspond to two competing methods of keeping time. Because they are compared both to the candles and to the stars, the woman's eyes function to create an artificial horizon for the symbolic limits of time: as candles, they illuminate Death, as stars they promise Eternal Life. In either case, however, they implicitly reflect the notion that the sun alone cannot carry out the full function of assuring that the daily passage of time be kept within symbolic limits. But because there are no stars in the sky, the poet needs the woman's eyes to replace the absent "aura" of the missing stars in order to contest and counteract the (implicitly) threatening quotidian temporality of the light of the sun.

Most often, however, one finds that Baudelaire delights in the absent light of the stars as long as the woman's body can both usurp their place and annul their damaged function. Therefore it follows that if, as we have seen, the presence of the stars indicates the language of memory, the absence of the stars can only be endured as long as memory and language are absolutely negated and contained. This is why when the woman takes the place of the stars, she becomes a vessel that contains pure silence. We can hear how the containment of this silence consoles the poet in the famous lines "Je t'adore à l'égal de la voûte nocturne/O vase de tristesse, ô grande taciturne" [I love you like the nocturnal vault/Oh vase of sadness, oh great taciturn]. In fact, the word "taciturne" itself contains within it a word for silence ("tacit") and a word for a sacred (often funereal) vessel: "urne." In "Le Possedé," the poet actually commands the woman to be "mute and dark" ("sois muette et sombre") before comparing her to a fallen star ("comme un astre éclipsé"). Furthermore, we find that when the absent stars are found in the woman's body, they are located either in her eyes, or in her hair, or even in the meeting point between eye and hair: the brow or the lash. In "Les Yeux de Berthe," the woman's eyes are a vessel containing an intoxicating night potion that douses the poet with soothing shadows:

> Beaux yeux de mon enfant, par où filtre et s'enfuit
> Je ne sais quoi de bon, de doux comme la Nuit!
> Beaux yeux, versez sur moi vos charmantes ténèbres!
>
> [Beautiful eyes of my child, whence filters and flees
> Something good, tender as the Night!
> Beautiful eyes, pour on me your charming shadows!]

Unlike the clear, speaking eyes of "Sonnet d'Automne" (that had to be forcibly "shut up"), these eyes are the very antithesis of both sight and speech. They do, however, recall the promise of drunken sleep cast by the shade of the lashes in the closing line of "Semper eadem." But since we now recognize that the woman's eyes (whether clear or dark) often function as surrogates for the absent stars, we can begin to understand why Baudelaire so often draws our attention to the hair that frames the woman's eyes and her face. The hair around the eyes provides a horizon for the proxy celestial lights while the hair around the face (or the sex) provides an intoxicating replacement for the missing firmament itself.

In the first stanza of "Les Promesses d'un visage," the poet praises both the lowered arch of the woman's eyebrows, from which flow welcome shadows, and her very black eyes that fill him with (lusty) dark thoughts. In the middle of the poem, these dark eyes begin to speak ("in accordance with the dark hair"), and together the hair and the eyes entice the poet to scan the woman's entire body in order to find the hair that lies under her belly. In the final stanza, we find that the hair on this dark place—the woman's sex—becomes the site of Baudelaire's most explicit mention of the absent stars:

> Une riche toison qui, vraiment, est la soeur
> De cette énorme chevelure,
> Souple et frisée, et qui t'égale en épaisseur,
> Nuit sans étoiles, Nuit obscure!
>
> [A rich fleece which, truly, is the sister
> Of that great head of hair,
> Supple and curled, your equal in depth,
> Night without stars, obscure Night!]

Only when the stars are entombed in the dark fleece of the woman's dark place can the poet extinguish the excruciating memory of the loss that is borne by the lost language of the stars. This is precisely what the poet cannot do in the only "star" poem in which no woman figures. In "Obsession," although the tormented poet expresses a longing for a "night without stars," his wish is thwarted by the very existence of the shadows themselves. As he explains,

> . . . les ténèbres sont elles-mêmes des toiles
> Où vivent, jaillissant de mon oeil par milliers,
> Des êtres disparus aux regards familiers.
>
> [. . . the shadows are themselves canvases
> On which, thousands springing from my eyes,
> Live vanished beings with familiar looks.]

Thus, where there is no feminine figure to contain the fallen stars and neutralize the shocking effect of the "decline of the aura," the poet becomes assaulted by his own, uncontainable (and alienated) memories, like a man buffeted by strangers in a crowd. Although this is not the place to pursue this reflection, we might add, in passing, that these uncontrollable memory ghosts recall the "phantom crowd of the words" that Benjamin uncovers in his famous derivation of the "shock" experience through his reading of "Le Soleil."

At this juncture, however, let us remark that although the "aura" section of the "Motifs" essay contains Benjamin's most extensive discussion of Baudelaire's relationship to a variety of feminine figures (nymphs, female satyrs, prostitutes, and sylphs), he does not fully examine the multiple ways in which those feminine figures mediate the experience of shock by incorporating the fallen stars and incarnating the "decline of the aura." The consequences of this (perhaps intended) oversight are triple: in the first place, this enables Benjamin to limit his analysis of the cultural effects of the "shock experience" to a "public sphere" dominated by men (the crowd, the factories, gambling, photography, journalism, etc.), and in the second place, it encourages him to underestimate the importance of the role that sexual fetishism and drugs—of all sorts—play in Baudelaire's conception of modernity, and finally, it permits him to overlook some of the most "expressive"—but far less "heroic" aspects of Baudelaire's description of the loss of experience in modern life.[17] We might gloss these remarks in pragmatic terms by observing that in all of Benjamin's extensive writings on Baudelaire, he expresses very little interest in the female body (apart from eyes and barren womb) and strictly no interest in the crucial place occupied by her hair. But is it really valid to ask *why* Benjamin isn't concerned with the fact that the poet's fetishistic fixation on (absent stars) in female hair is quite different from his fascination with the stars in her eyes? Why would one even think of asking Benjamin's readings to become accountable for the very figures he does not mention? We would certainly not be interested in subjecting Benjamin to this kind of analysis were it not possible to imagine that by examining some of the "feminine motifs" that he does not address directly, we might be able to read his essay in a different light and to reap new insights from it.

At this point, I would like to suggest that Benjamin needs to eliminate the mediating figure of the woman's body so that he can claim that the *defining* figure of Baudelaire's poetry is the poet/fencer's solitary "duel" (with language and against shock) that he locates in the first stanza of "Le Soleil." Benjamin writes: "This duel is the creative process itself. Thus Baudelaire placed the shock experience at the very center of his artistic work" (117). After suggesting that Baudelaire redefines *poetic labor itself* through this figure of the duel, Benjamin then argues that through his labor, the "dueling" fencer/poet bears conscious witness to the shocking impact that urban crowds, photography, and factory labor has had on modern experience.[18] One could not overstate the importance and the impact of Benjamin's insight into Baudelaire's poetic process and the shock experience. However, by extending Benjamin's analysis of the "shock experience" beyond the dueling fencer to the range of "motifs" associated with

Baudelaire's female figures, I would like to explore how Baudelaire's poetry might provide us with a slightly different lexicon for the various kinds of "temporal disorders" that pervade modern experience. As we have begun to see, Baudelaire's problematic relationships with his feminine figures engage us in temporal struggles that cannot be fully expressed in the figure of the poetic "duel." By showing how Baudelaire's feminine figures are virtually inextricable from his "temporal firmament," we can look more closely at the labor performed by these figures in order to regulate the problems of time and memory in his poems.

It should be clear by now that most of these female figures do not and cannot exist *in* the world as autonomous entities or even as human beings. Instead, these female figures are the essential, necessary supplements that mediate, express, and redress the poet's experience of temporality. One of the functions of the woman is to be a prosthetic extension of the sky or one of its heavenly lights. We have begun to see how Baudelaire often cuts up her body in significant ways to make those prime body parts (mouth, eyes, and hair) perform specific temporal tasks. By looking at the specific tasks he assigns to his female figures (or their various body parts), we can read the traces of a particular kind of description of the experience of modern life. Put in different terms, we would suggest that if Baudelaire so systematically inscribes the woman's body into the sky (while he recoils from the sound of the present moment in her voice), it is because something has interfered with his ability to "remember" the sky and something must be done to silence the sounds of the moment. Her presence in the sky indicates that, in some larger sense, for Baudelaire there is no sky and there is no woman. If there were still celestial lights in the sky, he would not need to hang her there. If he could still read the language of the stars, she might be able to assume her own place beside him in the world. However, when he replaces the sky with the woman, Baudelaire does not merely invoke her as a "mediating" presence; instead, he requires her presence to "correct" his temporal relationship to the world.

This "feminine" correction functions according to the law of the supplement. What this means is that her very presence in the poems automatically reveals an underlying temporal problem (in the language of the poem and in the language of the world) and simultaneously functions to veil and redress that problem. Put in still more radical terms (and we will attempt to prove this in the pages that follow), the figure of the woman in *Les Fleurs du mal* is commonly asked to incarnate (and contain) precisely those aspects of the shock of modern experience that the poet is unable to conquer through his "poetic duel." Here we would add that in his discussion of the duel in "The Sun," Benjamin never mentions that this poem provides us with one of the very few cases in which the poet actually *succeeds* in winning his duel against shock. In the final two stanzas of the poem (which Benjamin does not cite), we find that the poet/fencer has actually successfully transformed the shocking repetitive blows of the "modern urban sun" of the first stanza into a fertile, rejuvenating source of light, health, and life! However, this "poetic success" is recorded in two of the most insipid lines in Baudelaire's entire corpus: "C'est lui qui rajeunit les porteurs de bequilles/Et les rend gais et doux comme des jeunes filles" [He it is who rejuvenates the crutch-bearers/And makes them as happy and sweet as young girls]. In any case, the story of "poetic labor" in Baudelaire very rarely results in such a "happy" ending without being actively mediated by the body of a feminine figure. In very simple terms this means that when, for example, the poet cannot sleep, or he cannot remember, or he cannot forget, or he cannot block out the deafening sounds of the city—he divests himself of these losses by endowing his female figures with the (divine or infernal) power to represent and contain those losses in various ways. We might even say, paraphrasing Benjamin, that the figure of the woman is the primary "shock absorber" of *Les Fleurs du mal.*

In order for her to function as "shock absorber," she must become an image (preferably a dream, an illusion) or, even better, a lie that shields him from his own shattered perception of the world. We should recall that at the end of "Semper eadem," the poet begs the woman to become the material support of his *lie* ("mensonge") and he likens that "lie" to a beautiful dream ("beau songe"). But Baudelaire himself consistently reminds us that he *knows* that his very dependency on this lie is a function of the trauma produced by the shock experience. In "Semper eadem," the poet's final, desperate craving for the druglike lie that only the woman can give him is clearly a defensive response to the shock produced by her opening question. But, paradoxically, because the shock of her question throws him into a state of unbearable "hyper-consciousness," he must remain fully conscious of his own *need* for the lie. Thus, by definition, the needed lie always comes too late: it can never fully eradicate the traces of the trauma that rendered it necessary. In his depiction of the temporal void opened up between the moment of the experience of shock and the inevitably "belated" relief procured through the necessary lie, Baudelaire provides us with a stunningly elegant derivation of the temporal structure of certain forms of addiction. We will return to this question later through a discussion of "La Chevelure."

For now, we can observe that in "Semper eadem" the woman is given two different and apparently mutually exclusive functions: in the opening lines she becomes a "shock conductor" by speaking, while in the closing lines she becomes a "shock absorber" by supplying the poet with the promise of the drunken lie he craves. However, to sustain the illusion required for the position of shock absorber, the woman must either illuminate the poet's gaze (as sun, moon, or star) or annihilate that gaze (as soothing "shadow" or enveloping "head of hair"). Conversely, every time she opens her mouth, the woman threatens to mutate from "shock absorber" into "shock conductor." These are two of the primary functions ascribed to Baudelaire's female figures, and it is not uncommon to find them "dueling" with one another in a single poem.[19]

But in either function—be it as shock absorber or as shock conductor—Baudelaire reworks and challenges the limits of the lyric tradition through his feminine figures. Although the figure of "female beauty" clearly represents one of the most conventional elements in his poems, Baudelaire often explicitly endows that figure with a "traditional mask" only so that he can then expose the "modern visage" that lies underneath it. This is the explicit project of the allegorical poem "Le Masque." Subtitled "Statue allégorique dans le goût de la Renaissance," the poem was inspired by a statue sculpted by Ernest Christophe and it is dedicated to the sculptor. Like the form of the female beauty depicted inside it, the poem is precisely cut in half and has two faces. The shocking revelation of the woman's duplicity occurs in its central verses:

> O blasphème de l'art! ô surprise fatale!
> La femme au corps divin, promettant le bonheur,
> Par le haut se termine en monstre bicéphale!
>
> [O blasphemy of art! O fatal surprise!
> Divine-bodied woman, promising happiness,
> Ends at the top in a two-headed monster!]

The poem then goes on to explain that one of these two heads lies and the other tells the truth. Of course, it is the "beautiful face" that lies because it promises "bonheur." The word "bonheur" should be read literally here—as "good hour" or time made good. By contrast, the true face is distorted by shock and contorted by pain:

Et, regarde, voici, crispée atrocement,
La véritable tête, et la sincère face
Renversée à l'abri de la face qui ment.

[And look, here it is, horribly frozen,
The true head, and the sincere face
Turned over in the shelter of the face that lies.]

The shock is conveyed through the word "crispée." In his famous urban love sonnet, "A une passante," Baudelaire uses this same word to express the electric shock of erotic love that has no place in the modern world: "Et moi . . . crispé comme un extravagant" [And me . . . frozen like a madman]. Like the figure of Andromaque in the urban poem "Le Cygne," the woman in "Le Masque" sheds a river of tears. But whereas Andromaque weeps over an irrecoverable past, the beauty in "Le Masque" weeps over an unlivable present and an unbearable future. In the concluding lines of the poem, the poet explains her weeping:

—Elle pleure, insensé, parce qu'elle a vécu!
Et parce qu'elle vit! Mais ce qu'elle déplore
Surtout, ce qui la fait frémir jusqu'aux genoux,
C'est que demain, hélas! Il faudra vivre encore!
Demain, après-demain et toujours!—comme nous!

[—She weeps, you fool, because she has lived!
And because she lives! But what she deplores
Most, what makes her tremble to the knees,
Is that tomorrow, alas! She must live still more!
Tomorrow, and tomorrow and forever!—like us!]

In these final lines, Baudelaire subtly unmasks the traditional form of "Renaissance allegory" promised by the poem's subtitle and reveals its distorted modern face. In this "modern" allegory, there is no renaissance—no rebirth—but only the incessant shock of endless life with no relief in death. There is no future in the future but only more of the same thing. It is "Semper eadem" all over again and again and again.

Time Fragments, Body Parts, and Memory Implants

The only way to combat this eviscerated past, empty present, and endless future is by cutting up time and filling it with memories. But memory, in its fullest sense—in what Benjamin calls *Erfahrung*—is arguably the single greatest source of anxiety, doubt, and conflict in *Les Fleurs du mal.* Certainly, memory can never be taken for granted. Although it is extremely rare for a memory to form "naturally"—without willful provocation and/ or external stimulants—in those rare cases where this seems to occur, Baudelaire expresses the quasi-miraculous fragility of such an event through the felicitous fleeting beauty of the final moments of the setting sun. We see this clearly in "Le Coucher du soleil romantique." There, the poet is seemingly both amazed and stunned by his own momentary capacity to remember having been part of the world and having seen "everything" in it. His amazement, however, quickly gives way to anxiety as he chases after his own fading memory just as the last rays of the sun lapse into the falling darkness:

> Je me souviens! . . . J'ai vu tout, fleur, source, sillon,
> Se pâmer sous son oeil comme un coeur qui palpite . . .
> —Courons vers l'horizon, il est tard, courons vite,
> Pour attraper au moins un oblique rayon!

> [I remember! . . . I've seen all, flower, spring, furrow,
> Swoon beneath its eye like a throbbing heart . . .
> —Let us run toward the horizon, it is late, run quick,
> To catch at least one oblique ray!]

The poet's anxiety about losing his memory is everywhere palpable; it is thematized in the race toward the horizon, it palpitates in the image of the throbbing heart, and it reverberates in the poem's punctuation. The exclamation point following the announcement "I remember!" indicates that there already is a problem with the poet's claim on memory. The ellipsis (following the word "palpite") and the hyphen (preceding the word "courons") wordlessly confirm our sense that the future memory loss that the poet attempts to ward off has already occurred even before he sets out on his race with the light of the setting sun.

Baudelaire often uses the image of the setting sun to illuminate the last vestiges of fading memory.[20] The seasonal expression of this fragile grasp on memory is the autumn. If we pause here to recall our earlier discussion of the autumn poems, we are now able to see why, in "Chant d'Automne," the poet asks the woman "to be" either an autumn sky or a setting sun. The poet wishes that the woman would become either of these figures so that she could, perhaps, enable him to sustain a recollection his own former existence in the world. With the woman's help, the poet could hope to extend the duration of the fleeting act of memory that allowed the solitary poet in "Le Coucher du soleil romantique" to recall that he had, indeed, seen "everything."

As we have seen, however, the temporal firmament of *Les Fleurs du mal* is irreparably torn: the fabric of the sky cannot hold memory in place and the celestial lights have gone out of the sky. They cannot insure that time will be kept and divided into a cycle of livable seasons and meaningful days. Therefore, one finds that the only way of keeping time from lapsing into the infernal present is by actively cutting it up into inhabitable units. In section X of the "Motifs" essay, Benjamin cites Proust's writings on Baudelaire to elucidate these odd allocations of time.

Familiarity with Baudelaire must include Proust's experience with him. Proust writes: "Time is peculiarly chopped up in Baudelaire; only a very few days open up, and they are significant ones. Thus it is understandable why turns of phrase like 'one evening' occur frequently in his works." (139)

Benjamin declines to mention that Proust goes on to relate these peculiar segments of time to two other "peculiarities" found in Baudelaire's writings: his philosophy of elegant furniture and his perverse preference for certain female body parts. Proust writes:

Le monde de Baudelaire est un étrange sectionnement du temps où seuls de rares jours notables apparaissent; ce qui explique les fréquentes expressions telles que "si quelque soir," etc. Quant au mobilier baudelairien qui était sans doute celui de son temps, qu'il serve à donner une leçon aux dames élégantes de nos vingt dernières années, lesquelles n'admettaient pas dans "leur hôtel" la moindre faute de goût. . . . Monde baudelairien que vient par moment mouiller et enchanter un souffle parfumé du large, soit par réminiscences (*La Chevelure*, etc.). . . . Nous disions que l'amour baudelairien diffère profondément de l'amour d'après Hugo. Il a ses particularités, et, dans ce qu'il a d'avoué, cet amour semble chérir chez la femme avant tout les cheveux, les pieds et les genoux. . . . Évidemment entre les pieds et les cheveux, il y a tout le corps.[21]

[Baudelaire's world is a strange cutting up of time in which only rare notable days appear; which explains the frequency of expressions such as "if some evening," etc. As for Baudelairean furnishings which were no doubt those of his age, may they serve to teach a lesson to the elegant ladies of these last twenty years, who would not accept in "their mansion" the slightest failure of taste . . . Baudelairean world on occasion moistened and enchanted either by a perfumed breath from the open sea, or by reminiscences (*La Chevelure*, etc.) . . . We were saying that love in

Baudelaire is profoundly different from love in Hugo. It has its oddities, and, in what it expresses explicitly, this love seems to cherish above all in the woman her hair, feet and lap. . . . Of course between the feet and the hair, there is the whole body.]

Proust establishes a connection between the following seemingly unrelated things: time sections, interior decorating, perfume, and Baudelaire's predilection for female hair, laps, and feet. One possible way of understanding how these apparently incongruous items might be related is to observe that they all can be used as prosthetic devices that assist the creation of artificially produced "interiors." The poet then uses these "prosthetic interiors" to restructure time so that it can be made accessible for the production and storage of memories. Or, in more simple terms, we could say that in order to "chop up time," Baudelaire must first redefine space as enclosure and the female body as something that has no "openings": no mouth, no eyes, no hands, no fingers, sex or breasts.

Baudelaire often invokes enclosed spaces (bedrooms, alcoves) and small containers (armoires, perfume bottles, jewel boxes) in order to create the hermetically sealed environment needed to cut up time and fill it with memories. We find descriptions of these interiors throughout his writings and they are implicitly always conceived of as *defensive* places—the poet retreats into them because the noise, activity, and general reality of the external world is unbearable. As defensive places, their first function is to shut out the outside world to provide an escape from the temporality of everyday life. In some poems (like "Parfum exotique" and "La Chevelure") the poet's retreat from the world is depicted as a necessary precondition for the creation of an artificial "temporal firmament" through which memories of a "lost" world can be either mechanically retrieved or artificially reproduced. In those poems, the goal of the retreat is the reconstruction of a sense of duration. However, in other poems (like "Rêve parisien" and the prose poem "La Chambre double") the poet retreats into his room to create an imaginary dream world (that is invariably shattered in the poem) whose function is to annihilate memory so that he can forget the shocking sounds of the present day. Thus, in "La Chambre double," the intrusion of memory actively violates the poet and the act of remembering one's real place in life and time becomes the ultimate nightmare: "Horreur! Je me souviens! Je me souviens! . . . Oui! Le Temps règne; il a repris sa brutale dictature. . . ." [Horror! I remember! I remember! . . . Yes! Time rules; it has resumed its brutal dictatorship . . ."].

The poem which most comprehensively engages all of the issues raised by Proust and which brings them (so to speak) to a head is, of course, "La Chevelure." In this famous invocation of the evocative power contained in a woman's hair, Baudelaire provides us with perhaps the most complicated, ambivalent, and twisted expression of time, memory, and the female body in his entire corpus. This poem is so tricky that one hardly knows (for reasons that can be attributed to the intricate temporal structure depicted within it) where or how to begin speaking about it. Three of the first questions that confront any potential reader are: (1) how does one read the "hair" announced by the poem's title? Is it a synecdoche for the woman or a substitute for her? If the hair is a synecdoche, why is the "whole woman" reduced to this particular body part? If it is a substitute for the woman, what happened to the rest of her? Does she exist as a living being in the poem or not? (2) What is the poem about? Is it a love poem or not? If it is a love poem, how does the poem define love? If it is not a love poem, then why does it engage erotic themes and figures? (3) What is the relationship between time and memory in this poem? Is it about a triumph of memory or a failure of memory? Is the poet's goal to remember or to forget? Unfortunately, the constraints imposed by the scope of this chapter oblige me to restrict most of my remarks to a cursory examination of the poem and therefore prevent me from being able to provide a detailed response to all these questions here. Nonetheless, by pointing out that "La Chevelure" demands, in some sense, that one *ask* these questions (while refusing any clear certainty about their answers) we have already stumbled upon some of the central interpretative difficulties posed by and in the poem. Although my analysis will concentrate on the first and last stanzas of the poem, it is best to reproduce it here in its entirety:

La Chevelure

Ô toison, moutonnant jusque sur l'encolure!
Ô boucles! Ô parfum chargé de nonchaloir!
Extase! Pour peupler ce soir l'alcôve obscure
Des souvenirs dormant dans cette chevelure,
Je la veux agiter dans l'air comme un mouchoir!

La langoureuse Asie et la brûlante Afrique,
Tout un monde lointain, absent, presque défunt,
Vit dans tes profondeurs, forêt aromatique!
Comme d'autres esprits voguent sur la musique,
Le mien, ô mon amour! nage sur ton parfum.

J'irai là-bas où l'arbre et l'homme, plein de sève,
Se pâment longuement sous l'ardeur des climats;
Fortes tresses, soyez la houle qui m'enlève!
Tu contiens, mer d'ébène, un éblouissant rêve
De voiles, de rameurs, de flammes et de mâts:

Un port retentissant où mon âme peut boire
À grands flots le parfum, le son et la couleur;
Où les vaisseaux, glissant dans l'or et dans la moire,
Ouvrent leurs vastes bras pour embrasser la gloire
D'un ciel pur où frémit l'éternelle chaleur.

Je plongerai ma tête amoureuse d'ivresse
Dans ce noir océan où l'autre est enfermé;
Et mon esprit subtil que le roulis caresse
Saura vous retrouver, ô féconde paresse,
Infinis bercements du loisir embaumé!

Cheveux bleus, pavillon de ténèbres tendues,
Vous me rendez l'azur du ciel immense et rond;
Sur les bords duvetés de vos mèches tordues
Je m'enivre ardemment des senteurs confondues
De l'huile de coco, du musc et du goudron.

Longtemps! Toujours! ma main dans ta crinière lourde
Sèmera le rubis, la perle et le saphir,
Afin qu'à mon désir tu ne sois jamais sourde!
N'es-tu pas l'oasis où je rêve, et la gourde
Où je hume à longs traits le vin du souvenir?

[*Hair*

O fleece, rolling to the neck!
O curls! O perfume loaded with nonchalance!
Ecstasy! To people this evening the dark alcove
With memories sleeping in this hair,
I want to shake it in the air like a handkerchief!

Languorous Asia and burning Africa,
A whole world, distant, absent, all but extinct,
Lives in your depths, aromatic forest!
As other spirits sail on music,
Mine, o my love, swims in your perfume.

I will go away there where tree and man, full of sap,
Swoon long in the ardent heat;
Strong locks, be the swell that carries me off!

You contain, ebony sea, a dazzling dream
Of sails, of oars, of flames and masts:

A sounding port where my soul can drink
In great gulps perfume, sound and color;
Where vessels, gliding in gold and moire,
Open their wide arms to embrace the glory
Of a pure sky where eternal warmth trembles.

I will plunge my head, in love with drunkenness
In this black ocean where the other is enclosed;
And my subtle spirit caressed by rocking waves
Will know to refind you, o fertile indolence,
Infinite cradling of embalmed leisure!

Blue hair, tent of shadows spread,
You give me back the blue of the immense round sky;
On the downy shores of your twisted locks
I get ardently drunk on the mingled scents
Of coconut-oil, musk and tar.

For a long time! Forever! My hand in your heavy mane
Will sow ruby, pearl and sapphire,
So that to my desire you will never be deaf!
Are you not the oasis where I dream, and the gourd
In which I inhale in long draughts the wine of memory?]

Certainly, it is possible to assume that the hair in question is attached to an existing woman and that the poem is, indeed, a declaration of love addressed to her. In his book *Baudelaire and Freud*, Leo Bersani proposes a lucid and suggestive psychoanalytic interpretation of "La Chevelure." He opens his argument with the emphatic assertion that "the subject of 'La Chevelure' is desire."[22] This premise inspires Bersani's most compelling and provocative insight. He states: "Precisely because she is the object of desire, she initiates desires which remove the poet from her; the woman exists for Baudelaire, not in order to satisfy his desires, but in order to produce them" (39). In making this claim, Bersani implicitly relies on the psychoanalytic distinction between object and aim of desire. This means that although the woman is the *object* of the poet's desire, the *aim* of that desire is the activity of fantasy as a means of escaping from "present" reality—including the reality of her body and her presence in the sexual act. He writes:

Sexual excitement would be *identical to* a psychic movement which submits reality to the passionate interpretations of desire. This is dramatically illustrated in

Baudelaire's "La Chevelure" by the total absence of the woman from the fantasies evoked by her presence. If the pleasure which she has given the poet has always been inseparable from the operations of his desiring fantasies, the woman is best remembered when she is continuously being forgotten. (41)

Bersani's point here seems to be that the presence of the woman is required in order to facilitate the fantasy of her (desired) absence. Her actual sexual body then serves as nothing more than the material foundation of the poet's fantasy. Furthermore, Bersani implies that the reason the poet desires the woman's absence is so that she can become an object of "memory." In fact, after having posited the relationship between the woman's absence and the poet's memory, Bersani goes on to make some more general claims about the status of memory and time in the poem:

The objects of desire are not objects; they are creative processes. In a sense, this liberates memory from time. More precisely, desiring fantasies are by no means turned only toward the past; they are projective reminiscences. This is suggested in "La Chevelure" by the fact that the references to memory enclose several stanzas in which the dominant tense is, either explicitly or implicitly, the future. (40–41)

But is memory ever liberated from time in "La Chevelure"? Does the poem ever succeed in producing the sorts of "projective reminiscences" Bersani describes? Although all the issues Bersani raises are central to the poem's concerns, his interpretation of the creative "desire" of fantasy in the poem and the status of the so-called woman in it rely upon a set of questionable assumptions. Moreover, because his analysis is grounded in these assumptions, he overlooks any mention of the significant details in the poem that might challenge the validity of his conclusions.

A word of caution is needed here: by exploring the poetic foundations of Bersani's (mostly plausible) assumptions, we risk falling into the vertigo of "La Chevelure." A careful reading of this poem requires that one engage in the maddening (but necessary) activity of "splitting hairs." And once one starts splitting those hairs, they proliferate and become endlessly tangled. So perhaps it would be best to begin with the hair itself. Bersani never even mentions it in his reading. For him, it would seem that the matter of hair (named by the poem's title and invoked throughout it) is ultimately irrelevant or superfluous to his derivation of desire in the poem and hence has no bearing on it. From the start, he assumes that the hair is a "neutral" poetic device that stands in for a "real" woman with whom the poet is having sex. Furthermore, once he imagines (also a debatable point) that there is a sex act depicted in the poem (37), he automatically and immediately endows that "real woman" with a whole body and doesn't worry about the fact that she might, after all, exist for the poet as nothing more (or less) than a simple "head of hair"—a "chevelure." What are the implications of this? For starters, even if one were inclined to agree with Bersani's conviction that the "subject" of the poem is "desire," one would have to take into account that—at least until the final stanza—the poem explicitly, specifically, and relentlessly designates the "object" of that desire as "hair" rather than as "woman."

But can we really assume that the expression of a desire provoked by "hair" is identical to that produced by an actual woman? According to psychoanalysis (Bersani's own chosen method), the form of desire that could only be satisfied by or, following his own distinction, "produced" by a head of hair differs in significant ways from the desire that seeks to express itself through a relationship with another person. Psychoanalytic theory has described this particular expression of desire as a pathology (perversion) and has even given it a precise technical name: fetishism. Moreover, it is certainly no coincidence that the core psychic problems raised by and in the psychoanalytic theory of "fetishism" correspond closely to the questions raised by the hair in "La Chevelure." Although I examine the temporal ramifications of fetishism at great length later in this book, for the purposes of this discussion we can recall that psychoanalysis understands fetishism as a complicated and particular form of defense against reality: disavowal or *Verleugnung.* Disavowal manifests itself as a perceptual denial of the difference between presence and absence; its exemplary form is the denial of the fact that the mother does not have a penis. However, disavowal is not restricted to a denial of the existence of the maternal penis: it is often extended to a denial of differences of all sorts, including those between organic and inorganic material and between living and dead people. Furthermore, although the experience of the denial manifests itself perceptually (as a psychic compromise that gives a visual expression to an absent object), this perceptual "adjustment" is itself a response to a prior (or simultaneous) traumatic memory loss. As I suggest in "The Erasing of Modern Life," the perceptual denial of *sexual difference* found in fetishism depends upon and is related to a collapse of *temporal difference* that results in a particular form of impaired memory function. Freud indicates this in "Fetishism" when he writes:

It seems rather that when the fetish is instituted some process occurs which reminds one of the stopping of memory in traumatic amnesia. . . . The subject's interest comes to a halt half-way, as it were; it is as though the last impression before the uncanny and traumatic one is retained as a fetish.[23]

For Freud, then, although the fetish comes into being as a defensive response to shock, its psychic *function* is to parry the shock by "forgetting" it. Perception of the fetish object becomes a way of compensating for the memory loss and absorbing the shock experience. By filling the (present) visual field, the fetish object appears to close the temporal void opened up by the shock. The sight of the fetish object then becomes invested with a magical aura of presence that is seemingly endowed with the power to redeem all losses. Paradoxically, the aura of "presence" that saturates the fetish object is psychically manufactured out of a lost experience of loss.

Long before Freud, however, Baudelaire was writing his own theory of fetishism in "La Chevelure."[24] At virtually every level of its construction, this poem provides us with an extended meditation on the use of fetishism both as a defense against the shock of reality and as a means of expressing problems of time and memory, presence and absence, and anxious male sexuality. Fetishism is present at the thematic level in "La Chevelure" through the emphasis on the figure of the hair; it is present at the formal level through the use of apostrophe; it is present at the rhetorical level through the reliance on the trope of synecdoche.[25] Finally, it is present at the temporal level through the bizarre progression of verb tenses that run through the poem. One cannot help but imagine that there must be some sort of "denial" at work here if one looks closely—even for an instant—at the final lines of the poem. "La Chevelure" culminates in the emphatic assertion of an anxious wish couched in the subjunctive ("Afin qu'à mon désir tu ne sois jamais sourde"), rapidly followed up by an even more anxious question posed through a negative form of the verb to be ("N'es tu pas . . .") before then dissolving into what appears to be an oxymoron: "le vin du souvenir."

The poem's title, "La Chevelure," highlights the specific potency attributed to "hair." By endowing the woman's "chevelure" with the power to summon up an entire lost world, Baudelaire asks us to think about how and why this particular figure complicates the very questions about time and memory that are asked and enacted in the poem. It is certainly no accident that the desired object that gives this poem its title is also, at the conceptual level (if not at the empirical level), one of the exemplary objects of fetishism. Hair epitomizes the fetish because it incarnates a fundamental confusion about the limits between life and death and hence it negates the difference between presence and absence. Hair goes on growing for some time after the body to which it is attached has died. Conversely, hair renders the very life of the body uncanny because it represents that part of the (living) organic body that most resembles (dead) inorganic matter. Hair decomposes (if at all) far more slowly than the rest of the exposed body parts. Furthermore, hair is one of the few body parts that one can cut off (infinitely) without harming, damaging, or destroying the life of the body in any way. Finally, because hair can be detached from a living body without losing its form or color, it can be used to preserve a memory of that body even if that body has since died. In this way, hair is capable of supporting an absolute denial of death: although a lock of hair proves, without a doubt, that it was once "living," once it has been detached from a body, one cannot know whether or not the body from which it came still lives.[26]

If one reads the hair in the poem as an emblematic figure of *Verleugnung*, then one must consider the possibility that the desire in the poem is ultimately less "happy" than Bersani's reading would suggest.[27] Looked at from this perspective, the "desire" in the poem emerges as an anxious defense against loss rather than a simple affirmation of the poet's "creative" potential. Furthermore, Bersani's "happy reading" cannot account for the fact that while this poem seems to begin on a note of utter certainty, it certainly ends on a note of anxious, enigmatic doubt. The exclamations of ecstasy and declarations of desire for the hair that open the poem are radically put into question by the poem's concluding question to the woman who is suddenly addressed in the final stanza. Up until the final stanza, the poet never acknowledges that the hair might be attached to a person. Moreover, as the disembodied object of the poet's address, the hair revives lost memories, reanimates the dead, traverses time and space, and even restores the blue sky in the firmament. But in the final stanza, the poet finally concedes that the hair that performed all of these miracles might belong to a woman. The last stanza begins with the exclamation "Longtemps! Toujours!" Through these words (which conclude the poet's address to the hair and which introduce his address to the woman) we understand that the hair has been the ideal object of his desire because the aim of his desire is the recovery of lost time. It is hard to know exactly how to read the tone of this exclamation: Is it a final triumphant declaration of the temporal power of the hair or is it a quasi-hysterical plea—tinged with lament and anxiety—addressed to a woman who might not be willing or able to satisfy his desperate longing for duration and eternity?

The next line, however, clarifies the poet's position and fears. After finally admitting that the hair actually belongs to her through his use of the possessive pronoun ("ma main dans *ta* crinière lourde"), the poet initiates a linguistic exchange with the woman, in which he implicitly acknowledges (for the first time) the possibility of loss. The recognition of the possibility of loss becomes visible through the poet's attempt to circumvent it. His first direct address to the woman is a financial proposition designed to guarantee temporal satisfaction: he proposes to give her "jewels" to compensate for the loss of the past and to ward off the loss of the future. In return for jewels that he will deposit in her hair—rubies, pearls, and sapphires—he asks that she never be deaf to his "desire," that she consent to restore his sense of lost time. If we recall that Baudelaire often uses the hair as a replacement for the missing temporal firmament, then we can see that his offer to shower her with precious jewels can be read as an attempt to buy back time through this act of purchased love. By sowing her hair with jewels, the poet seeks to resow (artificially) the seeds of lost time with sterile matter. He proposes to buy back the lost celestial lights in the sky by placing precious earthly stones in the firmament of her hair: the rubies take the place of the sun, the sapphires replace the moon, and the pearls reflect the forgotten light of the fallen stars.

But the very act of speaking directly to the woman (instead of to her hair) appears to shatter the poet's dreamlike fantasy of denial. In the final two lines of the poem, he suddenly seems to wake up into the reality of the present moment and become semiconscious of the fact that despite his need for her to exist solely for the purpose of providing him with memory and time, she is, in fact, a woman endowed with consciousness and not merely a head of hair. In his final question to her, he abandons the fantasy of the future tense and the apostrophe of denial and slips into an anxious inquiry about the nature of her "being" in a negative interrogative present tense:

> N'es-tu pas l'oasis où je rêve, et la gourde
> Où je hume à longs traits le vin du souvenir?
>
> [Are you not the oasis where I dream, and the gourd
> In which I inhale in long draughts the wine of memory?]

The power, pathos, and beauty of this poem are due, in part, to the fact that this question can and must be read simultaneously as a "real" question and as a rhetorical means of disavowing its disturbing urgency. On one level, this question is as "real" as questions get. In these final lines, the poet implicitly recognizes that his fetishistic fantasies of visiting tropical islands and being cradled by the rocking of the ocean waters were but a denial of his essentially arid existence in a temporal wasteland. When he asks her if she "is" his oasis, we learn that he knows that he lives in the desert. By demanding whether she "is" a vessel that contains the "wine of remembrance," we understand that if he needs her to supply him with drunken memories it means that he has no other way of keeping his own memories intact and that he cannot retrieve them without the help of external, artificial intoxication.

The final enigmatic image of the poem, "le vin du souvenir," can be read in various ways. Some readers insist that one must read the figure of the wine of remembrance as a the expression of a desire to forget. Barbara Johnson, in *Défigurations du langage poétique*, argues that this is the case:

Le poème en vers, qui fait du souvenir un breuvage producteur de l'ivresse—d'ivresse qui, pour Baudelaire, est toujours un *oubli* du temps—finit en fait par affirmer que celui qui hume le vin du souvenir est en réalité un mangeur non de souvenirs mais de lotus: au fond du souvenir, c'est l'oubli qu'il boit. En affirmant une équivalence métaphorique entre souvenirs et oubli par la médiation du mot "vin", le poème en vers élimine ainsi rhétoriquement la temporalité elle-même.[28]

[The verse poem, which makes of memory a drink productive of drunkenness—drunkenness which, for Baudelaire, is always a *forgetting* of time—ends up in fact by affirming that he who inhales the wine of memory is in reality a lotus-eater rather than a memory-eater: in the depths of memory it is forgetting that he drinks. By affirming a metaphorical equivalence between memories and forgetting through the mediation of the word "wine," the verse poem thus rhetorically eliminates temporality itself.]

Such a reading is entirely possible. Furthermore, the desire to "eliminate" temporality is, as we have seen, one of the functions of the fetish of the hair. Baudelaire himself, however, suggests another way of understanding the phrase "vin du souvenir" in his writings on Edgar Allan Poe.[29] In a passage devoted to thinking about the meaning of Poe's drinking, Baudelaire writes:

Il existe dans l'ivresse non seulement des enchaînements de rêves, mais des séries de raisonnements, qui ont besoin, pour se reproduire, du milieu qui leur a donné naissance. Si le lecteur m'a suivi sans répugnance, il a déjà deviné ma conclusion: je crois que dans beaucoup de cas, non pas certainement dans tous, l'ivrognerie de

Poe était un moyen mnémonique, une méthode de travail, méthode énergique et mortelle, mais appropriée à sa nature passionnée. Le poète avait appris à boire, comme un littérateur soigneux s'exerce à faire des cahiers de notes. Il ne pouvait résister au désir de retrouver les visions merveilleuses ou effrayantes, les conceptions subtiles qu'il avait rencontrées dans une tempête précédente; c'étaient de vieilles connaissances qui l'attiraient impérativement, et, pour renouer avec elles, il prenait le chemin le plus dangereux, mais le plus direct. Une partie de ce qui fait aujourd'hui notre jouissance est ce qui l'a tué. (*OC* 2:315)

[Drunkenness has not only its linked chains of dreams but also its rational trains of thought, which, if they are to be repeated, need a repetition of the circumstances which gave them birth. If the reader has followed me as far as this without disgust, he will have already guessed my conclusion; I think that very often, though by no means always, Poe's drunkenness was a mnemonic device, a deliberate method of work, drastic and fatal, no doubt, but suited to his passionate nature. Poe taught himself to drink, just as a careful man of letters makes a deliberate practice of filling his notebooks with notes. He could not resist the desire to return to the marvelous or terrifying visions, the subtle conceptions, which he had encountered in a previous storm; they were old acquaintances which peremptorily called to him, and in order to renew relations with them he took the most perilous but the straightest road. One part of what delights us today was the cause of his death.]

The argument of this passage is both complex and telling. Baudelaire suggests that Poe actually employed his drinking as a mnemonic device and that his pursuit of drunkenness should be considered an integral part of his working method. He claims that by drinking Poe was able to restore two kinds of lost continuity necessary for his artistic production. According to Baudelaire, drinking produces the following productive effects: (1) it fabricates narrative continuity out of diverse dreamlike visions by linking these visions together into a chain, and (2) it facilitates the faculty of reason. The state of being drunk re-creates and simulates the state out of which thoughts are born; it then collects those thoughts and immerses them into a common medium so that they can be arranged according to logical, meaningful sequences. Although Baudelaire then compares Poe's drinking to the way other writers "take notes," he concludes, however, that Poe's "method" was both "more direct" and "more dangerous" than that practiced by other writers. He implies that one reason "recovered memory" through drinking is more direct (and more dangerous) than note taking is that the drinker, unlike the normal writer, actually expends vital resources in order to "reconnect" (renouer) with these past experiences instead of simply recalling or retrieving them.

Baudelaire's analysis of Poe's drunken re-creation of memory encourages us to wonder whether Baudelaire also implies that Poe was condemned to pursue the "direct and dangerous" method of remembering precisely because the "less direct" method was no longer available to him. Baudelaire seems to suggest that Poe (whom he celebrates elsewhere as the exemplary "poet" of modern life), was compelled to pay with his life in order to salvage memory from the shock experience. In any case, it seems clear that Baudelaire's poem "La Chevelure"—in its final invocation to the "vin de souvenir"—recalls Poe's struggle to reclaim memory through drinking. In "La Chevelure," however, the poet attempts to bypass the unhappy consequences of drinking (that killed Poe) first by producing memories through the intoxicating power of a woman's hair and then by trying to preserve those simulated memories by transforming her very "being" into a repository for them. It goes without saying that the poem must end before the woman has a chance to shatter the poet's illusions by voicing her own response to his final question.

As we have seen, the final stanza of this poem reveals that the poet's grasp on memory is fraught with uncertainty. The poet's anxious attitude toward memory at the end of the poem undermines his apparent mastery over memory at its beginning. After we read the poem's final stanza, the famous display of "voluntary memory" in its first stanza no longer seems quite as simple as it might have appeared to be on a first reading. Like the "boucles" in the woman's hair, this poem curls back upon itself and demands to be read in circular fashion—not only from beginning to end but from end to beginning. When read from start to finish the poem doesn't make much logical sense: if the poet really is capable of commanding memory at will at the beginning of the poem, then why does he need to bribe the woman into colluding with him at the end? If, however, we begin with the end, we understand that the poet must *simulate* memory production through intoxication.

Apostrophe paves the rhetorical road to inebriation; it is the exemplary poetic trope of a desired but impossible state of immediacy and pure plenitude.[30] In the opening lines of "La Chevelure," the poet initially uses apostrophe to increase the intensity of the "presence" of the hair in order to lose himself in its immediacy:

Ô toison, moutonnant jusque sur l'encolure!
Ô boucles! Ô parfum chargé de nonchaloir!
Extase! . . .

[O fleece, rolling to the neck!
O curls! O perfume loaded with nonchalance!
Ecstasy! . . .]

These apostrophes perform like poetic speech acts that actually seem to propel the poet into a state of intoxicated bliss. The three apostrophes that climax in "ecstasy" remind us that the voyage of memory in "La Chevelure" begins with this inaugural act of forgetting. Only after he has gotten high from the apostrophe-charged hair does the poet embark on his active pursuit of memory:

Extase! Pour peupler ce soir l'alcôve obscure
Des souvenirs dormant dans cette chevelure,
Je la veux agiter dans l'air comme un mouchoir!

[Ecstasy! To people this evening the dark alcove
With memories sleeping in this hair,
I want to shake it in the air like a handkerchief!]

But once we recognize that this very act of "voluntary" memory requires prior intoxication, we are compelled to wonder about the status of the poet's memory itself. Is the poet's active, forceful, "voluntary" pursuit of "sleeping memories" really a sign that his memory functions, or is it, paradoxically, the very evidence that the poet's (own) voluntary memory has, in fact, already failed him? We can interpret the poet's excessive insistence on manufactured "presence" (produced by apostrophe and sustained through the reduction of the woman to a semi-inorganic enveloping body part) as a defense mechanism and symptom of denial. By losing himself in the "presence" of the head of hair, the poet removes himself from the reality and temporality of the world around him. One can conclude, therefore, that the opening of the poem is itself both a product and a sign of disavowal.

The exclamatory apostrophes of "La Chevelure" are the fetishistic vestiges of a prior catastrophe. The poem is the poet's defensive response to this catastrophe. By founding the poem with apostrophe, the poet self-consciously invokes the performative power of poetic expression itself. He attempts to use his poem—and the poetic acts depicted in it—first to deny his temporal loss and then to redress it. By addressing his apostrophes to the (fetishized) hair, the poet creates an intoxicating medium of artificial "presence" from which the "memories" of the poem are subsequently generated. He then "rediscovers" an entire lost history of the world still "living" in that hair. This resurrection of "world history" through fantasy corresponds to a fantasy about the origins of the world. By treating the curls of the woman's hair as atemporal time capsules, the poet imagines that her hair retains the preserved remains of all of the lost primitive and prehistoric civilizations in the East:

> La langoureuse Asie et la brûlante Afrique,
> Tout un monde lointain, absent, presque défunt,
> Vit dans tes profondeurs, forêt aromatique!

> [Languorous Asia and burning Africa,
> A whole world, distant, absent, all but extinct,
> Lives in your depths, aromatic forest!]

The poet must actively deny all differences (between himself and the woman, between Paris and the East, between the present moment and ancient history, between his cosmopolitan urban experience and the distant cultures of Asia and Africa) and voyage to the ends of the earth in order to redeem his catastrophic sense of loss. Through this poetic voyage, he neutralizes all instances of alterity and transforms them into druglike memory implants that he then inhales as the "wine of remembrance."

The Shock of Modern Love and the Mechanics of Ecstasy

Our examination of "La Chevelure" has shown us that the poet's desire for "sexual ecstasy" is motivated by temporal anxieties. The desire depicted in the poem is both perverse and intoxicating. And, as we have seen, the perversion and the intoxication are codependent. "Ecstasy" is the name of the drug that is contained in the interior coils of a woman's hair. By ingesting the drug, the poet escapes from the world and denies both the reality of his loss and the loss of his reality. The woman's hair supplies him with the promise of an artificial temporal firmament: he needs to purchase ecstasy in her hair to imagine that he can redeem his sense of lost time and lost experience. In the poem, the poet offers the woman jewels in exchange for the temporal "ecstasy" procured by his perverse investment in her hair.

In "real life," however, Baudelaire describes sexual "ecstasy" as a manifestation of traumatic shock rather than as a source of intoxication. In *Fusées*, he writes:

Je crois que j'ai déjà écrit dans mes notes que l'amour ressemblait fort à une torture ou à une opération chirurgicale. . . . Entendez-vous ces soupirs, préludes d'une tragédie de déshonneur, ces gémissements, ces cris, ces râles? . . . Ces yeux de somnambule révulsés, ces membres dont les muscles jaillissent et se roidissent comme sous l'action d'une pile galvanique, l'ivresse, le délire, l'opium, dans leurs plus furieux résultats, ne vous en donneront certes pas d'aussi affreux, d'aussi curieux d'exemples. Et le visage humain, qu'Ovide croyait façonné pour refléter les astres, le voilà qui ne parle plus qu'une expression de férocité folle, ou qui se détend dans une espèce de mort. Car, certes, je croirais faire un sacrilège en appliquant le mot: extase à cette sorte de décomposition. (*OC* 1:651)

[I believe that I have already written in my notes that love strongly resembles torture or a surgical operation. . . . Do you hear those sighs, preluding a tragedy of dishonor, those moans, those cries, those rattles? . . . Those sleepwalker's in-turned eyes, those limbs whose muscles jut out and harden as though galvanized by a battery, the drunkenness, the delirium, the opium, in their most furied results, certainly could not give you examples as atrocious and as bizarre. And the human face, which Ovid believed to be fashioned to reflect the stars, here no longer can speak anything but an expression of mad ferocity, or one fading into a kind of death. For of course I would think it a sacrilege to apply the word "ecstasy" to this kind of decomposition.]

This description of the sex act is striking for a number of reasons. In the first place, Baudelaire depicts the sexual act as a theater of cruelty; it is more like a public event rather than a private experience. His attitude toward the act is neither that of an engaged participant in an act of love nor even that displayed by the drunken poet in "La Chevelure." Instead, Baudelaire here poses as an ironic "flâneur" of the bedroom. Despite the fact that Benjamin derives Baudelaire's response to the "shock experience" from his urban poems, it is in Baudelaire's personal writings about private sex acts that we stumble upon this most articulate analysis of the shock experience. Although Benjamin reads Baudelaire's response to shock in the "heroic" stance of the fencer/poet, we find that in his private writings Baudelaire's poetic "heroism" gives way to perversion: the description of the shock of sex is more than a little tinged with voyeurism and sadism. Furthermore, from this description we discover that the impact of shock is not restricted to the public sphere, nor does it remain there. The experience of the streets has entered the bedroom and left its mark on it. Baudelaire's description of the contorted bodies in the throes of the sexual act recalls Poe's description of the urban pedestrians in "The Man of the Crowd." All of the essential physical signs of the shock experience are present: electricity, drunkenness, disjointed movements, and disfiguring facial expressions.

Baudelaire concludes his description of the shocking aspect of sex with an explicit reference to the lost temporal firmament. By contrasting the disfigured faces in this contemporary sex act with the ancient face of "Ovid's man" (who recognized himself in the aura of the stars), Baudelaire implicitly gives a specifically modern face to this erotic act. This sex act has lost any "aura" of the experience of love because the experience of love requires the ability to experience time. Instead, Baudelaire derives "ecstasy" from the way the erotic act transforms the human face into a figure of death. In erotic ecstasy, the event of death is inscribed on the human face:

Et le visage humain, qu'Ovide croyait façonné pour refléter les astres, le voilà qui ne parle plus qu'une expression de férocité folle, ou qui se détend dans une espèce de mort. Car, certes, je croirais faire un sacrilège en appliquant le mot: exstase à cette sorte de décomposition. (*OC* 1:651)

[And the human face, which Ovid believed to be fashioned to reflect the stars, here no longer can speak anything but an expression of mad ferocity, or one fading into a kind of death. For of course I would think it a sacrilege to apply the word "ecstasy" to this kind of decomposition.]

In the "Motifs" essay, Benjamin alludes to this separation of sex and love in modern experience through his reading of the urban love sonnet "A une passante."

The delight of the urban poet is love—not at first sight, but at last sight. It is a farewell forever which coincides in the poem with the moment of enchantment. Thus the sonnet supplies the figure of shock, indeed of catastrophe. But the nature of the poet's emotions has been affected as well. What makes his body contract in a tremor—"crispé comme un extravagant," Baudelaire says—is not the rapture of a man whose every fibre is suffused with *eros*; it is, rather, like the sexual shock that can beset a lonely man. . . . [These verses] reveal the stigmata which life in the metropolis inflicts upon love.[31]

Benjamin suggests that the "urban poet" finds ecstasy in "love at last sight" because "love at first sight" is no longer possible. In order to experience "love at first sight" one needs to be able to imagine a future and rely upon the duration of experience. But in the city, and in the temporal existence determined by "shock," there is neither continuity nor duration. Under these conditions, death becomes eroticized because it and it alone can complete an otherwise fragmented experience of time.

If the private face of modern love is stamped with death, its public face bears the imprint of the commodity fetish. Benjamin devotes considerable attention to the figure of prostitutes in Baudelaire. The prostitute removes sex from the realm of inner experience and brings it into the street. Benjamin treats this "Woman of the Crowd" as if she were Baudelaire's postscriptum to Poe's "Man of the Crowd." For Benjamin, the whore incarnates the shock experience: by selling sex, she turns pleasure into work and her body becomes the ultimate commodity. In "Central Park," he writes:

Ever more callously the object world of man assumes the expression of the commodity. At the same time advertising seeks to veil the commodity character of things. In the allegorical the deceptive transfiguration of the world of the commodity resists its distortion. The commodity attempts to look itself in the face. It celebrates its becoming human in the whore.[32]

Benjamin credits Baudelaire for having transformed the prostitute into an allegory of "mass communication." She both makes herself available to the masses and is, in some sense, "mass-produced." These modern incarnations of the "oldest profession" expose "new forms" of alienated labor and mass production. According to Benjamin, the phenomenon of mass production affects both the worker and the object made. The worker begins to resemble an object while the object acquires the aura of a fetish.

In "Les Métamorphoses du vampire," Baudelaire invokes the figure of the vampire as a poetic allegory of the two faces of modern love. The vampire incorporates both the eroticized death of the bedroom and the impersonal, nightly work of the whore. Like the prostitute who extracts money from her johns in exchange for alienated ecstasy, the nocturnal vampire seduces the poet with the promise of love only to suck the blood from his body and the marrow from his bones. Through its use of allegory, its divided formal structure, and its temporal message, "Les Métamorphoses du vampire" resembles "Le Masque" and evokes the allegorical concerns of "La Beauté." Like the feminine statue in "Le Masque," the inhuman feminine vampire is a duplicitous creature who ultimately reveals an unbearable aspect of modern temporality. But unlike "Le Masque," "Les Métamorphoses du vampire" is situated in a modern world that has lost all contact with the past. In this poem, we find no reassuring figures of classical beauty, no allusions to statuesque perfection, and no viable or reliable form of memory. Instead, in the first stanza, the vampire speaks. The feminine voice of the vampire—speaking in the present tense—seduces the poet by promising to simulate the lost temporal firmament. She says:

> —"Moi, j'ai la lèvre humide, et je sais la science
> De perdre au fond d'un lit l'antique conscience.
> Je sèche tous les pleurs sur mes seins triomphants,
> Et fais rire les vieux du rire des enfants.
> Je remplace, pour qui me voit nue et sans voiles,
> La lune, le soleil, le ciel et les étoiles! . . .

> [—"Me, I have a moist lip, and I know the science
> Of losing deep in a bed the ancient conscience.
> I dry all tears on my triumphant breasts,
> And I make old men laugh like children.
> I replace, for he who sees me naked and unveiled,
> The moon, the sun, the sky and the stars! . . .]

By selling her body as a substitute for the entire temporal firmament—including all of its heavenly lights—this vampire promises to incarnate the ultimate ecstasy. Although she mimics the allegorical voice of "Beauty," the vampire claims to surpass the power of Beauty. Where Beauty relies on the "pure artifice" of her formal perfection to stop time and shield the poet from the pain of reality, the vampire professes to reverse the passage of time and eliminate pain altogether. In short, this allegorical figure for "drugs" impersonates and displaces the function of the allegorical figure for "art." Furthermore, where Beauty creates a beautiful "lie" in the service of an eternal truth (the notion of eternity itself), the vampire lures the poet into a drugged stupor only to shatter his illusions by assaulting him with the shocking image of an uncompleted, living death.

In the second stanza of the poem, after the vampire has sucked the marrow from the poet's bones, his dream vision turns into a horrific, waking nightmare. He sees the body of his beloved decomposing before his very eyes. Although he tries to close his eyes to the unbearable sight before him, when he opens them again he finds that she has now become transformed into an animated skeleton that sings and dances like an automated machine:

> Quand elle eut de mes os sucé toute la moelle,
> Et que languissamment je me tournai vers elle
> Pour lui rendre un baiser d'amour, je ne vis plus

Qu'une outre aux flancs gluants, toute pleine de pus!
Je fermai les deux yeux, dans ma froide épouvante,
Et quand je les rouvris à la clarté vivante,
A mes côtés, au lieu du mannequin puissant
Qui semblait avoir fait provision de sang,
Tremblaient confusément des débris de squelette,
Qui d'eux-mêmes rendaient le cri d'une girouette
Ou d'une enseigne, au bout d'une tringle de fer,
Que balance le vent pendant les nuits d'hiver.

[When she had sucked all the marrow from my bones,
And, languishing, I turned to her
To give her back a kiss of love, I saw no more
Than a sticky-sided bag, all full of pus!
I closed both eyes, in my cold horror,
When I opened them again to the living light,
At my sides, in place of the powerful mannequin
Who seemed to have stocked up on blood,
There trembled a rubble of skeletal debris,
Which all by itself gave out the shriek of a weathervane
Or of a sign hanging off an iron rod,
Swinging in the wind on winter nights.]

At the beginning of this stanza, we discover that the vampire is not the only undead creature in this poem. In the very instant he turns to give her a "love kiss," the poet becomes forced to bear witness to his own dead life. His last look of love coincides with his last look at life. Here Baudelaire explicitly plays with the ambiguity of the expression "je ne vis plus." Depending on context, these words can either mean "I saw no more" or "I no longer live." Although the grammatical context here clearly dictates that the phrase "je ne vis plus" must mean "I saw no more," the very meaning of vision in the poem suggests that when his vision collapses, his life elapses. Furthermore, this phrase occurs at the end of the line where it creates an echo out of its two possible meanings and tenses. One is tempted to hear the muted echo of its double meaning thus: "I saw no more: (I no longer live)." In order to be able to distinguish between the past tense of the verb "voir" and the present tense of the verb "vivre," one would have to be able to distinguish between completed past events and the present moment. In "Les Petites vieilles" Baudelaire uses the same confusion between these two verbs (and the present and past tenses) to establish an empathetic connection between the poet and the old women:

Je vois s'épanouir vos passions novices;
Sombres ou lumineux, je vis vos jours perdus.

[I see blossom your novice passions;
Sombre or luminous, I live, I saw your lost days.]

Here, by bearing witness to the women's experience, the poet relives their experience in the act of having seen it. By looking at them, he recalls the (past) sight of their lost days and recollects those lost days by reliving them in the present. But in "Les Métamorphoses du vampire" there is no analagous form of recovered memory: there is no sense of the past and hence no possible difference between past and the present moments. When the poet sees his own death in the decomposing body of the vampire, he renounces perception and consciousness and closes his eyes in shock.

When he reopens his eyes to the "living light," he discovers nothing but the living ruins of death. Although he "sees" the dancing rubbish of bones, this final vision blurs the distinction between perception and hallucination. At the end of the poem, the poet's "sight" seems to fade; his vision is disrupted by the jarring noises made by the vampire's bones that scream like a weathervane spinning in the winter wind. The weathervane's metallic shriek is an alarming sign that something has happened to time. Likewise, in the tinny clatter of the skeleton's mechanical bones, we hear the ticking of a clock that can no longer keep time. But unlike the "metal throat" of the clock in "L'Horloge," this clock doesn't even tell the poet that it is time to die. Its confused death rattle chatters like the cold and empty echo of a dreary series of winter nights. The iron sounds of this machine recall the sounds of all mass-produced machines; we can hear the tired echoes of factory machines in it. It is no accident that the vehicle for this mechanical voice is a feminine figure.[33] The alluring siren who seduced the poet with a dream of time now speaks in her true voice: she is a mechanical instrument who wakes him up to the reality of an undying day.

Wake-up Calls

At long last we are ready to hear the woman's confession. In "Confession," Baudelaire's poet recalls how—on only one occasion—his beloved suddenly began to speak. The poem's opening stanzas ironically set the stage for this remarkable event through the evocation of amorous interludes couched in romantic clichés: the poet and his beloved are alone to-gether, it is late, and the full moon watches over the sleeping city of Paris. The romantic setting does not lead the couple to tender lovemaking; in-stead, it incites the woman to open her mouth in speech. As the first words of the poem attest ("Une fois, une seule"), it is critical to the poet (and the poem) that the woman speaks "only once." By insisting on the singular na-ture of the event, the poet removes her disturbing speech from the realm of lived life and prosaic conversation. He transforms her speech act into a story by transposing it into lyrical form. Because this epic event occurred only "once," it becomes a poetic subject worthy of memory and music. He remembers the event by retelling it in a poem filled with musical figures and instruments. In his lyrical recollection of the event, the woman does not speak in words, but in musical notes. He compares her to a harmo-nious musical intrument that suddenly plays an odd and disquieting note:

> Tout à coup, au milieu de l'intimité libre
> Éclose à la pâle clarté,
> De vous, riche et sonore instrument où ne vibre
> Que la radieuse gaieté,
>
> De vous, claire et joyeuse ainsi qu'une fanfare
> Dans le matin étincelant,
> Une note plaintive, une note bizarre
> S'échappa, tout en chancelant
>
> [Suddenly, amidst the intimate confidence
> Opened to the pale light,
> From you, rich resounding instrument ringing only
> With radiant gaiety,
>
> From you, clear and joyous as a trumpet-call
> In the sparkling dawn,
> A plaintive note, a note bizarre
> Escaped, staggering]

This poem is not, however, as "singular" as it appears to be. Its lyri-cal surface masks the fact that at the level of its plot, "Confession" retells the very same story we just encountered in "Les Métamorphoses du vam-pire." In both poems, the woman suddenly drops her mask of "joyous beauty" to reveal a figure ravaged by time. Both poems represent the voice of time as a shrill shriek that violently interrupts the erotic moment. In both poems, the feminine bodies become instruments of the shrieking sound of time. The inhuman voice of time is played on the female bodies; it passes through them, but does not actually belong to them. In "Les Métamorphoses du vampire," the iron voice of time vanquishes the poet and usurps his voice at the end of the poem. The poet in "Confession," however, parries the shock of this "scream" by metamorphosing it into a musical memory in the poem's first stanza. This poem appears to show Baudelaire's poet in the act of succesfully transforming the shock experience of *Erlebnis* into poetic *Erfahrung*.

But the confessional voice in the poem tells a slightly different story. The woman's confession exposes the fragility of the poet's command over the reality of time and the time of reality. Her message is quite prosaic, even mundane. The woman "confesses" that she can no longer continue to uphold the temporal firmament by incarnating an image of eternal "Beauty." The poet transcribes her voice thus:

> Pauvre ange, elle chantait, votre note criarde:
> "Que rien ici-bas n'est certain,
> Et que toujours, avec quelque soin qu'il se farde
> Se trahit l'égoïsme humain;
>
> "Que c'est un dur métier que d'être belle femme,
> Et que c'est le travail banal
> De la danseuse folle et froide qui se pâme
> Dans un sourire machinal;
>
> "Que bâtir sur les coeurs est une chose sotte;
> Que tout craque, amour et beauté,
> Jusqu'à ce que l'Oubli les jette dans sa hotte
> Pour les rendre à l'Éternité!"
>
>
> [Poor angel, she sang, your strident note:
> "Nothing is certain here below,
> And always, however carefully disguised,
> Human selfishness itself betrays;
>
> "A hard job it is to be a beautiful woman,
> And it is the menial work
> Of the mad and frigid dancer who swoons
> With a mechanical smile;
>
> "Building on the heart is a foolish thing;
> All cracks, love and beauty,
> Until Oblivion tosses them in his sack,
> To return them to Eternity!"]

Through her confession, the woman reveals that "being beautiful" is darned hard work. It doesn't come naturally, nor does it have anything to do with nature. She shows that she knows that the poet needs her to work at being beautiful so that he can keep time in place. But like a prostitute who is worn out after a long night's labor of giving pleasure to the masses, this beauty is exhausted. Being beautiful is a real grind; it is a "dur métier" and a "travail banal." In the confession of this tired woman, we can hear a remote echo of the unsung labor of modern workers: prostitutes and wage laborers. Like the woman who speaks here, neither the prostitute nor the worker can escape from the incessant shocks of daily experience. For the prostitute, pleasure has been deformed by work; for the laborer, work is devoid of substance and there is no time for pleasure. The job of the beautiful woman is not only hard work, but it is compared to a form of mechanical labor that mechanizes the worker. The image of a dancer coldly going through the motions of her dance with a "mechanical" smile plastered on her face recalls the automated dance of the mechanical bones in "Les Métamorphoses du vampire."

Like the lying vampire in that poem, this tired beauty not only fails to replace the poet's lost temporal firmament, but also exposes the fact that the vocation of being a modern poet is as tiring a job as that of being a beautiful woman. The traditional lyric is worn out and cracked at its foundations. Its two most cherished subjects—"love" and "beauty"—are as exhausted as she is; they have become figures of ruins and are destined to be forgotten until the end of time. Moreover, she is not the only tired figure in this poem, nor does the poem's "confession" belong solely to her. The poem's title, after all, is "Confession." Despite his attempts to parry the shock of her confession by setting it to music, Baudelaire's poet is, as we have seen, as tired as she is. Throughout *Les Fleurs du mal*, he wants nothing more than to go to sleep. As he puts it famously in "Le Léthé": "Je veux dormir! Dormir plutôt que vivre!" [I want to sleep! To sleep rather than live!].

But he can't sleep. And he can't die. When "vivre est un mal" and daily life is a living hell that is indistinguishable from death, death no longer offers the promise of repose. That is why, for Baudelaire, the antidote to life is not death, but sleep. So he takes drugs to forget and drinks to remember. But he never quite manages to forget enough; he never manages to forget that he can't remember the past. Nor can he ever stop hearing the shrieking voice of the present moment. Whenever a woman opens her mouth, no matter what she says, he always hears the same thing: "semper eadem," the sounds of the present moment ticking away. The vocal woman in Baudelaire's poems is not, as he claims in his journal, natural "comme des animaux." When she speaks, he cannot help but hear the pounding sounds of daily life in progress. Even the most flowery voice of the most beautiful woman always sounds to him like the metallic ticking of an infernal clock. So all he can do is tell her to "shut up."

By invoking a long lyric tradition founded upon the trope of the beloved beauty's remote silence, Baudelaire relies on classical poetic devices to close her mouth and transform her body into the shining star of his lost temporal firmament. Because he needs her to contain the voice of time, he injects that inhuman voice into her body precisely so that he can tell it to shut up. Baudelaire is able to do this because he finds the idea that she might have a voice of "her own" absurd. His diaries make clear that for him, a "speaking woman" is an oxymoron. This is why her body makes an ideal vessel ("vase" or "gourde") with which he contains the sound of that voice. But neither the poet, nor his poetry, can entirely shut up the voice of the present day that passes through her. Although he attempts to silence the voice of time through the figure of the woman's body, that same repressed voice returns to haunt his poems through the figure of the talking clock.

The chatter of clocks can be heard throughout *Les Fleurs du mal.* Always anthropomorphic figures, clocks cough, rattle, sigh, scream, and scold. In "Spleen (IV)" angry church bells—abandoned by the gods—address their exiled rage to the empty sky:

> Des cloches tout à coup sautent avec furie
> Et lancent vers le ciel un affreux hurlement,
> Ainsi que des esprits errants et sans patrie
> Qui se mettent à geindre opiniâtrement.

> [Bells suddenly leap with fury
> And hurl heavenwards an awful howl,
> Like souls wandering with no homeland
> Arise stubbornly to moan.]

In "Spleen (I)," a sick clock plays a part in a discordant musical ensemble:

> Le bourdon se lamente, et la bûche enfumée
> Accompagne en fausset la pendule enrhumée.

> [The great bell tolls, and the smoking log
> Accompanies in falsetto the wheezing clock.]

In "Rêve parisien," the sounds of the noonday clock shake the poet from his blissful dream. This clock rings in the tired collapse of the temporal firmament:

> La pendule aux accents funèbres
> Sonnait brutalement midi,
> Et le ciel versait des ténèbres
> Sur le triste monde engourdi.

> [The clock, with funereal accents,
> Brutally sounded noon,
> And the sky shed shadows
> On the sad benumbed world.]

Thus, it is certainly no accident that the cycle of poems called "Spleen et Idéal" concludes with the allegorical voice of the clock in "L'Horloge." In that poem, the moment the poet invokes the clock through the emphatic apostrophe "Horloge! dieu sinistre," he loses control over his own voice. The clock starts ticking like a *machina ex deo*. The voice of this machine tells time instead of keeping it. For Baudelaire, telling time is a speech act from hell. The act of telling time makes it both unusable and unbearable. When time is told, it multiplies and divides into smaller and smaller units of a "present moment" that speed toward death without moving:

> Trois mille six cents fois par heure, la Seconde
> Chuchote: "Souviens-toi!"—Rapide, avec sa voix
> D'insecte, Maintenant dit: Je suis Autrefois,
> Et j'ai pompé ta vie avec ma trompe immonde!

> [Three thousand six hundred times an hour, the Second
> Whispers: "Remember!"—Quick, with its
> Insect voice, Now says: I am Past,
> And I have sucked out your life with my foul prong!]

Although the present moment that thus repeats itself mechanically orders one "to remember" to live, the very velocity of its actuality makes life impossible. The clock's incessant imperative "remember" leaves no time for memory. Without a temporal firmament to hold the past in place, the present moment falls out of time and cannot be remembered. The diabolical voice of this fallen present can only remind us that when the temporality of "life" is reduced to an empty stutter, it has already passed over into death. Every minute tick of this clock conveys the shock experience: it is an unstoppable alarm clock that keeps us awake in order to remind us to die.

In the final poem of the "Tableaux parisiens," Baudelaire depicts how the shock experience leaves its mark on the living inhabitants of Paris. Not surprisingly, "Le Crépuscule du matin" begins with a "wake-up" call intoned by a feminine voice:

> La diane chantait dans les cours des casernes,
> Et le vent du matin soufflait sur les lanternes.

> [Daybreak sang in the barrack yards,
> And the morning wind blew on the lamps.]

This daybreak call, however, does not usher in a new morning. There is nothing new about this day—it follows the "nuit blanche" of a sleepless night and is the continuation of it. The garish night light of the illuminated street lamp is compared to a bloody, tired eye that cannot bear the bright light of the morning sun:

> Où, comme un oeil sanglant qui palpite et qui bouge,
> La lampe sur le jour fait une tache rouge

> [Where, like a bloody eye which throbs and moves,
> The lamp makes a red stain on the day]

Like an eye that winces in pain, the light of the lamp deposits a bloody bruise on the light of the day.

"Le Crépuscule du matin" is filled with extraordinary images of ordinary people who experience fatigue, grief, and anxiety in their daily life. Baudelaire depicts the nocturnal dreams of adolescent boys who attain solitary ecstasy in their beds:

> C'était l'heure où l'essaim des rêves malfaisants
> Tord sur leurs oreillers les bruns adolescents;

> [It was the hour when the swarm of nasty dreams
> Twists on their pillows the dark young men;]

He expresses the lonely sadness of these nocturnal contortions through the verb "tord." Throughout *Les Fleurs du mal*, Baudelaire often uses the word "tordre" in place of the verb "dormir."[34] No one finds rest here. Even in sleep, through their open mouths, the whores expose the mute obscenity of their lives to the light of day:

> Les femmes de plaisir, la paupière livide,
> Bouche ouverte, dormaient de leur sommeil stupide.

[The women of pleasure, with livid lid,
Open mouthed, slept their stupid sleep.]

As the rest of the city prepares to go to work, the night revellers return wearily to their homes, exhausted by their laborious pursuit of pleasure: "Les débauchés rentraient, brisés par leur travaux." In this old morning, everyone is tired. The man is sick of writing and the woman is sick of love: "Et l'homme est las d'écrire et la femme d'aimer."

But underneath this fatigue, we can hear the muffled sounds of grief. The poem depicts these sounds as the sobs of a person who wakes up crying. As Benjamin observes, "'Le Crépuscule du matin' is the sobbing of an awakening person reproduced through the material of a city."[35] The people who are awakened by their own sobs no longer remember why they are crying. The atmosphere of the city is saturated with these tears of forgotten loss:

Comme un visage en pleurs que les brises essuient,
L'air est plein du frisson des choses qui s'enfuient.

[Like a face in tears dried by the breeze,
The air is aquiver with fleeting things.]

Les Fleurs du mal transcribes Baudelaire's complicated response to this collective memory loss. We have seen that Benjamin derives his description of the memory loss of modernity through the figure of Baudelaire's dueling poet who redefines poetic labor by using the form of the lyric to parry the shock of urban experience and contemporary modes of communication. But in his poetic depiction of women, Baudelaire redefines the work of the modern lyric in different ways. By looking at how he requires that his female figures uphold his sense of time, we can appreciate the range—and the extent—of his exhausting labor to surmount the shock experience. Furthermore, we have seen that Baudelaire's feminine figures reveal the failures of his labor as well as some of the more dubious consequences of his apparent successes. Paradoxically, it is through these failures that he speaks most clearly to us today. In his attempt to ward off the shock of lost time by denying it, Baudelaire provides us with a resonant poetic description of how fetishism, addiction, and latent misogyny have been woven into the temporal fabric of contemporary culture and experience. Through the strains of his speaking women, he gives a poetic voice to the quotidian dimension of shock. In his need to suffuse sex with death, he asks us to look at the temporal foundations of our erotic lives. The inhuman voice of time that passes through the body of Baudelaire's women wakes us up and reminds us not to forget to think about how failed expressions of time and memory continue to speak through the lived experiences of our present day.

2

Flat Death: Snapshots of History

Simply put, we might be tempted to call history that which has passed away—but any reflection on and of history encounters the trauma of how to be present not only to what has passed, but also to the activity of its passing. Both Baudelaire's "A une passante" and Roland Barthes's *Camera Lucida* are motivated by an impossible address to a female figure who has, as we say, "passed away." Baudelaire's sonnet "A une passante" is a lyric poem addressed to the figure of a woman who, having already "passed," cannot be present to receive the poem's address. *Camera Lucida*, Barthes's "note" on the ontology of photography, is centered and decentered by his attempt to speak about the death of his mother through a reflection on a photograph of her and on photography more generally. In both texts, the attempt to be present to a passing through the activity of mourning opens up the problem of how to represent history. The deaths which precede these two works are not figured by a passage, but rather by a ghostly, perpetually repeated and even mechanical "passing." In both these works, the activity of passing is repeated to the point of immobility and history is represented as "cliché." But instead of looking at these two works directly, we shall begin by looking at how Walter Benjamin sees the representation of history in "A une passante." By examining the traces of a "hidden figure" in Benjamin's reading of "A une passante," read through a series of relayed looks, we shall find that Benjamin uncovers a figure of history buried in this poem.

The Widow

One should not read Walter Benjamin's writings on Baudelaire with-out being startled by his reading of the sonnet "A une passante." His presentation of the poem occupies a pivotal position in the 1938 essay "The Paris of the Second Empire," as well as in the 1939 revision "Some Motifs in Baudelaire." In both essays, "A une passante" is the only poem from *Les Fleurs du mal* that Benjamin quotes in its entirety. But although he reproduces the entire poem in both texts, his discussion of it concentrates primarily on a figure that the poem never directly names or represents. In order to understand what is at stake in his reading of this poem, as well as why it remains the cornerstone of all of his work on Baudelaire, we must begin by understanding that Benjamin's reading strategy is inextricable from the conclusions it enables him to reach.[1] As Benjamin insists incessantly, "A une passante" must be read as a negative image, in relief, as it were, through the absence of its central figure—the crowd. In "Some Motifs in Baudelaire" he introduces the poem by claiming that "the masses had become so much a part of Baudelaire that it is rare to find a description of them in his works. His most important subjects are hardly ever encountered in descriptive form."[2] To say that Benjamin reads the poem "as a negative image" is to claim that his specificity as both reader and thinker must be traced through this peculiar insistence on traces of absent figures. As the example of the crowd illustrates, Benjamin often bases his exegesis of Baudelaire by pointing out, with remarkable precision, the importance of specific details that Baudelaire leaves out of his poems.[3] Like the ancient prophets who attempted to read the future in the entrails of certain animals, Benjamin reads "modernity" in the traces of poetic history that Baudelaire leaves in his wake. In the "Motifs" essay he writes: "This crowd, of whose existence Baudelaire is always aware, has not served as the model for any of his works, but is imprinted on his creativity as a hidden figure [*als verborgene Figur eingeprägt*]."[4] By tracking the imprints of a "hidden figure" in Benjamin's reading of "A une passante," we shall be able to read traces of a conception of the relationship among allegory, modernity, and history that Benjamin might have made more explicit had he lived to complete the project of the *Passagen-Werk*.

Why, we might begin by asking, does Benjamin insist on reading this particular poem as a medium for his presentation of the motif of the crowd? As he himself points out, "In the sonnet 'A une passante' the crowd is nowhere named in either word or phrase. And yet the whole happening hinges on it, just as the progress of a sailing-boat depends on the wind."[5] Through his analogy, Benjamin implies that the action depicted in the poem, like the progress of the ship to which he compares it, is primarily a medium for rendering visible an ineffable force that motivates it. Without a ship's sail, one can neither see the wind nor measure its velocity. For Benjamin, the action of the poem, like the sailboat's "progress," is read in its resistance to the force of the crowd through which the passing figure passes. Instead of focusing on the figure of the passing woman, he looks at the force (the mass of the crowd) through which her passage can be marked. By looking past her to the crowd, Benjamin turns our attention to what must have been passing around her and hence "present" to the eyes of the one who watches her. He goes on to discuss how the erotic encounter between the passing woman and the one who watches her is facilitated, rather than hindered, by the force of the crowd. It is the presence of the crowd itself that engenders this experience of modern love. In the "Motifs" essay he writes: "The delight of the urban poet is love—not at first sight, but at last sight. It is a farewell forever which coincides in the poem with the moment of enchantment. Thus the sonnet supplies the figure of shock, even of catastrophe . . . like the kind of sexual shock that can beset a lonely man."[6] Throughout his reading, Benjamin is consistently less concerned with the figure of the passing woman than with the impact that her passage produces on the one who watches her. For him, the force of the erotic encounter, as well as the poem it produces, can only be read in the aftershock of that encounter. His reading relies upon a dual structure of delayed action and relayed looks—Benjamin looks at the imprint of the wake of her passage reflected in the eyes of the one who watched her pass.

But it is curious that Benjamin appears to bypass the description of the passing woman almost altogether. While he does point out that she is in mourning (and we will return to this point in some detail later), he never refers to the poem's descriptions of her movement, "Agile et noble, avec sa jambe de statue,"[7] nor, more surprisingly still, to the fact that the final two tercets of the poem are, however impossibly, addressed to her. In his belated address to her (she is gone before he starts to speak), the poet calls out to the woman by calling her "fugitive beauté." The phrase "fugitive beauté" immediately links the figure of the "passante" to Baudelaire's definition of modernity in the essay "The Painter of Modern Life." Why does Benjamin choose not to comment on the obvious echoes between the invocation of a "fleeting beauty" in the poem and Baudelaire's definition of modernity as "fleeting beauty" in "The Painter of Modern Life"? Not only does Benjamin know the essay extremely well (he quotes from it constantly), but he uses that very essay as the foundation for his discussions of the flâneur, the crowd, and Poe's story "The Man of the Crowd" in both of his own essays on Baudelaire. We can only assume (and this assumption will be borne out by what follows) that Benjamin's silence concerning the figure of the "fleeting beauty" in the poem marks the site of a trace of a reading of Baudelaire's definition of modernity. By choosing to focus on this particular poem and by refusing to present it according to the paradigms that would be familiar to any reader of Baudelaire's discussion of modernity, Benjamin effectively *preempts* a reading that would claim that "A une passante" should be read as a poetic incarnation of Baudelaire's definition of modernity. The hidden figures embedded in Benjamin's reading of "A une passante" will allow us to read how, instead of relying on this poem in order to demonstrate Baudelaire's definition of modernity, Benjamin uses this poem precisely in order to challenge it.

In the 1938 essay "The Paris of the Second Empire in Baudelaire," Benjamin launches a direct attack on Baudelaire's definition of modernity in "The Painter of Modern Life." But the logic of this attack is so opaque that it provokes a critic as astute as Hans Robert Jauss to accuse Benjamin of a "violent" misreading of Baudelaire. Jauss begins his essay "Reflections on the Chapter 'Modernity' in Benjamin's Baudelaire Fragments" with the bold assertion that "it is paradoxical that Baudelaire's theory of modernity should have been misunderstood by the very critic whose work has done the most to propel us toward a new understanding of that poet."[8] While it would be impossible to enter into the specifics of Jauss's argument without presenting a systematic analysis of the Baudelaire essay in relation to both Jauss and Benjamin, and while I believe that Jauss is wrong in his assessment that Benjamin "misunderstood" Baudelaire's theory of modernity, I point to Jauss's claim in order to stress the fact that Benjamin's argument is anything but self-evident. In the section entitled "Modernism" in "The Paris of the Second Empire," Benjamin quotes and glosses Baudelaire's definition of modernity as follows:

And in the final passage on Guys he says: "Everywhere he sought the transitory, fleeting beauty of our present life, the character of what the reader has permitted us to call *modernism*." In summary form, his doctrine reads as follows: "A constant, unchangeable element . . . and a relative, limited element cooperate to produce beauty. . . . The latter element is supplied by the epoch, by fashion, by morality and the passions. Without this second element . . . the first would not be assimilable." One can hardly say that this is a profound analysis [*Man kann nicht sagen, dass das in die Tiefe geht*]. In Baudelaire's view of modernism, the theory of modern art is the weakest point. . . . None of the aesthetic reflections in Baudelaire's theory of art presented modernism in its interpenetration [*Durchdringung*] with classical antiquity, something that was done in certain poems of the *Fleurs du mal.*[9]

It is rare, to say the least, to find Benjamin passing judgment on Baudelaire's thinking with a one-line verdict like "This is not a profound analysis." It is equally rare to find him abdicating the position of Baudelaire's ideal reader; when Baudelaire invokes the reader's permission to call the "transitory, fleeting beauty of our present life . . . modernism," Benjamin refuses to accord him that permission. In short, it would seem that Benjamin accuses Baudelaire-the-theorist of having a superficial appreciation of Baudelaire-the-poet's articulation of modernity. Benjamin's dissatisfaction would seem to lie in the way in which Baudelaire isolates the "constant, unchangeable element" from the "transitory, fleeting . . . element supplied by the epoch." For Benjamin, these two elements can never be understood as discrete entities—each element exists only in relation to the other—in the structure of what he calls here *Durchdringung*. By understanding *Durchdringung* as a forceful permeation, we understand that modernism exists for Benjamin only to the degree that it is thoroughly stamped with the marks of classical antiquity.

In the very next paragraph, Benjamin explains that the more precise name for this penetrating process is allegory.

Among these the poem "Le Cygne" is paramount. It is no accident that it is an allegory. The city which is in constant flux grows rigid. It becomes as brittle and as transparent as glass—that is, as far as its meaning is concerned—"The form of the city, alas, changes more quickly than a mortal's heart. ". . . The stature of Paris is fragile; it is surrounded by symbols of fragility—living creatures (the negress and the swan) and historical figures (Andromache, "widow of Hector and wife of Helenus"). Their common feature is sadness about what was and lack of hope for what is to come. In the final analysis, this decrepitude [*Hinfalligkeit*] constitutes the closest connection between modernism and antiquity. Whenever Paris occurs in the *Fleurs du mal*, it bears the signs of this decrepitude.[10]

In the 1935 "exposé," "Paris—Capital of the Nineteenth Century," in letters to Horkheimer, Scholem, and Adorno, as well as in numerous fragments of the *Passagen-Werk*, Benjamin reiterates that his interest in

Baudelaire is first and foremost motivated by Baudelaire's distinctive use of classical allegory in his depiction of modernity. In the 1935 outline, the chapter on Baudelaire bears the epigraph "Tout pour moi devient allé-gorie" (Everything for me becomes allegory) from "Le Cygne" (The Swan), and in the first sentence of the outline he writes: "Baudelaire's ge-nius, which drew its nourishment from melancholy, was an allegorical one."[11] In a letter to Horkheimer dated 16 April 1938, Benjamin describes his project on Baudelaire as follows:

The work will be in three parts. Their projected titles are: "Idea and Image"; "Antique and Modern"; "The New and the Immutable." The first part will demonstrate the crucial importance of allegory for *The Flowers of Evil*. . . . The sec-ond part develops the fade-in/fade-out effect as a structural element of the alle-gorical vision [*der allegorischen Anschauung die Uberblendung*]. As a consequence of this effect, antiquity is revealed in modernity, and modernity in antiquity.[12]

Moreover, it was precisely in relation to the question of allegory that Benjamin claimed that Baudelaire had been consistently misread. In the *Passagen-Werk* he notes: "Baudelaire's allegorical way of looking at things was not understood by any of his contemporaries and, consequently, ulti-mately failed to be noticed altogether."[13] Keeping these examples in mind, we can now understand that Benjamin's critique of Baudelaire's articulation of modernity in the "Painter of Modern Life" is primarily concerned with the absence there of an articulation of the role of allegory in Baudelaire's definition of modernity.

Benjamin's systematic invocation of the poem "Le Cygne" as the priv-ileged example of allegory in Baudelaire is *not* fundamentally based, as one might expect, on the fact that the word "allegory" actually appears in the poem. For Benjamin, the allegorical quality of the poem resides in the poem's depiction of the city. As he remarks in his discussion of "Le Cygne," the city "becomes as brittle and as transparent as glass. . . . The stature of Paris is fragile; it is surrounded by symbols of fragility—living creatures (the negress and the swan) and historical figures (Andromache, 'widow of Hector and wife of Helenus')." The invisible but overpowering presence of the ruins of Troy in the poem shatters the newly built city of Paris at the level of its mythic foundation.[14] The image of the modern city is superim-posed on the rubble of the ancient one—thus the modernity of the new city must be read through the figure of its past and future decrepitude. In a fragment from the *Passagen-Werk*, Benjamin revises Baudelaire's definition of modernity by invoking the figure of "ruins" to collapse Baudelaire's distinction between a "constant, unchanging element" and a "fleeting, transitory" element. He writes: "The experience of allegory, which holds on to ruins, is, actually, that of the eternally transitory."[15] Benjamin reads Baudelaire's allegory to show that history is not the site of solid foundations but of ruins—it is no less fleeting than modernity. History is as fleeting as a bad dream that never fails to recur and allegory is the form that that bad dream takes. In the *Passagen-Werk* he writes: "Modernity has antiquity as one has a demon, which came over one in sleep."[16]

Thus, Benjamin invokes "Le Cygne" to prove that Baudelaire's poetic use of allegory challenges his own definition of modernity in "The Painter of Modern Life." How does Benjamin's discussion of allegory and modernity in "Le Cygne" relate to our initial question concerning the "hidden figure" in his reading of "A une passante" in the "Motifs" essay? And why, given his repeated claims (in the 1935 exposé, in the *Passagen-Werk*, in the letters, and in the 1938 essay "The Paris of the Second Empire") that Baudelaire's use of allegory is the determining factor in his poetic depiction of modernity, does Benjamin make no explicit reference in the "Motifs" essay either to allegory or to the poem that can be read as its insignia, "Le Cygne"? The most obvious explanation for this omission is, of course, that the 1939 "Motifs" essay was conceived as a revision of only the "Flâneur" portion of the 1938 "Second Empire" essay: the passages that we examined from the "modernity" portion of the earlier essay were never intended to be part of the "Motifs" revision. Nonetheless, one tiny but significant trace of Benjamin's discussion of allegory, modernity, and history emerges in the "Motifs" essay in his presentation of the "passante" poem. As I said at the outset, "A une passante" is the only poem from *Les Fleurs du mal* that Benjamin quotes in its entirety in both the "Second Empire" and the "Motifs" essays. In both essays Benjamin presents the poem in order to introduce a discussion of the hidden figure of the crowd. By adding one significant detail to his reading of the poem in the "Motifs" essay, Benjamin directs us to read "A une passante" through his reading of "Le Cygne." In the opening lines of his analysis of "A une passante" in the "Second Empire" essay, he writes:

This sonnet presents the crowd not as the refuge of a criminal but as that of love which eludes the poet. One may say that it deals with the function of the crowd not in the life of the citizen, but in the life of the erotic person.[17]

But in the "Motifs" essay, he adds:

In a *widow's* veil, mysteriously and mutely borne along by the crowd, an unknown woman comes into the poet's field of vision. What the sonnet communicates is simply this: far from experiencing the crowd as an opposed, antagonistic element, this very crowd brings to the city dweller the figure that fascinates.[18] (italics mine)

Benjamin's invocation of the word "widow" is surprising because while the poem does refer to the fact that the passing woman is in mourning ("en grand deuil"), there is nothing in the poem to indicate that the mourning woman is a "widow." It could be argued that one of the most compelling aspects of the poem is the fact that the passing woman mourns a death that is itself shrouded in mystery. Why does Benjamin, who is the very epitome of the meticulous reader and who had previously referred to the "passante" as "a female apparition in mourning,"[19] now decide to give a name to the source of her mourning?

The simplest explanation would be to recall that Benjamin reads the erotic encounter depicted in the poem as an encounter characterized by loss. He argues that the poem does not speak of love at first sight, but rather "love at last sight." For Benjamin, "A une passante" is not merely a poem about love, but rather a poem about looking for love in all the wrong places (the street) and about losing it in the very moment it has been found. In the *Passagen-Werk* he repeatedly comments on the fact that Baudelaire modernizes the lyric by suffusing the love poem with images of sexual perversion.[20] By claiming that the mourning woman is a widow, he suggests that the erotic loss narrated in the poem was already figured in the widow's prior loss of her husband. The figure of the "lost husband" would thus stand as a synecdoche for the specifically *erotic* nature of the loss (as distinct from the loss of a non-eroticized object).

But another explanation for Benjamin's decision to cast the mourning woman in the role of a widow brings us back to our discussion of the relationship between antiquity and modernity in "Le Cygne." For while there is no explicit mention of a widow in "A une passante," in "Le Cygne," the apostrophe to the widow, Andromache, constitutes the poetic source of the poem.[21] The entire poem emerges out of reflections cast in the stream of the widow's tears:

> Andromaque, je pense à vous! Ce petit fleuve,
> Pauvre et triste miroir où jadis resplendit
> L'immense majesté de vos douleurs de veuve,

Ce Simoïs menteur qui par vos pleurs grandit,
A fécondé soudain ma mémoire fertile. . . . (*OC* 1:85)

[Andromache, I think of you! This small river,
Sad and meager mirror where long ago,
The boundless majesty of your widow's grief glittered,
This lying Simois, which swelled with your tears,
Has quickened my memory. . . .]

Read through the widow's veil, Benjamin encourages us to read "A une passante" as a palimpsest superimposed upon the ancient ruins of "Le Cygne." The bustling streets depicted in the first poem are haunted by the rubble of Troy invoked in the second one. Seen in this light, "A une passante" presents a vision of modernity that is permeated by the decay of history. In both poems, the city only becomes visible when it is seen through the veil of a mourning woman. Through the widow's veil, Benjamin invites us to read the stasis of modernity across the transitory flight of history.

In the *Passagen-Werk* Benjamin defines the figure of the crowd as an allegory of modernity and the figure of the city as an allegory of antiquity: "In Baudelaire, Paris stands as an emblem of antiquity, in contrast to his crowd, as emblem of the modern."[22] But, as our reading of Benjamin's reading of "A une passante" demonstrates, there is no simple historical progression *from* antiquity *to* modernity; they are frozen together in the form of a kind of static repetition. Instead of presenting history as a fluid movement, Benjamin conceives of Baudelaire's depiction of history in architectural terms: history is seen as the rigid scaffold which binds allegorical antiquity to modernity. In one of the most opaque fragments of the *Passagen-Werk*, Benjamin suggests that this construction of history, in Baudelaire, can only be understood nondialectically: "The correspondence between antiquity and modernity is the only constructive conception of history in Baudelaire. Through its rigid armature, it excluded every dialectical one" [Die Korrespondenz zwischen Antike und Moderne ist die einzige konstruktive Geschichtkonzeption bei Baudelaire. Durch ihre starre Armatur schloss sie jede dialektische aus].[23] If we recall Benjamin's discussion of the function of allegory in "Le Cygne," we remember that, for Benjamin, history becomes visible when modernity is petrified by antiquity: "The city which is in constant flux grows rigid. It becomes as brittle and as transparent as glass." The very rigidity of this structure renders it both brittle and fragile. If history cannot be conceived of in dialectical terms here, it is because the petrification process cancels out the possibility of movement. Rather than appearing as the movement through which progress can be marked, this historical construction recalls the ossification of ruins. And it is no accident that the widow is the privileged witness to this model of history: the death that she mourns is, as Barthes will later say of the photograph, nondialectical; it is as irrevocable and static as the image of history that appears refracted through her veil.

The Widow's Veil and the Photographic Cliché

In a letter dated 2 August 1935, written in response to the (1935) draft of the exposé for the Arcades Project, Theodor Adorno writes to Walter Benjamin: "I find the passage about the crowd as a veil wonderful." In that early text (which makes no mention of "A une passante") Benjamin had written: "The crowd was the veil from behind which the familiar city as phantasmagoria beckoned to the *flâneur.*"[24] Given his later reproach that Benjamin's "Second Empire" essay suffered from an excess of "immediate . . . materialism" compounded by the absence of a mediating theory,[25] it is not surprising that Adorno should have particularly appreciated the figure of the crowd as veil. In the "Motifs" essay Benjamin writes: "The mass was the agitated veil; through it Baudelaire saw Paris."[26] In attributing the figure of the veil to Baudelaire, instead of to the flâneur, Benjamin links this veiled vision to the experience of shock. At the end of the "Motifs" essay, he argues that while the flâneur is seduced and "bedazzled" by the "lustre of the crowd," Baudelaire "was no flâneur"; he "singled out his having been jostled by the crowd as the decisive, unique experience. . . . This is the nature of something lived through (*Erlebnis*) to which Baudelaire has given the weight of an experience (*Erfahrung*)."[27] Paradoxically, the veil intensifies, rather than filters, the shock of experience.

But the figure of the veil also serves as the medium through which Benjamin links the structure of repetition and relayed looks in "A une passante" to Baudelaire's place in literary history. In "A une passante," the veil—the mark of death which separates the face of the woman from the look of the other—becomes the bearer of a relayed reflection of everything that passes around it. The mourner's veil functions like a mechanical mirror—or photographic apparatus—that turns our gaze away from the (perhaps nonexistent) face of the woman and back onto the amorphous crowd which is "present" all around her. It is via our gazing at the veil that the "present" is represented. Through her veil, which is itself the mark of a prior passage, we can see that which could never otherwise be seen: the experience of the present.

Benjamin addresses the historical figure of Baudelaire in terms that recall those employed by the narrator of "A une passante" in his address to the figure of the passing woman. "Some Motifs in Baudelaire" attempts to speak about the historical passing of lyric poetry by staging an encounter with Baudelaire, whom Benjamin calls the last lyric poet. In the final section of "Some Motifs in Baudelaire," Benjamin enumerates the factors that contribute to Baudelaire's privileged position in relation to both lyric poetry and history. He writes:

Les Fleurs du mal was the last lyric work that had a European repercussion; no later work penetrated beyond a more or less limited linguistic area . . . , it cannot be denied that some of his lyric motifs—and the present study has dealt with them—render the possibility of lyric poetry questionable. These . . . facts define Baudelaire historically. They show that he imperturbably stuck to his cause and single-mindedly concentrated on his mission. He went so far as to proclaim his goal "the creation of a cliché."[28]

Benjamin's essay both begins and ends with this reiteration that Baudelaire was the "last lyric poet." But because Baudelaire is the last lyric poet, he is not merely historicized within the context of lyric poetry, but speaks of and to the problem of history. One might even say that Benjamin's essay is nothing other than an attempt to develop (as one develops a photograph) an image of history that he finds reflected in the relayed gaze of the figure of its last lyric poet.[29] Benjamin reads the passing of lyric poetry by looking through the veil of Baudelaire's experience of the city and the crowd. Baudelaire cannot simply be the "last lyric poet" because that position would imply the possibility that lyric poetry is still "present" in Baudelaire, a claim that Benjamin disputes when he writes that "some of his lyric motifs . . . render the possibility of lyric poetry questionable." Instead of being the last lyric poet, Baudelaire becomes lyric poetry's first simulacrum—its first stuttering ghost.

It is at this juncture that we can begin to understand why Benjamin ends his essay by insisting that Baudelaire proclaimed his goal to be the "creation of a cliché." But what does the word "cliché" literally mean and where does it come from? The word that is translated in English as "cliché" appears as the word "poncif" in Baudelaire's original French text.[30] While the connotations of the word "poncif" are almost identical to those of the

English word "cliché," the French word "poncif" has a very long history (the *Petit Robert* gives it the date 1551), whereas the word "cliché" (imported from French into English) relates directly to the technological advances (the printing press) and inventions (photography) of the nineteenth century.[31] But unlike the English word "stencil" (which is what a *poncif* is), the French word "poncif" carries the connotation of a piece of work that lacks all originality. That Benjamin should have placed so great an emphasis on Baudelaire's characteristically perverse desire to "create a cliché" is a testimony to his insight into Baudelaire's position in literary history.[32]

Paradoxically, a look at the history of the word ("cliché") that appears in the English translation of Benjamin's text may bring us closer to Benjamin's understanding of history than either the word "poncif" used in the Baudelaire's original French text or the word "*Schablone*" used in Benjamin's original German one. The English word has itself become a cliché—meaning that it has been endlessly reproduced and reiterated (keeping its French voice as it passes into English) to the point where the traces of its material history have been effaced. But embedded in the history of this word is a condensed history of the evolution of mechanical reproduction. The French word "cliché" first emerges at the outset of the nineteenth century and its meaning evolves throughout the nineteenth century and into the beginning of the twentieth century. *Le Petit Robert* informs us that the word "cliché" first appears around 1809 and it was initially used in the context of typography.[33] Then, in 1865 (eight years after the first publication of *Les Fleurs du mal* and corresponding with the growth and emergence of photography), a new definition appears: "negative image. see negative." The word "negative" presumably denotes the noun "photographic negative"—the inverted image through which we are able to make endless "positive" copies. In 1869 (according to the dubious chronology of the dictionary), we find that "cliché" finally assumes the definition through which we know it today: "Figurative and pejorative. An idea or expression that is used too often. A banality, a *Lieu commun*." What we find buried in the history of the word "cliché" is a certain passage from the mechanical reproduction of letters to that of photographs, coupled with an emphasis upon an image which is cast in relief—what I have referred to as a "negative image." It is this model of "cliché," in which the notion of mechanical reproduction is linked to that of a negative image, that determines both Benjamin's reading of Baudelaire and his articulation of history. Like the frozen passage between modernity and antiquity that we found embedded in Benjamin's reading of "A une passante," the word "cliché" condenses the history of the development of mechanical reproduction and freezes the representation of that history into the rigid scaffold of a single imprinted word. Furthermore, the activity of that freezing process is precisely that of the photographic "click." As Benjamin writes in the "Motifs" essay:

> Of the countless movements of switching, inserting, pressing, and the like, the "snapping" of the photographer has had the greatest consequences. A touch of the finger now sufficed to fix an event for an unlimited period of time. The camera gave the moment a posthumous shock, as it were.[34]

Not only does Benjamin claim that Baudelaire wanted to "create a cliché," but he supports that claim by focusing his reading of Baudelaire on images presented in "cliché": he reads the *lieu commun* or common space (the street) that is presented in Baudelaire through its negative images. Only by reading "A une passante" as a negative image, presented in relief, can Benjamin read the crowd as the primary (albeit negative) figure of the poem. And it is only by reading Benjamin's reading of "A une passante" as a "cliché" that we understand how the modernity of "A une passante" is imprinted with the traces of the allegorical antiquity of "Le Cygne."

If we retain the memory of the notion of the "negative image" in the word "cliché," we can begin to see how Benjamin reads history, through the figure of Baudelaire, as cliché. In the most complex and enigmatic lines of the "Motifs" essay, Benjamin attempts to describe how to read a change in the structure of experience. In an attempt to describe how history is represented in the passage from Bergson's supposedly ahistorical account of the structure of memory to Baudelaire's poetic "cliché" of history, Benjamin writes:

> It is, however, not at all Bergson's intention to attach any specific historical label to memory. On the contrary, he rejects any historical determination of memory. He thus manages to stay clear of that experience from which his own philosophy evolved or, rather, in reaction to which it arose. It was the inhospitable, blinding age of big-scale industrialism. In shutting out this experience the eye perceives an experience of a complementary nature in the form of its spontaneous after-image, as it were [Dem Auge, das sich vor dieser Erfahrung schliesst, stellt sich eine Erfahrung komplementärer Art als deren gleichsam spontanes Nachbild ein]. Bergson's philosophy represents an attempt to give details of this after-image and to fix it as a permanent record. His philosophy thus indirectly furnishes a clue to the experience which presented itself to Baudelaire's eyes in its undistorted version in the figure of his reader [Sie gibt derart mittelbar einen Hinweis auf die Erfahrung, die Baudelaire unverstellt, in der Gestalt seines Lesers, vor Augen tritt].[35]

Benjamin's reading of the view of history that can be developed in the passage between Bergson's philosophy and Baudelaire's reader mirrors the structure of a photographic apparatus and recalls his reading of the negative image of history in "A une passante." Benjamin locates the imprint of history on Bergson's philosophy in the very gesture through which Bergson attempted to blot it out. It is "the blinding age" that forces Bergson to shut his eyes to the historical dimension of memory. But because he shuts his eyes in response to the blinding flash of history, his shut eyes perform the role of a photographic shutter: they retain the blotted image and allow it to be recorded (negatively) despite the fact that the recorded image was never seen directly. The trace of history that Bergson's philosophy records can only be seen when it is "developed" through the gaze of the figure of Baudelaire's reader. In order to read the trace of this photographic cliché of history, we shall return, once again, to "A une passante."

If we have not yet looked directly at "A une passante," it is because it is not clear what one can see by looking directly at it. The central event in the poem occurs in the ellipsis of a blinding flash: "Un éclair . . . puis la nuit!" (A flash . . . then night!). But by following Benjamin's attempt to develop the negative image of history that is represented in it, we shall read this poem as Baudelaire's written photograph of history as cliché.

> La rue assourdissante autour de moi hurlait.
> Longue, mince, en grand deuil, douleur majestueuse,
> Une femme passa, d'une main fastueuse
> Soulevant, balançant le feston et l'ourlet.
>
> Agile et noble, avec sa jambe de statue.
> Moi, je buvais, crispé comme un extravagant,
> Dans son oeil, ciel livide où germe l'ouragan,
> La douceur qui fascine et le plaisir qui tue.
>
> Un éclair . . . puis la nuit!—Fugitive beauté
> Dont le regard m'a fait soudainement renaître,
> Ne te verrai-je plus que dans l'éternité?
>
> Ailleurs, bien loin d'ici! Trop tard! *Jamais* peut-être!
> Car j'ignore où tu fuis, tu ne sais où je vais,
> O toi que j'eusse aimée, ô toi qui le savais! (*OE* 1:92–93)

> [The deafening street around me was screaming.
> Long, slim, in deep mourning, majestic grief,

A woman passed, raising, with a delicate hand,
The trim and hem of the flounces of her gown;

Graceful and noble, with her statue's leg.
And I drank, frozen like a madman,
In her eye, livid sky where the storm breeds,
The softness that fascinates and the pleasure that kills.

A flash . . . then night!—O fleeting beauty
Whose look made me suddenly be reborn
Shall I not see you again but in eternity?

Elsewhere, far from here! Too late! *Never*, perhaps!
I know not where you flee, you don't know where I go,
You, whom I would have loved, you who knew it was so.]

The structure of the sonnet (which divides the poem into two quatrains followed by two tercets) also divides the action depicted in the poem. In the first half of the poem the narrator makes a desperate attempt to represent the presence of the passing figure. The tercets in the second half of the poem reiterate the event represented in the quatrains—but they take the form of an impossible address relayed through a kind of photographic afterimage. The pathos of the apostrophe resides in the fact that the poet's futile address to the woman coincides with and collapses into an equally futile attempt at recollecting the encounter. The fulguration or "lightning flash" that separates the two halves of the poem is, as Benjamin has indicated, precisely not the "coup de foudre" of love at first sight, but rather like the flash of a camera, which explodes after the moment has vanished and through which the image of that moment is retained: "Un éclair . . . puis la nuit!" The lightning flash—the very mark of instantaneity—occurs long after the figure has presumably passed. What produces this flash? What is reiterated in it?

One of the greatest difficulties this poem presents to the reader is how to read the various grammatical tenses of the verb "passer" that appear in the poem. The verb "passer" is intransitive here and it cannot have a simple present: How does one think the present tense of the verb that means "to pass"? The title of the poem, "A une passante," transforms the present active participle of the verb "passer" into a (almost proper) name that is given to the feminine figure.[36] In the designation "passante," the figure of the woman clings to the present tense of the verb "passer" and vice versa. In the poem's title, the woman and the verb cannot be construed as separate entities: hence it would be an error to read "passante" synonymously with a phrase like "celle qui passe" or "she who passes." The present tense of the verb *adheres* to the figure of the woman, in the way that, as Barthes will later claim, the photographic referent *adheres* to the photograph.[37] It is only through its incarnation in the woman's body that the verb "passer" can be represented in the present tense and that a moment of "passing" can appear as presence. The moment that the poem attempts to arrest can be read in the "décalage" between the time when the woman's body clings to the verb in the present active participle and the time of the separation between the body of the woman and the action of the verb, that occurs in the line: "Une femme passa" (a woman passed). Before she is called a woman, this embodied feminine present is named "passante" and *as* "passante" she is always perpetually passing. She is only called a "femme" (woman) in her absence, *after* she has already passed away. The poem attempts to arrest, photographically, the impossible temporal disjunction evoked by her passage.

So, let us ask naively, exactly *when*, in the poem, does the "passante" pass? The first line of the poem situates the narrator in the deafening presence of a noisy street. It would seem that it is the passante's silence, in contrast to the noisy street, that first catches the narrator's attention. He does not notice her by chance; she stands out from the crowd. And it is *not* her beauty that draws the poet's attention to her: the poem does not refer to her beauty until after she has passed away. It is the fact that she is "en grand deuil," dressed in mourning, that catches the poet's eye. But if he notices her because she is in mourning, in the very moment he looks *at* her, he has already looked past her—to the death which preceded her presence and which marks her passage. This poem presents a relay of deaths: the first death precedes the poem and the woman's veil is a figure of its passage; then she, in turn, passes away. It is this relay of perpetual passings, layered upon one another, that the poem repeatedly mourns.

So when does she pass? In the moment of her "arrival" she is hardly distinguishable from the description of the street itself. The figures for the street and for the woman converge in the adjectives through which she is introduced: "longue, mince." The figure for the woman detaches itself from the passing crowd only through the invocation of her mourning: "en grand deuil, douleur majestueuse." The third line presents us with the poem's central paradox: "Une femme passa, d'une main fastueuse\soulevant, balançant le feston et l'ourlet." Une femme passa. A woman passed. The verb tense that recounts her passage is the *passé simple*, the simple past. But in this poem this past tense is anything but simple. It is immediately

followed and contested by the re-emergence of two verbs in the present active participle: "soulevant" and "balançant."

The continuous repetition of this passage, as an immobilized and
even petrified "present," characterizes the remainder of the poem. The
figure of the "passante" becomes literally petrified; she is a walking tomb-
stone with "sa jambe de statue." It would seem to be this image of a
petrified present that shocks and freezes the narrator: "Moi, je buvais,
crispé comme un extravagant." It is only after this reciprocal petrification
that the narrator looks specifically at her eye: "Dans son oeil, ciel livide où
germe l'ouragan/La douceur qui fascine et le plaisir qui tue." The look that
they presumably exchange (as the closing lines of the poem would appear
to suggest) is only reconstructed after the event—after she has already
passed. And it is doubly impossible: not only is she gone before he gazes in
her eye, but if she is "en grand deuil" she is veiled—and although she can
see through her veil, her "eye" may not be visible through it. The veil becomes a one-way mirror, a screen onto which the narrator projects a hallucination of the reciprocated gaze that can never take place but which he is
eternally condemned to repeat. Furthermore, in the act of looking her "in
the eye," he has the revelation (and this revelation is already figured by the
notion that he "lifts her veil" to look her in the eye) that the eros "in her
eye" is, like the veil it bypasses, imprinted by the mark of death. "In her
eye," he reads the trace of a "pleasure that kills." The mark of a past death
that was imprinted in the veil returns through the mark of a future death
impaled "in the eye" of the hallucinated look.

Although it is bizarre enough that this hallucinated look takes place
at all, it is even odder that the lightning flash which should logically precede or coincide with the look follows it, thereby transforming the flash
into a posthumous shock of the event rather than as the sign of the event
itself. The flash marks the aftermath of the encounter: it repeats the ex-
changed look in a cliché ("Un éclair . . . puis la nuit—fugitive beauté/Dont
le regard m'a fait soudainement renaître, ne te verrai-je plus que dans l'é-
ternité?"). It would seem that the narrator is "reborn" in the flash of the mechanical reproduction of a look that is repeated without ever having actually occurred.

In the final tercet of the poem, the narrator's desperate attempt to
conjure up the experience of this passage as "presence" terminates in cliché.
The temporal disjunction that the poem has already set in motion returns
in spatial terms: "Ailleurs, bien loin d'ici." Although, in the previous stanza,

the word "eternité" invoked the clichéd hope that there might be an "eternal" temporal and spatial utopia in which the poet could recover his lost object, in the final stanza, all hope of restitution is abandoned. In apparent despair, the poet calls out to the lost woman by invoking more and more negative images of time and space: "Ailleurs, bien loin d'ici! Trop tard! *Jamais* peut-être!" (Elsewhere, far from here, too late, *never* perhaps!). As Benjamin remarks in the "Second Empire" essay, "The *never* marks the high point of the encounter, when the poet's passion seems to be frustrated but in reality bursts out of him like a flame. He burns in this flame, but no Phoenix arises from it."[38] Although, as Benjamin indicates, there can be no future rebirth from the passion ignited by and in this *never*, we are reminded once again that the stuttering repetition of loss recounted in "A une passante" is itself a vertiginous replay of the losses depicted in "Le Cygne." The italicized word "*jamais*" in "A une passante" functions like a citation of the stuttering repetition of the word "jamais" in "Le Cygne." In "Le Cygne" Baudelaire writes: "A Quiconque a perdu ce qui ne se retrouve/Jamais, Jamais!" (To whoever has lost that which is not re-found/Never, Never!).

This depiction of an empty repetition of a death that can never be assimilated, transcended, or put to work is reminiscent of what Roland Barthes calls photographic death. Barthes's reflections on "his" photograph recall the crisis experienced by the narrator of "A une passante."

The Photograph—my Photograph—is without culture: when it is painful, nothing in it can transform grief into mourning. And if dialectic is that thought which masters the corruptible and converts the negation of death into the power to work, then the photograph is undialectical: it is a denatured theater where death cannot "be contemplated" reflected and interiorized.[39]

Through its attempt to capture the movement from "passing" to "past" which is figured by repeated images of frozen movement, "A une passante" becomes a photograph in the Barthesian sense. This poem cannot get past the passing of its central figure: the symbolic pathos of the mourning figure collapses into a disarticulated repetition. The dead are neither buried nor put to rest; ghosts of history return in the form of stuttering clichés.[40] "A une passante" stages a strangely embodied, immobilized, and undialectical death where private mourning meets the banality, the *lieu commun*, of the public space. The passing woman never quite dies, but rather becomes a figure for death's immobile movement.

In the opening lines of *Camera Lucida*, Roland Barthes narrates an anecdote through which (as he later says explicitly) we understand that he sees himself, historically, as the last witness to an amazement provoked by the sheer ontological fact of the photographic image.

One day, quite some time ago, I happened upon a photograph of Napoleon's youngest brother, Jérôme, taken in 1852. And I realized then, with an amazement I have not been able to lessen since: "I am looking at eyes that looked at the Emperor." Sometimes I would mention this amazement, but since no one seemed to share it, or even understand it (life consists of these little touches of solitude) I forgot about it. My interest in photography took a more cultural turn.[41]

Recalling that in the "Motifs" essay Benjamin situates the shock of photography in the context of a study devoted to "the last lyric poet," we can begin to appreciate what might be at stake in Barthes's lonely amazement. Writing of staring at the photographic or clichéd face of Napoleon's brother, Barthes implies that his amazement stems from the sense that he is staring history in the face. This impression (that he is looking directly at the face of history) could not have been produced, one understands, by a photograph of the emperor himself, even if such a photograph were possible. If Barthes sees "history" in the photograph of the emperor's brother, it is because he reads that photograph as a negative image, and thus perceives the absent face of the emperor that is depicted, in relief, through the relayed gaze of his brother. History, once again presented as cliché, can only be seen here by looking at a photographic representation of someone for whom the face of the emperor would be something other than merely a figure for history. It is through the suggestion of an absent "familiar look" (which recalls Benjamin's discussion of Baudelaire's use of the term "regards familiers") at the emperor that Barthes perceives the trace of history.

Toward the very end of *Camera Lucida*, Barthes gives another name to that relationship among history, death, and photography that we have been calling "cliché." If, in reading Baudelaire through Benjamin, we have seen how the look of history is sent back as "cliché," in Barthes's text the operative word is "platitude." It is through the use of this word that Barthes explains, obliquely, why he insists upon staring at the ontological fact of photography rather than by addressing the question of its history directly. Barthes explicitly chooses *not* to write a history of photography but instead to look at how photography both produces and reproduces our contemporary conception of the image of History. History, as Barthes understands it here, is itself a product of the nineteenth century. He writes: "A paradox:

the same century invented History and Photography."[42] The history that Barthes sees in photography is a certain history of death. The word that he uses for the history of death read through the photograph is "platitude":

With the photograph, we enter into *flat death*. One day, leaving one of my classes, someone said to me with disdain, "You talk about death very flatly."—As if the horror of Death were not precisely its platitude![43]

It is in relation to this vision of death as platitude that photography assumes its own, historical perspective. He writes:

For photography must have some historical relation with what Edgar Morin calls the "crisis of death" beginning in the second half of the nineteenth century; for my part I should prefer that instead of constantly relocating the advent of photography in its social and economic context, we should also inquire as to the anthropological place of Death and the new image. . . . Contemporary with the withdrawal of rites, Photography may correspond to the intrusion, in our modern society, of an asymbolic Death, outside of religion, outside of ritual, a kind of dive into literal Death. Life/Death: the paradigm is reduced to a simple click, the one separating the initial pose from the final print.[44]

The photograph is the veil of this asymbolic death. Its platitude lies in the fact that this asymbolic death can never be transcended, can never be put to work. It is nothing but a cliché, a stutter, a repetition, platitude.

Flat death: it is this inability to "go beyond" the passing of the past—the being caught in the relay of an infinite mechanical reproduction which we do not transcend—that is the cliché that is contemporary history.

3

The Erasing of Modern Life

C'est que je devine l'avenir, moi.
—Flaubert to Louise Colet, 6 or 7 August 1846

Memory Loss and Consciousness

Neurotics are often very reliable prophets. This is hardly surprising since they base their sense of the future upon their internal, unconscious convictions about the truth of the past. But when, in a letter to Louise Colet, Gustave Flaubert declares that *he* can predict the future, we must conjure up a slightly different psychic logic—and a different logic of the psyche—in order to explain the specific nature of the prophetic powers he claims to possess. Indeed, Flaubert accurately predicted the fate of his future love affair with Louise Colet in his earliest letters to her. As early as his second letter, he is full of dire warnings and threats written in tortuous verb tenses. For Flaubert, their foretold future is always already the story of what will not have happened. He leaps through untenable temporal postures with the dexterity of the acrobat to whom he compares himself in the same letter. He evokes, for example, the tender future memory of him that Louise will never have: "J'aurais voulu passer dans ta vie comme un frais ruisseau qui en eût rafraîchi les bords altérés et non comme un torrent qui la ravage. Mon souvenir aurait fait tressaillir ta chair et sourire ton coeur" (*Correspondance* 1:276) [I should have wanted to pass in your life like a fresh stream that would have refreshed its damaged banks and not like a torrent ravaging it. Your memory of me would have made your flesh tremble and your heart smile]. Toward the end of the letter, Flaubert attempts to explain his own impossible relation to time and experience through a curious fable about tribal customs from the ancient past:

Les Numides, dit Hérodote, ont une coutume étrange. On leur brûle tout petits la peau du crâne avec des charbons pour qu'ils soient ensuite moins sensibles à l'action du soleil qui est dévorante dans leurs pays. Aussi sont-ils de tous les peuples de la terre ceux qui se portent le mieux. Songe que j'ai été élevé à la Numide. (*Correspondance* 1:279)

[The Numidians, says Herodotus, have a strange custom. When they are very small, they burn the top of their heads with coals so that later they will be less sensitive to the heat of the sun which is overwhelming in their country. Thus they are, of all the people of the earth, the ones who are the most fit. Remember that I was raised as a Numidian.]

Flaubert ostensibly tells Louise this story about how a distant and archaic culture protects itself from its natural environment in order to protect her from the future damage he will cause her. Implicit in this parable, however, is a remarkable description of Flaubert's paradoxical relationship to time and reality. The little story has a compelling and complicated moral. While it would appear that burning the children's heads is an act of cruelty and sadism, we discover that the ritual act is an ingenious protection from an intolerable aspect of reality. The story posits a threatening and problematic relationship between the self and the world. In it, the very literal physical encounter between self and world, that is, between the top of the head and the rays of the sun, becomes the central site of conflict. At the tenderest age, as the fable goes, the skulls of children are ritually burned with coals so that they will lose their capacity to feel the effects of being burned. The point of the story is that what appears to be a violent act of mutilation is, in fact, a necessary means of self-protection and self-preservation. By using the art and artifice of a ritual, one prevents an inevitable natural disaster from occurring. The painful act through which one attempts to ward off the experience of a future pain avoids that pain only by anticipating it. By anticipating the pain of life through artificial means that pre-produce (rather than reproduce) the effects of that future pain, one erases the pain of the future. In order for this act of self-defense to work, the pain that is inflicted must be precisely calibrated to the future threat. The implied lucid view of real and not imagined dangers in the external world renders this gesture and its implications strangely powerful. The act acknowledges and records indelibly, on the skull, the very damage that it is designed to avoid. The scarring on the burnt skulls becomes a visible memory trace—almost a physical photograph—that marks the very traces of the future pain that will not be felt and records them. More than anything else, this story points to the terrible paradox that propelled Flaubert and fascinated Freud after him: the notion that our sense of reality derives from our need to defend ourselves from reality. Psychoanalytically speaking, the notion of an unmediated encounter with the external world— if such a thing were possible—would be both a sign and cause of illness. Melancholics, notes Freud in passing, often have "a keener eye for the truth than other people who are not melancholic."[1] But the unavoidably compromised relationship to reality can take many forms. In the story that Flaubert tells Louise, he implies that ritual, artifice, or his word "Art," is the means through which one preserves life by protecting one from the unbearable pain of life. In order to be able to confront and withstand the reality of the future sun, one creates an appropriate form of artificial pain. In order for the ritual to function effectively, however, the very flight from reality must be able to pre-record as traces the very unbearable aspects of reality that will no longer be perceived consciously, or felt as such. It is in this radical sense, I would like to argue, that we must consider Flaubert to be a "realist."[2]

By understanding Flaubert's so-called realism not as an attempt at a mimetic transcription of the external world, but rather as a highly specific and unusual form of defense against it, we can resolve the apparent contradiction between the fact that literary history persists in viewing him as a founder of "realism" despite the fact that Flaubert—and his best readers— vociferously deny the validity of such a designation.[3] Victor Brombert begins his important study *The Novels of Flaubert* by attempting to prove that Flaubert was *not* a realist, in part because he hated reality and did everything to flee from it. "Flaubert," writes Brombert, "always considered that the highest and purest pleasure of literature is its power to liberate those who practice it from the contingencies of life. Art was for him quite literally an escape. Its superiority over life was precisely its ability to transcend the conditions of living."[4] But what happens to our conception of both "Life" and "Art" if "Art" is no longer seen as being *opposed* to life, but rather as a necessary continuation of it by other means? If we read Flaubert's little warning to Louise as an allegory of his own articulation of the relationship between Life and Art, we are confronted with a paradigm in which the flight from reality through Art simultaneously shapes, records, and paradoxically "forgets" that reality in unusually telling ways. "Reality" is forgotten because it is perceived and recorded in such a way that it bypasses both consciousness and memory.

Flaubert warns Colet about their unviable personal future by invoking an ancient tribal past. However, in the temporal hiatus created by this curious collapse of distant past and anticipated future, we can read the shadowy impressions of Flaubert's response to his experience of the present time. Paradoxically, Flaubert's obvious fascination with the story of the Numidians is motivated by specifically modern preoccupations. The ancient parable provides him with a concrete example in which a real threat from the external world is as self-evident and natural as the heat of the sun. Thus the very peculiar structure of the pre-recorded defense against reality appears as a salutary, necessary, and legitimate response to pressures from the environment. But Flaubert modernizes the narrative in the act of appropriating it for his own personal and artistic ends. In the specific way in which he turns to "Art" as a prophylactic defense against the pervasive, albeit highly ambiguous and unlocatable dangers posed by contemporary reality, Flaubert joins his contemporary Baudelaire in helping to refine one of the defining emergent paradigms of nineteenth-century modernity: the notion that defensive measures against external stimuli often produce a decrease in the function of memory.

Both Flaubert and Baudelaire respond to the experience of their time by creating new literary figures that show how the time of experience has been threatened by failures in memory functions. But in order to clarify how the distinctive forms of defensive forgetting that we will encounter in Flaubert's work are subtly different from the complicated forms of disabled memory that we have been examining in Baudelaire, it would be useful at this juncture to recall how Baudelaire treats the relationship between consciousness and memory. Walter Benjamin devotes a good part of his reflections on Baudelaire to describing this phenomenon.

In an attempt to explain why the shocks of the modern world widen the gap between consciousness and memory, Benjamin invokes Freud's remarks on how trauma affects the psychic apparatus. For Benjamin, following the Freud of *Beyond the Pleasure Principle*, the explosion of stimuli in the modern world results in an increase of defensive consciousness along with a corresponding decrease in the unconscious receptivity necessary for memory.

The greater the share of the shock factor in particular impressions, the more constantly consciousness has to be alert as a screen against stimuli; the more efficiently it does so, the less do these impressions enter experience (*Erfahrung*), tending to remain in the sphere of a certain hour in one's life (*Erlebnis*). Perhaps the special achievement of shock defense may be seen in the function of assigning to an incident a precise point in time in consciousness at the cost of the integrity of its contents. This would be a peak achievement of the intellect; it would turn the incident into a moment that has been lived (*Erlebnis*). Without reflection there would be nothing but the sudden start, usually the sensation of fright which, according to Freud, confirms the failure of the shock defense. Baudelaire has portrayed this condition in a harsh image. He speaks of a duel in which the artist, just before being beaten, screams in fright. This duel is the creative process itself. Thus Baudelaire placed the shock experience at the very center of his work.[5]

In his discussion of the "shock experience" in Baudelaire's work, Benjamin establishes a temporal distinction between *Erfahrung* and *Erlebnis*. *Erfahrung* (experience) is related to memory and temporal continuity. For Benjamin the sense of temporal continuity requires that impressions be able to become stored in the psyche as unconscious memory traces. But when the external shocks increase, consciousness retains those impressions as immediate perceptions and prevents them from entering the psyche in the form of unconscious memory traces. This creates a paradoxical situation in which consciously perceived impressions become capable of fixing a specific moment in time while being simultaneously removed from the organizing temporal function of memory. Baudelaire's poetry provides numerous examples of this effect. We can extend Benjamin's argument by observing that it occurs most often in poems narrated by a first-person speaker in a state of excessively heightened consciousness. In many of these poems, specific fixed moments—*souvenirs*—become detached from the organizing fabric of memory. Frozen perceptions overwhelm the speaker who becomes petrified and burdened by their weight. One thinks, for example, of the lines: "Et mes chers souvenirs sont plus lourds que des rocs" [And my dear memories are heavier than rocks] from "Le Cygne," or the lines from "Spleen (II)":

> Un gros meuble à tiroirs encombré de bilans,
> De vers, de billets doux, de procès, de romances,
> Avec de lourds cheveux roulés dans des quittances,
> Cache moins de secrets que mon triste cerveau.
> C'est une pyramide, un immense caveau,
> Qui contient plus de morts que la fosse commune.

[A great chest of drawers stuffed with lists,
Poems, love letters, lawsuits, romances,
With heavy locks of hair rolled in receipts,
Conceals fewer secrets than my sad brain.
It is a pyramid, an immense vault,
Which contains more dead bodies than the common grave.]

In both of these poems, the speaker's conscious awareness of these "souvenirs" only reveals to him that his preserved memories have themselves become lifeless. As the speaker becomes more and more conscious of his "memories" they, in turn, become "heavier than rocks." These "souvenirs" are heavy because they are dead; they are dead because they are conscious. As consciousness of them increases with their weight, they become deadly. Since they inhabit the realm of consciousness, dead memories have the power to haunt. The more these dead memories haunt the consciousness of the speaker, the more isolated and lonely he becomes. According to Benjamin, it is *Erfahrung*, "experience," that gives us a sense of community: we become bound to one another through the shared experiences which are transmitted through unconscious memory traces. By contrast, the preserved bits and shards of lived moments—*Erlebnis*—are severed from any form of commonality or sense of duration. Since they are preserved in time but remain devoid of temporal duration, these "souvenirs" or "conscious memories" ultimately engulf the life of the speaker and transform him into a walking graveyard—a lonely witness who, by becoming the conscious repository for what once was but is no longer, loses his capacity to live in time. Many of the prose poems in *Le Spleen de Paris* dramatize this phenomenon by endowing a first-person narrator with the lonely and burdensome task of recording—through a conscious visual perception—the failure of collective memory and the dissolution of all bonds of community. Thus, the poem "Le vieux saltimbanque" ends with the lines: "Je viens de voir l'image du vieil homme de lettres qui a survécu à la génération dont il fut le brillant amuseur; du vieux poète sans amis, sans famille, sans enfants, dégradé par sa misère et par l'ingratitude publique, et dans la baraque de qui le monde oublieux ne veut plus entrer!"

To resume: we find that a powerful source of Benjamin's particular interest in Baudelaire stems from the fact that Baudelaire's poetry occupies a privileged relationship to modernity because of its engagement with transforming the shock experience into poetic figures. When the shock experience of modern memory loss takes a poetic form—rather than another form—it becomes capable of describing the very process of heightened consciousness as a response to memory loss. Baudelaire's lyric poetry becomes the privileged access to the impact of the shock experience because the intrinsic "unconscious memory traces" embedded in the lyric tradition render it capable of transforming the increased consciousness of perception into a heightened consciousness of reflection. In other words, Baudelaire's poetry does not merely "record" the experience of modernity, but it provides a language through which one can describe and analyze what has been seen.

But the loss of memory functions through the shock experience of modernity can take other forms as well. For Benjamin, and Barthes after him, photography provides the most powerful incarnation of the process of heightened perception accompanied by memory loss. But in photography, unlike Baudelaire's lyric poetry, the heightened perception that is produced becomes even more detached from the realm of reflection. For both Benjamin and Barthes, photographs paradoxically reflect the impact of the shock experience because they produce precise, visual perceptions of a moment in time—but these visual perceptions cannot be transformed into the realm of memory, language, and thought. Baudelaire's poetry is associated with photography because they share a relationship to the shock experience. Hence Benjamin includes a discussion of photography in his essay on Baudelaire. He writes:

Of the countless movements of switching, inserting, pressing, and the like, the "snapping" of the photographer has had the greatest consequences. A touch of the finger now sufficed to fix an event for an unlimited period of time. The camera gave the moment a posthumous shock, as it were. Tactile experiences of this kind were joined by optic ones, such as are supplied by the advertising pages of a newspaper of the traffic of a big city.[6]

Benjamin's remark that the "camera gave the moment a posthumous shock" reminds us of what we saw earlier in Baudelaire's poetry: the detached "souvenir" is lifeless. Photography does not provide the duration of memory; rather it provides duration for the already dead detached perception.

Like Benjamin, Roland Barthes devoted considerable time and energy grappling with the counterintuitive notion that photography destroys memory instead of becoming an extension of it. Toward the end of *La Chambre claire*, Barthes writes:

Non seulement la Photo n'est jamais, en essence, un souvenir . . . , mais elle le bloque, devient très vite un contre-souvenir. Un jour, des amis parlèrent de leurs souvenirs d'enfance: ils en avaient; mais moi, je venais de regarder mes photos passées, je n'en avais plus. Entouré de ces photographies, je ne pouvais plus me consoler des vers de Rilke: "Aussi doux que le souvenir, les mimosas baignent la chambre": la Photo ne "baigne" pas la chambre: point d'odeur, point de musique, rien que *la chose exorbitée*. La photographie est violente: non parce qu'elle montre des violences, mais parce qu'à chaque fois *elle emplit de force la vue*, et qu'en elle rien ne peut se refuser, ni se transformer.[7]

[Not only is the photograph never, in essence, a memory . . . , but it actually blocks memory, quite quickly becomes a counter-memory. One day, some friends were talking about their childhood recollections; they had plenty; but I, who had just been looking at my old photographs, no longer had any. Surrounded by these photographs, I could no longer console myself with Rilke's line: "Sweet as memory, the mimosas steep the bedroom": the Photograph does not "steep" the bedroom: no odor, no music, nothing but the *exorbitant thing*. The photograph is violent: not because it shows violent things, but because on each occasion *it fills the sight by force*, and because in it nothing can be refused or transformed.]

Although Barthes's critical terminology and conceptual framework are quite different from Benjamin's, we find, once again, a correlation between overwhelming and excessive perception and loss of memory function. Barthes's commentary seems to echo Benjamin's reading of Freud by implying that the sheer force of photographic perception actually creates a shield that prevents memory traces from being formed. Through his invocation of Rilke, Barthes provides a physical, spatial metaphor to describe how the experience of memory ought to work. Like Benjamin's *Erfahrung*, memory ought to be released into the room from an outside place—the elsewhere of the unconsciously guarded past. Memories, like the mimosas, come from outside, but when brought in, their odor creates a unifying atmosphere within the borders of the room. The smells released into the room permeate the inside with active, living traces from the outside. Memories release bits of past time into the present, and through this process, they transform the passage of time into an inhabitable place, a place to live. Only when space is figured as actively responsive to time, marked and imbued with time, can it function as place, *habitus*. By contrast, the "shock experience" permits no interiority: its defensive function is to keep the outside "outside" and it is for this reason also that Benjamin alludes to "the traffic of a big city" when he writes about photography.

But although the trauma of the shock experience can account for important aspects of the structure of memory loss in Baudelaire and in photography, in Flaubert's writing we find a more subtle and more insidious form of failed memory. As we said earlier, in the context of the parable of the Numidians, Flaubert posits the possibility of a creative act that defends against an intolerable aspect of reality by circumventing consciousness as well as memory. The heightened consciousness of memory loss we found in Baudelaire is completely absent in Flaubert's work. Instead, Flaubert produces a structure of forgetting that is so engrossing that it erases most of the traces of its own activity. I would like to suggest that the form of forgetting we find in Flaubert's work provides us with a descriptive symptom of modernity as potent as that of the shock experience Benjamin reads through Baudelaire's work.

Hence, one of the hypotheses of this book is that Flaubert continues to speak to us about undescribed aspects of modern experience in part because of his intimate engagement with this highly modern form of forgetting. If we examine *Madame Bovary* from this perspective, we find that in the opening pages of the novel, Flaubert returns to the issues raised by the Numidian fable—the creation of a defensive act in order to define and regulate the boundaries between self and the world—and radically recasts them into a modern form and context. But where the Numidian fable gave us a natural conflict between the heat of the sun and the top of the head, in *Madame Bovary* we find that the cultural collision between self and world is mediated not by a communal ritual, but by an unnatural description of a singularly unconventional cap. One cannot overstate the outrageousness of the fact that Flaubert begins the novel that defines him as a "realist" by devoting the better part of the first chapter to the vicissitudes of an object that has neither any practical use nor any apparent narrative function. Only by interrogating how and why this thing both conceals and reveals something about the way memory and consciousness function in the novel do we have any way of explaining what it is doing there in the first place.

That object so dazzles the reader that it compels us to forget that the novel's bizarre beginning effaces the conventional ways in which people and things normally rely on language's capacity to name in order to claim a discrete place in either consciousness or memory. The entire opening sequence of the novel is devoted to transforming a description of a cap into an event that becomes so memorable that it makes us forget that we have forgotten that we have no other way of remembering the character that the cap recalls. That character defies being recalled through memory because he has no access to his proper name. He fails to speak under the sign of his proper name and hence never manages to make that name remembered by others. The text establishes a direct correlation between the presentation of the cap and the character's failure to speak as well as to name himself or be called by name by others. When we allow the unforgettable description of the cap to speak for this character (as most critics do), we tend to forget that this entire scene systematically omits any specific description of his face and repeatedly erases any retention of his name. More strangely, the scene about that character and his cap is never again remembered by him or by any other character in the book or by any other event or aspect of the novel. Its unique appearance—in every sense—in both space and time, renders it the most memorable object in *Madame Bovary* and arguably the most notable accessory in all of literary history. If we too quickly succumb to the urge to invoke the presence of the cap as a convenient way of remembering the beginning of the novel, we run the risk of overlooking the fact that the cap compels us to forget more than it allows us to remember. That cap paradoxically reminds us to forget that it itself instigates and enacts a bizarre function of forgetting. In the pages that follow, we will look more closely at the ways in which this memorable object undermines the faculty of memory by unnaming everything it touches, including the poor boy for whom it supposedly speaks.

Striptease

For all the (deserved) attention showered upon Charles Bovary's inaugural headgear, Flaubert's readership has, dare I suggest it, remained rather discreet—one might even say tactful—concerning the obscenity of the thing in question. The strange physical description of the boy on the first page of the novel sets the stage for the stupefying object that appears a page later. Let me rehash the critical elements of the scene once again. An unidentified witness, speaking in the first person plural, opens the novel by announcing the arrival of the as yet unnamed Charles Bovary into the classroom. The designated *nouveau* is described, from head to toe, in a kind of reverse striptease—his fully clothed body transforms the ordinary and quotidian nakedness of his wrists into a spectacle—"son habit-veste de drap vert à boutons noirs devait le gêner aux entournures et laissait voir, par la fente des parements, des poignets rouges habitués à êtres nus."[8] We are asked to look at this meeting point of body part, covering, and cleft. But what, exactly, is being revealed or covered over in this scene? Or, more precisely, what drama between covering and exposure does this image both present and obscure to our gaze? Although his naked wrists expose themselves to us, the initial description turns our attention away from the fact that the *nouveau* lacks the two most essential characteristics of human figuration—he has neither a name nor a face. Furthermore, this inaugural lack, or "fente" to use Flaubert's word, is simultaneously reconfirmed and denied through the description of the distinctive cap that comes to supplant and supplement the inadequate being of this figure on the following page. Although I will offer my own remarks on these lines later on, for the time being let me allow the description of the cap to speak on its own behalf:

C'était une de ses coiffures d'ordre composite, où l'on retrouve les éléments du bonnet à poil, du chapska, du chapeau rond, de la casquette de loutre et du bonnet de coton, une de ces pauvres choses, enfin, dont la laideur muette a des profondeurs d'expression comme le visage d'un imbécile. Ovoïde et renflée de baleines, elle commençait par trois boudins circulaires; puis s'alternaient, séparés par une bande rouge, des losanges de velours et de poil de lapin; venait ensuite une façon de sac qui se terminait par un polygone cartonné, couvert d'une broderie en soutache compliquée, et d'où pendait, au bout d'un long cordon trop mince, un petit croisillon d'or en manière de gland. Elle était neuve; la visière brillait. (294)

[It was one of those headgears of the composite kind in which one can rediscover elements of the fur hat, the shako, the bowler, the sealskin cap and the cotton nightcap; in short, one of those poor things whose mute ugliness has depths of expression—like an idiot's face. Ovoid and stiffened with whalebone, it began with three rolls; next followed an alternating sequence of lozenges of velvet and rabbit fur separated by a red band; then came a sort of bag which was topped off by a cardboard polygon covered with complicated braiding from which hung, at the tip of a long and too thin cord, small gold threads twisted into the shape of a tassel. It was new; its peak was shiny.] (my translation)

This delirious description of Charles Bovary's cap presides over the opening pages of *Madame Bovary* like an insidious insignia that promises to reveal, in miniature, the secret language of the novel's substance, style, and structure. Charles's misbegotten headpiece is like an oracular obstacle that never fails to fascinate and frustrate its readers. The colossal challenge posed by reading this object invariably pushes readers to the very limits of their critical capacities. One often has the queasy sense that this cap is more capable of reading its reader than is the reader in reading it. As Jonathan Culler aptly remarks, "The cap, one might say, is, in its excessiveness, a parody of the symbolic object, in that by throwing down a challenge it calls into play interpretative operations that are inadequate to the task it appears to set."[9]

Understandably, critics are so seduced by the lure of the *description* of this object that they tend to focus more on what the cap signifies (or doesn't as the case may be) rather than on the way it functions to incite the schoolroom drama that erupts around it. For this reason, although almost all of the hat's many readers observe that the cap is *inherently* an impossible object, they continue to assume, nonetheless, that Charles's cap bears some relation, however remote, to the realm of wearable clothing. Thus, even a reader as astute as Culler asserts that "at the empirical level we can say little more than that a silly hat denotes a silly wearer." With all due respect to Culler's eloquent gloss on the cap (to which I will return in a moment), I would like to quibble about the deceptive clarity of the so-called empirical level. At the "empirical level" of the events narrated, Charles never ever succeeds in "wearing" that hat. Instead, as the text rigorously, insistently, adamantly repeats, Charles consistently places his cap not on his head but on his lap, nestled between his knees. While this quintessentially foolish gesture can be read as an appropriately ridiculous use for an object that has been clearly designated at the very least as a "fool's cap," Charles's piteously tenacious struggle to keep his hat firmly planted on his lap raises important questions about the entire relationship between words, things, and bodies in Flaubert's work.

Let me restate the problem in slightly different terms. Critics, either implicitly or explicitly, tend to agree that Charles's cap functions simultaneously on two levels: on the one hand, the cap as "empirical object" can be said to belong, however pathetically, to the world of things, whereas the cap as description or "parody of the symbolic object," to use Culler's term, belongs to the world of words. Culler's reading beautifully sketches out how Flaubert forces the distinction between these two levels into conflict. He argues, quite convincingly, that "the discrepancy between the prose and the object grows, displaying the ludicrousness of language spinning itself out in clauses piled one on the other, all in an attempt to comprehend an unworthy hat."[10] It is, however, in Culler's concluding remarks about the hat that he comes closest to articulating what is at stake here. Comparing Flaubert to Balzac, he writes:

In the case of Balzac, . . . there is a nice fit between the world and language . . . therefore, the visual is always material for knowledge, a flesh that can be made word through his mediation. Everything is subject to thematic elaboration and nothing need escape him. But here in Flaubert we can witness the escape; flesh made word is singularly grotesque, with all the flaws of incomplete metamorphosis. There is none of the existential coziness, derived from a faith in the intelligibility of the world, which reassures the readers of Balzac's descriptions: only an emptiness, in the guise of linguistic despair.[11]

Although I readily espouse all of the terms that Culler invokes to describe this peculiar phenomenon, I would suggest that his argument might be even more resonant if turned on its head, or cap, as it were. The activity that Culler describes as the "incomplete metamorphosis" of "flesh made word" works as often in inverted fashion: in lieu of "flesh made word" Flaubert offers us the even more grotesque transformation of "words made flesh." Therefore, as we shall see in a moment, the cap behaves more like body part rather than like body covering. Where Culler concludes that Flaubert's lack of faith in the "intelligibility of the world" leaves us with "only an emptiness, in the guise of linguistic despair," I would argue that the despair in question is not limited to the "linguistic" register and cannot be said even to reside there. The "despair" that Culler points to (and he has said as much) is linked to the incommensurate relationship between words and things. But, and this marks one of Flaubert's precise and perverse contributions to the world of letters and literary theory, this "incommensurate relationship" is calibrated into an elaborate economic calculus. One thinks, for example, of the following formula from *L'Education sentimentale*": "la misère des propos se trouvait comme renforcée par le luxe des choses ambiantes."[12] The fissure between words and things is always carefully meted out in economic terms; the consequences of this rift incur risks and losses both erotic and financial. And, when his characters are libidinally invested, the price exacted gets tallied on the body. In Flaubert's world, the recourse to excessive language—rich words—speaks to the poverty—a kind of ontological lack in being—of the things they stand in for. Thus, words function rarely as "representations" of things—but rather as a kind of compensation for a latent and shadowy doubt concerning the thing's claim on existence or meaning. Thus, quite often (as is the case with the cap) one finds that the "poorest things" are described with the "richest words." Let us recall at this juncture that the cap is literally described as "une pauvre chose."

But what, after all, is a "poor thing"? Someone, somewhere, ought to do a complete inventory of the use of the adjective "pauvre" in Flaubert's writings: it is one of his most tender words. Although I am getting ahead of myself, I would quickly point out that when the word "pauvre" modifies a person it is reserved for the bereaved or for those who are stricken with desire. Recall, for example, that in the chapter where Emma deduces (because he is unable to tell her) that Leon is in love with her, Flaubert kindly places this word in Emma's thoughts:

Assis sur une chaise basse, près de la cheminée, il faisait tourner dans ses doigts l'étui d'ivoire; elle poussait son aiguille, ou, de temps à autre, avec son ongle, fronçait les plis de la toile. Elle ne parlait pas; il se taisait, captivé par son silence, comme il eut été par ses paroles.
　　　　—Pauvre garçon! pensait-elle.
　　　　—En quoi lui déplais-je? se demandait-il. (387)

[Seated on a low chair near the fire, he kept turning the ivory thimble case with his fingers. She stitched on, or, from time to time turned the folds of the cloth with her nail. She did not speak; he was silent, captivated by her silence, as he would have been by her speech.
　　　　"Poor boy!" she thought.
　　　　"Why doesn't she like me?" he asked himself.] (translation modified)

Emma's silence divests Leon of his words and sends him into a state of mute, enthralled rapture. The adjective "poor" is like a verbal voucher that shows that Emma has received his unspoken desire even if neither of them can cash in on it. Although Flaubert uses the word "pauvre" here, let us remember that for him "impoverished silence" is the richest and least damaging (because least alienated) possible incarnation of desire. Flaubertian desire demands silence not because words are lacking, but because they are too full, too rich. Only in the silence of a desire which causes words actively to fail can the body find a place in the space normally furnished, all too lavishly, by words.

All of which brings us round, circuitously, to the narrator's declaration that the cap is "une de ces pauvres choses, enfin, dont la laideur muette a des profondeurs d'expression comme le visage d'un imbécile." When faced with this cryptic utterance, critics have a tendency to skip over the reference to the "mute ugliness of poor things," as if to say that those words about ugly, poor things do not deserve to be read because they are themselves too poor in signification. Almost everyone seems to prefer the rich simile about the depths of expression of the imbecile's face to the reference to those poor, ugly things. The image of a human face—even if it is only the product of a verbal hallucination stitched into the folds of an impossible hat—seems to reassure the reader that there is, indeed, a limit to the seemingly infinite process of disfiguration at work in this passage. But is there? Significantly, this rhetorical gesture of prosopopoeia—giving face to an inanimate object—is often read as if it could simply be transformed into a representation of the still unnamed Charles Bovary's still missing face. When the face rhetorically given to the mute ugliness of the cap is read as if it were Charles's face, this "poor thing" is implicitly elevated from being an impoverished and inadequate signifier and made to become a transparent (and readable) *signified* of Charles himself. Thus, critics very often interpret the hat either as a metaphoric or metonymic representation of Charles Bovary's character and/or mental capacities. For Victor Brombert, the hat is a totalizing metaphor that "sums up" Charles's stupidity: "But it is above all the boy's headgear, a pitiful, unsightly combination of shako, bearskin, billycock hat and cotton nightcap, which sums up, in its tiers and superstructure, the layers and monumentality of the wearer's unintelligence."[13] In a sense, Brombert's chosen verb "sums up" says it all. For even a cursory reading of the description of the hat tells us that mathematically speaking, although the hat adds and adds, it never quite "adds up" to a whole. Part of its obscenity derives from this—it is a colossal partial object made up of a seemingly arbitrary set of assembled parts. It is technically monstrous in that it indiscriminately mixes different genres of hats and removes them from their separate wearable contexts. It is an edifice of hat citations that become ruinously meaningless because they are literally unaccountable (there are too many of them to count as one hat) and hence the hat can never really "sum up" anything at all. But who is counting? By contrast, for Ross Chambers, the hat can be made to speak for its wearer through metonymy: "By metonymic transference, the new student's cap will shortly be described as having 'les profondeurs d'expression du visage d'un imbécile.' . . . But already Charles appears here as the village idiot come to be educated in town—and as a Gilles-like buffoon mocked by the crowd."[14] I hope no one will be offended that I have decided to split hairs concerning the critical terminology used when speaking about the hat. By insisting that Flaubert's text resists our capacity to read it according to our available models of meaning-making, I hope to read this "new cap" on this "new boy" in a new way and to show, along the way, that the disquieting relationship between Charles and his cap reveals something novel about the way words and things function in Flaubert.

Before moving forward, I want to re-place the appearance of the hat's description back into its narrative context. In the passage that directly precedes the description of the hat, we are told by the novel's infamous first-person narrator that all of the other boys have caps that they throw against the wall before entering the classroom. Here is how Flaubert's narrator describes this important schoolboy ritual:

Nous avions l'habitude, en entrant en classe, de jeter nos casquettes par terre, afin d'avoir ensuite nos mains plus libres: il fallait, dès le seuil de la porte, les lancer sous le banc, de façon à frapper contre la muraille, en faisant beaucoup de poussière; c'était là le *genre*. (294)

[We had this habit, when we came into class, of throwing our caps on the ground so that we could free up our hands; as soon as we reached the threshold of the door, we were supposed to toss them under the desk, so that they hit the wall and made lots of dust; that was really quite the *thing*.] (my translation)

"Schoolboys" define themselves as schoolboys and form a community of schoolboys by establishing the convention that hats must be thrown against the wall before entering the classroom. The use of the striking word "genre"—highlighted by Flaubert himself—would thus conventionally be understood to mean "fad," "custom," or any such token of gestural communication defined through time-bound site specificity. In other words, any mode of communication that marks its user as being "trendy" and "with it." It goes without saying, of course, that our new boy doesn't get it. In fact, as the text explicitly specifies, after Charles watches the other boys throw their caps, he literally hangs on to his hat—keeping it firmly where it belongs—on his lap: "Mais, soit qu'il n'eût pas remarqué cette manoeuvre ou qu'il n'eût osé s'y soumettre, la prière était finie que le *nouveau* tenait encore sa casquette sur ses deux genoux" [But—either because he didn't notice the move or because he didn't dare try it—even after the prayers were over, the *new boy* was still holding his cap on his lap] (294). The point is not merely that the new boy doesn't get it, but why he doesn't get it. In any case, it should be noted that well before Charles's inappropriate attachment to his own unbecoming headpiece makes him the laughingstock of the class, the new boy has already transgressed the law of hats. By looking a bit more closely at this boyish ritual, we discover that like Charles's hat, cap throwing seems to have something to do with words, things, and bodies.

When the boys toss their hats against the wall, they treat things like words. Throwing hats, after all, is an activity that has a meaning as well as a practical purpose. The gesture of throwing caps simultaneously does something (frees the hands to work) and means something (we are, here and now, boys who want to have fun instead of just being schoolboys). But something rather special occurs when the boys use these wearable things in place of words. The gap between words and things appears to narrow for a moment. And the body—momentarily—is relieved of the burden of signifying. Thus, there is something like a brief discharge of pleasure that can be heard in the delightfully noisy sounds made by the hats as they strike the wall, raising dust. This moment provides a small respite during which the boys' hands are set free before they succumb to the deadening effects of the language of the schoolroom. There, in school, those same hands will be put in the service of turning words into things: they are taught to copy out verses of a dead language in such a manner as to empty them of meaning altogether. These are the two extreme poles of the language of conventions: when things become words, the body is given the space to emerge; when words become things—commodities that have exchange value—they uphold the social order. Both of these operations function relatively well because they are immune to the sorts of losses that occur when particular human beings try to use language in order to say something particular.

But we are not there yet. For the moment, let us return to the description of our hat-throwing boys. Here, the studied insouciance of Flaubert's prose seems to match the innocent boyish gesture it describes. To my knowledge, no critic has ever paid any attention to these lines. They are, presumably, mere throwaway lines that serve to render Charles's cap all the more visibly present. Who would imagine that the insipid phrase, "c'était là le *genre*," actually exposes, in its bare simplicity, one of the central, underlying questions posed by the many rhetorical layers that cover up Charles's poor thing? A note of grave anxiety subtends this innocent clause. This anxiety can be traced to the fact that the conjunction of the words "là" and "le" is a homophone for the impossible combination of the feminine and masculine definite articles ("la" and "le"). Only a diacritical mark, the *accent grave* that covers the "a" in "là" like a cap, keeps the masculine and feminine genders from becoming brought into uncomfortable and confusing proximity. Even though the word "là" here means "this" or "here," this very mark of deictic presence is marked as feminine. Looking back to what we said about the small moment of pleasure experienced by the cap-throwing boys, we might say that at the very moment they toss their caps, the word "là" loses its cap and the body escapes signification in jouissance.[15]

Not coincidentally, this linguistic inscription of gender confusion is itself coupled with the polyvalent word "genre." In French, the word "genre" is used to designate grammatical gender of nouns, the sexual gender of persons, and is also used to designate any type or category within a taxonomic system. The phrase "c'était là le genre" is the hinge that simultaneously closes the description of the cap-throwing boys and opens up the discussion of Charles and his cap. When read as a descriptive utterance placed in the mouths of boys who throw caps, "c'était là le genre" denotes a meaningful, ludic moment; but when read as a herald of the description of the new boy's abnormal attachment to his freakish hat, this same phrase starts to make us wonder whether Flaubert has done something new (or "nouveau") to the very concept of *genre* itself. Here, I would point out that Flaubert himself puts both the word "*genre*" and the word "*nouveau*" into italics, thereby calling attention to both words and setting up a possible relationship between them.[16]

If we pause to look back at what we have seen and said up to this point, we can make the following remarks. We have shown that the cap cannot be read as a material, empirical, usable object. It fails to function as a cap in and of itself; it fails to have any obvious hatlike use-value for Charles; it fails to function as an object of exchange in a social contract between Charles and the other schoolboys. As a hat, in its hatness, it is an ontological monstrosity. Furthermore, once the text calls the cap a "poor thing," it indicates, by the same token, that it is not a thing at all. Only a thing that is already endowed with the capacity of speech can be called "mute." In the empirical, "real world"—if there is such a place—objects are not "mute"—that is to say deprived of speech—they are silent—they are devoid of speech. So from the very moment that the cap is called a "poor thing" with "mute ugliness" we understand that the specificity of this thing is that it is more than a thing and less than a viable symbol, signifier, metaphor, metonymy, anthropomorphism, or any other available figure of speech. It is too rich in words to be a thing and too poor in speech to be a word; thus it fails to be at the same time that it fails to speak.

It is now time to take another look at the famous headdress. As we have already seen, this hat violates all possible laws of *genre* that govern hats. It not only combines different hat elements from different hat types but also, more radically, confuses the distinction between hat parts and things that normally have no relation to hats. Dennis Porter shows how this double violation of genres produces a particularly monstrous effect:

The hat that is produced at this early point in the novel faces the reader with the category of the monstrous. . . . Flaubert imagines a hat that is five different hats in one. In its composition, he knowingly confuses a variety of shapes and orders; it is familiar and exotic, organic and inorganic, formless and geometric. The description combines references to three animals—a rabbit, an otter, and a whale—to food, fur, gold, and an acorn. In other words, largely as the result of the juxtaposition of disparate elements, a verbal context is established such that beyond the derived meanings of *baleine* ("whalebone stiffeners"), *boudin* ("roll") and *gland* ("tassel") their concrete sense reasserts itself.[17]

Porter's remarks concerning the impossible mixture of animal, mineral, and vegetable are gratifyingly precise and astute. It is puzzling, however, that despite the fact that he makes these observations in a (wonderful) article entitled "*Madame Bovary* and the Question of Pleasure," he does not mention how the hat also confuses masculine and feminine genders. Or, finally to put it baldly: male and female genitalia. The entire formal description of the hat culminates, tellingly, in an invocation to something "in the manner" of a "gland" that hangs from a "long cordon trop mince," which in turn is suspended from a kind of a "sac." Porter's own text directs our attention to two of the possible meanings of *gland*: "acorn" and "tassel." But the word *gland*, derived from *glans*, the Latin word for the tip of the penis, can also mean the tip of the penis in French. The placement of the word *gland* at the tip of the hat certainly tilts the word in this direction. And as if this isn't enough, we find that the tip of this penis/hat is made of shiny gold thread: "d'où pendait, au bout d'un long cordon trop mince, un petit croisillon de fils d'or en manière de gland." On the female side of the thing, we find nothing less than the word "ovoïde," which derives from the Latin word for egg ("*ovum*"), accompanied by fleshy, round "boudins," "rolls" that are decorated with velvet and fur. These Latinate names for sex organs occur, I hasten to add, in the context of a schoolroom class in which boys are being taught Latin. The figure of genitalia is imprinted into the cap in two divergent ways. On the one hand, we are led to derive the existence of the inscription of a "penis" in the cap by following the *signifying* etymological and anatomical associations of the word "gland," while on the other hand, the presence of a "penis" in the cap is rendered visible in the very description of the shape of the object itself. In other words—at the most literal level, if we try to imagine what this cap looks like, it looks more like a penis than like any of the hats that it cites as its points of reference. It is covered in fur, has a bag, a hanging cord, and a glistening rounded tip like a shiny cap. Thus, the cap conjures up, or stages the hallucination, of a penis by using two different forms of representation that although different, both *circumvent* conventional laws between signifiers and signifieds. In other words—the hat/penis association is made possible *either* by recalling the chain of signifiers that allows us to read "gland" as penis rather than as "tassel" or by succumbing to the illusion that the words of the description paint a visual picture—something that can be perceived by the eye. The hallucinatory "presence" of the form or image of a penis in the cap is further substantiated by the fact that the cap in question is, as we have said, located on the boy's lap. But although its physical location would seem to indicate that its function is to *cover* the genitals, this cap exposes in hallucinatory fashion the very thing that it is seemingly designed to veil.

The final words in the description complete the strange metamorphosis that completely blurs the distinction between the male human subject and the feminine inanimate thing. The very word formerly used to designate the masculine boy, "le nouveau," now comes to be used to designate the feminine word-thing that has usurped his place: "Elle était neuve; la visière brillait." Although the modifier "new" that first applied to the boy has now been transferred to the shiny brilliant "newness" of the cap, we are still at a loss to know exactly how to assess the nature of the "newness" of the description itself. We can begin by observing that the unnamed "new boy" has now become denoted by a feminine pronoun rather than by a proper name. There is a further gender confusion inscribed here: although the gender of the word for the "cap" is feminine, the thing that the cap appears to reveal is a male sex organ. As a sexual emblem, then, the cap radically confuses any possibility of marking a division between a feminine word and a masculine thing, between a piece of clothing and a body part, between a subject and an object, between the exterior of the world and the interior of the self. So what is this thing? Why is it there? What does it do?

In order to be able to address the first two questions, we must begin by answering the last one: What does the cap do? The quick response to this question is that the cap "makes a scene" and, in so doing, reveals the extent of its obscenity. The obscenity of the thing is perversely double-edged: it is excessively exhibitionistic and relentlessly taciturn. On the one hand, it always shows too much: things that either should not be shown (like the genitals) or things that are not there (the acorn, the whale, and the otter), while on the other, it says too little and literally becomes a speech impediment that causes the boy to be publicly exposed and humiliated.

Since the scene of humiliation is also the scene in which the cap prevents
the boy from being named, we must pause here to examine the way
Flaubert stages it. The spectacle truly begins when the professor asks the
boy to relieve himself of his helmet. But in the striptease that follows, as the
boy hangs onto his cap, he loses his face and his name instead:

> —Débarrassez-vous donc de votre casque, dit le professeur qui était un
> homme d'esprit.
> Il y eut un rire éclatant des écoliers qui décontenança le pauvre garçon, si
> bien qu'il ne savait s'il fallait garder sa casquette à la main, la laisser par terre ou la
> mettre sur sa tête. Il se rassit et la posa sur ses genoux.
> —Levez-vous, dit le professeur, et dites-moi votre nom. Le *nouveau* articula,
> d'une voix bredouillante, un nom inintelligible.
> —Répétez. Le même bredouillement de syllabes se fit entendre, couvert par
> les huées de la classe.
> —Plus haut! cria le maître, plus haut!
> —Le *nouveau*, prenant alors une résolution extrême, ouvrit une bouche
> démesurée et lança à pleins poumons, comme pour appeler quelqu'un, ce mot:
> *Charbovari.* (294)

["Relieve yourself of your helmet," said the teacher, who was a witty guy. There
was a burst of laughter from the boys which so thoroughly put the poor boy out
of countenance that he didn't know whether to keep his cap in his hand, leave it
on the ground, or put it on his head. He sat down again and placed it on his lap.
"Stand up," said the teacher, "and tell me your name." The *newcomer* enunciated,
in a stammering voice, an unintelligible name. "Say it again!" The same sputter-
ing of syllables made itself heard, covered by the hoots of the class. "Louder!"
screamed the master, "louder!" The *newcomer* then made a huge effort; opened up
his mouth way too widely and shouted, at the top of his lungs, as if he were trying
to call someone, this word: *Charbovari.*"] (my translation)

The professor, that refined joker, hits the nail on the head when he refers
to the poor boy's feminine "casquette" (cap) with the older, more robust
"masculine" noun "casque" (helmet). The word itself is curious. It seems to
be derived from a popular Latin expression that combines the word "casser"
(to break) with the very word "crâne" (head, or skull) which we encountered in the Numidian fable. A "casque" is thus the military armor that protects the head from being shattered by external blows. It appears to be a
perfectly appropriate form of protection for the kinds of dangers that
might threaten the average sixteenth-century warrior.

But where the "casque" presumably protects a man from external
blows without disrupting his relationship to memory, consciousness, or, by

gosh, the status of his sex, one cannot say the same of this bizarre, newfangled "casquette." The dictionary tells us that the feminine "casquette" only enters the French language in 1817, presumably less than a decade before the new boy appears on the scene with his new "casquette." Fancy that: a shiny new word for the new boy's shiny new thing! Furthermore, unlike the functional "casque," it appears that the diminutive casquette does not really function as "protective" headgear, but rather like a semiotic index that turns an individual into part of a recognizable, organized social group or class. The "casquette" is thus the crowning element of a "uniform"; it confers identifiable rank and uniformity onto its wearer. One speaks of "casquettes" in the context of army officers, police officers, postal workers, and the like. As a mark of distinction, the "casquette" paradoxically designates uniformity; it automatically "serializes" its wearer by turning him into one of many in a given social class or rank.[18] The "casquette" is thus related to the rise of the proletariat in the postrevolutionary era. It is a word/thing that confers a new meaning to the rising power of social groups and institutions that function by creating a unified class out of a series of individuals. At the risk of sounding glib, one might even go so far as to suggest that the word "casquette" conveniently comes into being as a proleptic index of the social forces at work that prepared the ground for the revolutions of 1830 and 1848. And, implicitly, this includes the figures of the press. For as part of a uniform, as one in a series, the "casquette" is also related to the rise of all the other forms of mechanical reproduction that began to flourish in the mid–nineteenth century—including the newspapers, stereotypes, factories, photography, and, Flaubert's favorite bête-noire, the linguistic cliché. The link between "casquette" and "newspapers" is particularly resonant because, as several critics have noted, Flaubert was inspired to write the description of Charles Bovary's "casquette" based on a drawing he saw in the June 1821 issue of the newspaper *Charivari*. Through this association, we find that the "casquette" has, once again, further undermined the specificity of the proper name the new boy never manages to assume.

If we return to the passage cited above in order to ask what actually happens to the boy's proper name, we discover that in response to the professor's demand for a name ("dites-moi votre nom"), the newcomer is not able to produce a name, but only a simple *word*: ("ce mot: *Charbovari*"). Since the word is only a word and not a name, and since that word sounds more like the name of a newspaper than like the name of a person, the word the boy utters empties him out into the world instead of recalling him. In perhaps one of the most poignant lines of the entire novel, Flaubert describes how, in the boy's vain attempt to say his own name, his gaping mouth becomes an obscenely disfiguring figure for the void of verbal connection between him and the world: "Le *nouveau*, prenant alors une résolution extrême, ouvrit une bouche démesurée et lança à pleins poumons, comme pour appeler quelqu'un, ce mot: *Charbovari*." Flaubert challenges us to hear the lonely desolation, emptiness, and futility in the boy's attempt to carve out a unique place for himself in a world in which language has lost the capacity to name particular beings.

But unlike Baudelaire who, as we have seen, bears witness to such moments by charging them with heightened consciousness, in the world Flaubert presents to us, there is no mediating witness, nor any consciousness on the part of the boy or anyone around him. Though this brief moment is one of the rare occasions in *Madame Bovary* where anyone actually tries to give meaning to something as specific and momentous as one's own name, the moment is gone as soon as it occurs and leaves absolutely no traces on the memory or the consciousness of its characters. But even though the characters—and the narrative voice—fail to remember this experience, it is repeated by the text in a nightmarish way. The image of an obscenely gaping mouth emptied of speech recurs two more times in the novel: on each occasion, the would-be speaker is dead and hence devoid of consciousness or memory. Although I will discuss these moments in detail in a later chapter of the book, it is important to note, in this context, that the figure of the gaping mouth is the defining image of *Madame Bovary*; it opens the novel with the new boy's attempt to say his own name and reappears significantly on the last page. Furthermore, the void opened up by this open mouth is precisely what the casquette both covers and reveals. The excessive, apparently verbal plenitude of the hat is a disavowal of the emptiness that it attempts to veil. Thus, the casquette paradoxically situates and records the site of the dysfunction of memory and consciousness through failed naming while, at the same time, it inaugurates the repetitive form of language use that overtakes the novel at this point. Let us recall, after all, that the spectacle initiated by the casquette terminates in an act of mechanical reproduction. At the very end of the scene, the new boy— whose name has already been forgotten by the very professor who was apparently so intent on learning it—is now ascribed a generic identity and a mechanical means of reproducing that identity in a dead language. He is sentenced to copy the verb "ridiculus sum" [I am an idiot] twenty times.

The further irony of this gesture is, of course, that the verb "ridiculus sum" has been stripped of its activity and temporality. It is a verb that has been turned into an empty label. Like the gesture required to "copy it," this verb cannot really be conjugated; it is a verb with no tense except a stuttering present that repeats itself indefinitely.

But even before the boy becomes disfigured by trying to say his own name, he has become significantly disfigured in other ways as well. By using the word "décontenança" to describe the effect of the boys' laughter on the boy, Flaubert implies that the poor thing has literally lost his face. More tellingly still, this passage makes it startlingly explicit that the "poor boy" has indeed become, like his cap, "a poor thing." Here, for the first time since the beginning of the novel, Flaubert finally uses the common noun "garçon" (instead of the relentlessly italicized term "le *nouveau*") to designate the boy. But before the word "garçon" even appears on the page, it is undermined by the dubious adjective "pauvre." Like the modifier "new," which began by being associated with the boy and later became transferred onto the hat, the adjective "poor" begins by modifying the hat and now becomes attached to the boy. Because both hat and boy are exiled from language in its traditional form—that is, in its capacity to confer discrete names onto specific beings—Flaubert creates another kind of linguistic bond between them. The boy and the hat are related because—as speaking beings and as figures of speech—they are both "new" and "poor." And their poverty is directly related to their newness. For want of a better word, we are calling this the "casquette-effect." By transforming the linguistic connection between the poor boy and his new cap into a scandalously obscene spectacle, Flaubert permits this emergent "casquette-effect" to become visible so that it can be read and analyzed. Through the peculiar connection between the "new thing" and a "poor boy," Flaubert has provided us with a perversely "realistic" and realistically perverse way of thinking about the impoverished novelty of the language of the experience of the modern world.

Although I have just argued that the obscene spectacle occasioned by the hat *enables* this modern form of forgetting to become visible, it is critical to note that the inverse is also equally true. As we have seen, the cap is so brilliantly "new" that it both shines with newness and blinds us to it. The very "shiny brilliance" that seduces the reader into a fascinated fixation on the hat also prevents the hat from being read in the same moment that it is seen. Therefore, it might be best to recap some salient points about the

cap in order to take a final look at what we have seen. Throughout the preceding pages, we derived the "casquette-effect" by tracing how it is constructed through a rhetorical twisting of three terms that are braided together in novel ways: the face, the name, and the flesh. We can further
understand how these terms are related by observing that faces and names
have similar and related functions: they are two different mechanisms for
establishing marks of difference so that people and things can be consciously perceived as specific beings and thereby become accessible to
memory. Our very ability to perceive specific people relies upon our capacity to identify them through their distinctive facial features, gestures,
and expressions; hence, if the initial perception is impaired, that perception
cannot be retained as memory trace. Naming is the primary way language
organizes the world so that it can be remembered. We observed that the
novel begins by glossing over the fact that the boy is initially presented as
having neither a name or a face. However, we then saw that the boy's "missing" face reappears—in quasi-hallucinatory form—through an imaginary
simile that modifies the term "poor thing" in the description of the hat.
Because the hat is so distinctive, it makes a scene that compels the boy to
become shamefully visible and strangely memorable.

Although the hat compensates for the boy's missing face and name up
to a point, it is an inadequate and excessive substitute for them. The cap
becomes spectacular and memorable precisely because of its monstrous violation of every possible differentiating system, including all grammatical
and cultural laws of gender and genre. The excessive proliferation of words
and things that accrue in the description of the cap ultimately render it a
monstrous thing with no name. Furthermore, imbedded in the description
of this monstrous thing with no name, we discovered the presence of the
figure of a penis. On the one hand, like the inscription of the face in the
cap, the figure of the penis can be read as a supplementary hallucination of
the very mark of difference that the boy seemingly *lacks*. In other words, if
we read the figure of the penis *in* the hat, it appears to be fabricated from
its rhetoric as a reactive disavowal—a fantasmatic counter "proof" of the
very "masculinity" that the hat has already put into question. But if we read
the penis *through* the hat—as the thing that the cap "points to" or "indicates" by its location on the boy's lap—we are confronted with a hallucination of a different sort. Read in this way, the cap appears to make visible
some access to the materiality of the body as flesh that is normally completely concealed by language. The penis—and most particularly the flaccid

penis—is arguably the part of the material world that is most strenuously veiled by conventional systems of representation.[19] In stark contrast to the erect "phallic symbol" that dominates world culture in all kinds of forms, the penis as simple body part—relieved of its burden to signify—is almost never visible. When things assume names, the penis is certainly one of the first objects to be lost. But when it has no name, when it is nothing but a "poor thing," the penis allows the body to assume a different place in the world. In order to be able to "decide" between these two readings of the hallucinated penis, we would need to be able to decide whether the hallucinated "penis" emerges as a defensive projection onto the world motivated by anxiety concerning a failure to establish gender difference, or whether the hallucinated penis is like a material trace, a nonlinguistic impression that delivers data from the world that is normally repressed through conventional systems of representation. But Flaubert's text does not allow us to decide between these two readings. The very mode of representation through which the question arises does not allow us to establish clear boundaries between the boy and his cap, between the supposed interiority of the self and exterior "reality" of the world. Although we cannot "decide" between these two readings, Flaubert has, nonetheless, provided us with the figure of the "casquette-effect" that creates a textual *place* for an interrogation of its temporal ramifications.

This place is, as we have seen, related to the place of speech and memory in the text. In an extraordinary article entitled "Les Innocents," Marie Depussé asks us to look at how the peculiar visibility of Charles's body is the price he pays for his inability to speak in the opening pages of the novel:

Flaubert a placé Charles dans un en-deçà de la parole que creusent les premières pages du roman. A la différence du corps de Marie Arnoux, le corps de Charles n'est pas laissé en repos par des mots, mais laissé pour compte. Il rejoint la visibilité de tout ce qui est, pour Flaubert, hors d'usage; tout ce qui montre sa trame, s'entrouvre pour "laisser-voir": choses abandonnées par le langage, échappant au grand effacement du bon usage, visibles comme le sont les déchets. . . . Charles n'est pas loin de ce point ultime de l'innocence où l'on est délivré de la bêtise parce qu'on est exclu de l'usage des mots.[20]

[Flaubert has put Charles in a place below speech, which the first pages of the novel hollow out. In contrast to Marie Arnoux's body, Charles's body is not left in peace by words, but left aside. This body takes on the visibility of everything that is, for Flaubert, beyond use; everything that is worn threadbare, that falls open and "lets itself be seen": things abandoned by language, escaping the great erasure of correct usage, visible like detritus. Charles is not far from this ultimate point of innocence at which one is delivered from stupidity because one is excluded from the use of words.]

For Depussé, Charles's body becomes visible as a waste product excreted by language. But through the exhibition of his body as "poor thing," the poor boy escapes the fate of being exposed to the annihilating forms of speech that would otherwise reduce him to the bêtise of a cliché. In relation to the argument being presented here, we can contrast the "newness" of the casquette with the implicit "obsolete" quality given to the body here. We note that Depussé argues that Charles's body is not described here as being merely "beneath" language, or "prior" to it in some simple fashion, but rather discarded by language as a "useless" thing that it has used up and tossed off. Although I suspect that I may be twisting her argument in directions that she did not intend, Depussé's insistence upon the outmoded quality of this specific Flaubertian body encourages us to wonder about its role as a memorial relic. The new boy's shiny new cap appears to offset a paradoxically prematurely ruined body, a body that has presumably survived its ability to function in the world but that bears some unspoken trace of its own unremembered past. Read in this way, we could conclude, for example, that the new boy is not simply lacking a face, but that his face was "worn off" or "erased" before the beginning of the novel. This is, in fact, curiously and literally true. In earlier drafts of the novel, Flaubert had provided the following two detailed depictions of Charles's head and face:

La couleur [des cheveux] . . . était d'un blond sale, entre le brun et le châtain, de même que les longs poils clairsemés, qui garnissaient ses mâchoires, calmaient la violence de son beau teint rose et donnaient à l'ensemble de sa tête un ton général gris, indécis et comme poussiéreux. . . .
    . . . Les longs poils fins qui veloutaient ses joues comme une moisissure blonde, tamisant l'éclat vif de ses pommettes, estompaient d'un duvet incolore, sa figure tranquille.[21]

[The color [of his hair] . . . was a dirty blond, between brown and chestnut, as were the long sparse hairs which adorned his jaws, calmed the violence of his fine pink complexion and gave to his head as a whole a general tint that was gray, indecisive and as though dusty. . . .
    . . . The long fine hairs that velveted his cheeks like a blond mold, filtering the vivid burst of his cheekbones, blurred with a colorless down his tranquil face.]

We have known for some time that Flaubert often "rewrote" his early drafts by eradicating the very details that he had researched and inscribed with painstaking care, but this particular case of erasure is particularly striking. When we look closely at the deleted details, we find that these two "erased descriptions" of Charles's face both describe that very face as being actively engaged in a process of effacement. The first description culminates in the assertion that Charles's face has a gray quality that is indistinct and "dust-like." He is, in other words, described as being "burnt out," extinguished; his face is as gray as ashes and dust; it is already a ruin. In the second version, Charles's face is described as being covered in a kind of "blond mold" that "blurs" or smudges his features into a nondescript tranquility. Thus, we find that the "blankness" of Charles's face that appears in the final version of *Madame Bovary* is not the "blankness" of "novelty" but an acquired "blankness" caused by a particular failure to assimilate the passage of time. The lack of specificity of the features of the "blank face" is an effect of some activity in and of time. The perversity of this description of the passage of time is, of course, that it leaves no specifically readable traces. Although we shall discuss this point later on in the book, I will point out that this mode of "effacement" is exactly what happens systematically to all of the subsequent "faces" that appear in the book. Instead of imprinting faces with "wrinkles" that reflect the depths of expression and experience that have been accumulated and recorded over the course of the passage of time, the curious temporality at work in *Madame Bovary* causes faces to be rubbed off, worn down, and effaced by time. These blank figures do not recall the past; they merely bear mute witness to the fact that the past has been forgotten.

Finally, we can relate the way Flaubert accentuates the decrepit newness of these "blank figures" to the way in which he introduces a new literary vocabulary for the worn-out quality of modern speech. By calling our attention to the serialized language of "casquettes," Flaubert shows how the modern world has specialized in inventing new genres of "blankness." Like the language of clichés or received ideas, these new genres of representation function as empty placeholders for meanings that have been eroded by time rather than remembered by it. As I hope I have shown, we must begin to read this new writing of time by recalling the ways in which the "casquette-effect" reminds us to forget that it is a sign of forgetting. Only by accounting for the poverty of this "poor thing" can we understand the extent to which the cap provides the new linguistic material out of which the rhetorical and temporal capital of the novel is fabricated. We can cap off this discussion by remembering that if the novel is spun out of the shiny threads of Charles's new cap, those "new threads" in the first pages of the novel announce the "poor threads" of its end. In the final paragraphs of the novel we learn that Charles's daughter has become destitute. The novel ends when that feminine "poor thing"—sole surviving bearer of the Bovary name—is condemned to "earn her living" by joining the serialized ranks of the mechanized labor force in a newly minted cotton factory.

Hysteria, Fetishism, and Amnesic Souvenirs

Perhaps nothing is more difficult than reading one's own time. But whenever we encounter heightened interest in a prevailing pathology we are invited to learn something about the specifically historical preoccupations that have helped to produce it. Thus, to the extent that the nineteenth century devoted itself to defining "hysteria," it has become partly defined, in turn, by the questions and problems raised by hysteria. As a number of feminist literary critics and cultural historians have conclusively shown, "hysteria" was the name the nineteenth century gave for its reigning anxieties concerning sexual difference and the place of women in society.[22]

Given *Madame Bovary*'s thematic depiction of a socially ambitious and sexually adventurous woman, it is not surprising that it has become one of the most enduring and oft-cited examples of hysteria as a social, medical, class-bound, literary, and cultural concern. As we approach the end of the twentieth century, however, recent reflections on Flaubert have taken a seemingly different turn. Dating roughly from the late 1970s (and perhaps inspired by the issues raised by the volume *Flaubert and Postmodernism* published in 1980), critics have increasingly and insistently become intent on examining Flaubert's relationship to another more modern, or perhaps postmodern, pathological structure: fetishism. Perhaps more than any other modern writer, Flaubert's work seems to place these two pathological structures in a kind of ongoing, active, and semiconscious dialogue with one another and with our time. Although there is a long critical history of documented interest in Flaubert's hysteria and hysteria in Flaubert (by figures as diverse as Baudelaire, Sartre, Naomi Schor, and Janet Beizer), in recent years there has been a veritable irruption of attention given to fetishism in Flaubert (notably by Charles Bernheimer, Tony

Tanner, Emily Apter, Naomi Schor, Louise Kaplan, and Marc Redfield). These critics have all astutely observed that Flaubert's work provides us with an almost encyclopedic catalogue of fetishism in all its various theoretical guises. As Marc Redfield puts it: "Particularly in the wake of Sartre's *L'Idiot de la famille*, critics have frequently construed Flaubert's texts in terms of linguistic, libidinal or socio-ideological fetishism. To such construals the texts respond with such alacrity that a closer look at the notion of the fetish holds considerable promise."[23] Feminist critics Naomi Schor and Janet Beizer understand Flaubert's "fetishism" in relation to his stylistic use of irony. They claim, in short, that Flaubert often uses his irony as a reactive and ultimately reactionary defense against representations of sexual difference in his texts.[24] Although their work on sexual difference has been invaluable, my approach to the problem will be slightly different. By examining how "fetishism" is an expression of a "temporal disorder" as well as a denial of sexual difference, I hope to be able to reframe the problem of sexual difference in Flaubert in relation to the question of time. I would like to suggest that if "hysteria" has become a symptomatic *representation* of the concerns of the nineteenth century, "fetishism" can be understood as one of the twentieth century's perverse *responses* to the unassimilated residue of the impact of questions produced by and in the nineteenth century. In other words, to the extent that fetishism can be read as a defining pathology of the twentieth century, it recapitulates the very questions raised by hysteria (sexual difference and psychic repression) as well as those of the shock experience (overwhelming stimuli that decrease memory function) and reorganizes them into a different formal and psychic representational framework. If, as Freud has famously suggested, hysterics suffer mainly from "reminiscences," by which he meant repressed memories that fail to be integrated into the psyche (and hence impeded those who suffered from them from conforming to the accepted sexual roles made available to them by society), the issues raised by "fetishism" include a denial of sexual difference (rather than a repression of its consequences) accompanied by a curious form of concretized, regressive "forgetting."

In the last several decades, psychoanalytic theory, like literary criticism, has also become increasingly attuned to the importance of reexamining the status of fetishism. Upon reflection, it becomes apparent that this renewed interest in fetishism is implicitly, if not explicitly, historically motivated and engaged with questions of temporality. On the most banal level, it seems clear that fetishism provided an obvious starting point for a

re-evaluation of many of the cultural and clinical concerns that began to
gain prominence in the post–World War II period. For example, it became
increasingly clear that it was necessary to refine the classical understanding
of the "perversions" in order to be able to respond to the urgent need for a
more general social recognition and acceptance of homosexuality. More recently, we have begun to witness the emergence of increasingly visible
forms of other still less conventional forms of sexual practice such as trans-
vestism and ritualized dominance and submission. But these thematic
manifestations of the historical link between what has been called perversion and contemporary culture are not, to my mind, the most compelling
articulations of what is ultimately at stake here. In the clinical literature of
the same period, however, we find evidence that thinking about fetishism
asks us to think about our time by asking us to rethink our conception of
time. Without going into all of the specifics of the psychoanalytic literature
on the subject, I would point out that recent work on the "borderline
states," "concreteness," and even the literature pertaining to the psychic
meaning of addiction is haunted by the conceptual and metapsychological
problems raised by fetishism.[25] Although I am moving far too quickly, the
salient point I want to make is that many of the contemporary pathologies
that were "discovered" and "defined" in the latter half of this century share
two common features: they are motivated by regressive tendencies rather
than by repression and hence often produce symptoms that are explicitly or
implicitly engaged in attempts to ward off the movement of time by "stopping it" or by reversing its movement. The term "regression" here refers to
a backward movement through time to a point that is, psychically speaking, prior to temporal differentiation. In his seminal paper, "The Waning
of the Oedipus Complex," Hans Loewald speculates that "modern life"
may be characterized—paradoxically enough—by the emergence of a new
(structural but not necessarily pathological), perverse form of a "return to
the archaic" in place of the more familiar, nineteenth-century (structural)
neurotic mode of a "return of the repressed." Loewald writes:

In the psychosexual and social life of the present day "archaic" currents are more
in evidence, less repressed, I believe. They consequently make for different trou-
bles, often closer to "perversion" than "neurosis." Our own views on what is to be
considered as perversion are changing, for example, in regard to homosexuality.
Modern life, partly moved by and partly moving psychoanalysis, is redrawing the
outline of normality, of what is archaic in mental life and what is advanced, ma-
ture mentality.[26]

In the final pages of his essay, Loewald seems to suggest that rapid changes in the temporal and organizational structures of the external world have sensitized us to those aspects of psychic reality that resist change and challenge all forms of differentiation—including time itself. In recent years (and inspired, in part, by Loewald's reflections on the relationship between time and reality), psychoanalyst and literary critic Alan Bass has been exploring the temporal dimension of fetishism through what he calls "the problem of concreteness." Bass defines "concreteness" as:

a compromise formation between any form of differentiation that represents the threat of too much tension and a set of fantasies that replace this unconsciously registered differentiation within consciousness. The basic properties of hallucinatory wish fulfillment and the disavowal and ego splitting intrinsic to fetishism are the dynamic underpinnings of this particular kind of compromise formation. . . . Another way of thinking about "concreteness," . . . is that the patient has difficulty with symbolization per se.[27]

In his discussion of "concreteness," Bass returns to Freud's discussion of fetishism and "ego splitting" by thinking about how the "defense against reality" described in these texts takes on a specifically temporal dimension. He explains how a fetishistic disavowal of reality necessitates a fetishistic disavowal of time itself.

As a defense, concreteness makes it clear that there is no such possible relief from the tension of differentiation. Every new moment renews the threat, for the simple reason that time itself implies possible change. Thus, the fetishist for Freud and the concrete patient in general lead one to think about the *process* of defense directed against what can be called the *processive* aspects of reality. Such processes produce real effects, but are not readily perceivable. The most salient example is time itself. Time, as just stated, is intrinsic to all change, to all differentiation. The idea that wish fulfillment implies perceptual identity is so important because it allows one to understand that by using negative hallucination to conflate reality and fantasy in the *now* of perception, wish fulfillment can be used defensively to ward off the process of differentiation over time . . . The entire problem is situated at the level of the regressive, defensive cathexis of consciousness and perception which uses these habitual guarantors of reality to suspend reality testing.[28]

Although we cannot take the time to work through all the complexities of Bass's argument, it should be clear that his work on "concreteness" resonates, in significant ways, with the terms we invoked in our discussion of Charles Bovary's cap. Bass suggests that in "concreteness" *perception* is used defensively in order to stop the process of time. He argues that the fantasy that time has been stopped is sustained by the apparent immutability of the "nowness" of perception. The very act of *perceiving* then functions as an active means of denying that there is any discrepancy between inner, "psychic" reality (in the form of unconscious wishes) and the dynamic—hence changing—aspects of external reality. In one of his most radical gestures, Bass suggests that this overinvestment in perception *requires* that the experience of time itself be erased and eliminated. This occurs, Bass implies, both *because* time cannot be grasped through perception and *so that* time can be successfully denied. Fetishistic perception then becomes a subtle defense against the temporal dimension of reality. Furthermore, when (false) perception is used to intercept reality testing in this way, memory no longer functions in normal fashion.

In "Fetishism," Freud repeatedly relates the phenomenon of fetishistic disavowal to a very specific form of failed memory. He introduces the problem of failed memory when he says, in what might appear to be an aside to his main argument about the disavowal of sexual difference, that "when the fetish is instituted some process occurs which reminds one of the stopping of memory in traumatic amnesia."[29] This "stopping of memory" which is likened to a "traumatic amnesia" seems to have a very different metapsychological status than the forms of forgetting that are the normal consequences of material that becomes unconscious by way of repression. In repression, "*Verdrängung*," unwanted bits of reality are removed from consciousness by being stored as unconscious memories. Thus, although such (former) perceptions are not available to consciousness they are, nonetheless, retained as memory traces in the unconscious. Repression, as Freud reiterates constantly, is the result of a conflict between inner, instinctual demands and the pressures coming from the outside world. But something very different seems to occur in fetishistic disavowal ("*Verleugnung*"). In disavowal, perception functions as a kind of active screen or shield between the subject and the external world that filters out unwanted realities before they can even be transformed into memory traces. Disavowal prevents these perceptions from entering into the fabric of the psyche in any kind of symbolic form. These disavowed, fetishistic perceptions fail to form "memories" in the traditional sense because they remain relegated to a realm untouched by language functions. Unlike "repressed" unconscious material, which is constantly reworked in the unconscious and which returns (partially) to consciousness through the distortions inherent to symbolic substitutions in the form of words, dreams, and symptoms, disavowed material is "registered"—somewhere—in the famously "split" ego, but rendered radically inaccessible to language, meaning structures, memory, and time itself.[30]

In the preceding pages, I coined the term "casquette-effect" to describe the operation whereby Charles Bovary's cap functions as an object that reminds us to forget that we have forgotten something. It should be apparent by this point that what I have been calling the "casquette-effect" is, by any other name, a mise-en-scène of the structure of fetishism. If I have somewhat coyly (and perhaps disingenuously) delayed calling this operation by the technical name by which it could be most easily recognized, it is in part because the term "fetishism" risks becoming as deceptively familiar to us as Charles Bovary's cap. But by coming to the problem of fetishism through the figuration of the hat and by looking at the links between them, I have tried both to describe the "cap" in new ways and to put Freud's discussion of fetishism into the context of a historical shift in the way we have come to think about the relationship between temporality and representational structures. In a felicitous formula, psychoanalyst Robert Stoller has written that a "fetish is a story masquerading as an object."[31] In the context of this discussion, we might use our reading of the cap to embellish his description as follows: "A fetish is a story (replacing a forgotten but unassimilated event) masquerading as an object (or 'poor thing') that makes a scene in order to ward off an unbearable aspect of reality by stopping time."

It should be apparent by this point that Charles's cap is a quintessentially fetishistic thing. On one level, the self-evident nature of this revelation can only render it disappointingly anticlimactic. To say that objects of clothing function as fetishes in Flaubert is hardly news. As Charles Bernheimer puts it: "Of the numerous structures of substitution that abound in Flaubert's writing, fetishism is surely one of the most evident. What reader has not noticed the way Frédéric focuses on Madame Arnoux's shoes, the hem of her dress, the fur trim of her black velvet coat? These objects of clothing classically fulfill the Freudian description of the origin of the fetish."[32] Certainly, even if one limited oneself uniquely to hats, shoes, gloves, and accessories, the evidence is overwhelming and the verdict conclusive: fetishistic descriptions of objects constitute the norm, rather than the exception, in Flaubert's writing. It is important to note here that although the terms fetishism and Flaubert have begun to go together like hand and glove, Charles Bovary's cap has, somewhat surprisingly, escaped being catalogued with the other, more readily recognizable fetish objects that adorn nearly every page of *Madame Bovary*.[33] And, in some sense, this is as it should be. The cap is not simply a fetish object among other fetish objects for, as we have seen, it can hardly be viewed as an object at all. As we saw in the preceding pages, it is a prosthetic cornucopia that bears witness not simply to the loss of one specific object, but rather the loss of all objects—the loss of the world as such. As the figure through which the very relationship between inner and outer, name and thing, male and female, singular and serial is articulated, the cap must be understood as a literary incarnation of a theoretical speculation about fetishism rather than a fetish in its own right. What does this mean? It means that the cap initiates, encapsulates, and enacts a drama about the highly unusual and specific organizing assumptions about language, sexual difference, and time that constitute the entire system of representation that unfolds, in myriad ways (including the proliferation of more authentically fetishistic objects), throughout the remainder of the novel. It is critical to note that the cap appears *in place of* the inauguration of the narrative. It is the novel's First Thing. This First Thing is nothing other than an anti-clock. In place of a series of narrative events, the hat freezes the beginning of this "story" into the thing. The hat does not merely appear, is not merely described, but it "happens." It is not merely an object, but also an event.

Effacements

As the novel's originary fetish, the hat announces the perverse antichronological nature of the narrative itself. Paradoxically, the very same eventful object that gets the story started functions—simultaneously—to stop the passage of time. The story that the hat fails to tell—that it displaces and replaces—concerns the ability of the narrative—and the characters within that narrative—to retain events and to assimilate them into a meaningful temporal structure. Here, we must recall that after the fetishistic "primal scene" created and sustained by the presence of the cap, the first chapter of *Madame Bovary* subsequently re-recounts Charles's life story through a stunningly rapid summary of a series of thoroughly generic "events" punctuated by bizarre moments of evacuated consciousness. The scrupulous attention given to the role that *temporality* plays in Charles's preschool education by the priest is a case in point. Charles receives what can only—and ironically at that—be called a "temporal education." Prior to this education, Charles's childhood existence is described as one long happy atemporal romp in the fields. This pastoral and temporally Edenic existence reaches its apotheosis and abruptly ends with a description of how Charles quite literally fuses with time, nature, and experience by swinging on the church bells in order to make them ring: "Il . . . suppliait le bedeau de lui laisser sonner les cloches, pour se pendre de tout son corps à la grande corde et se sentir emporter par elle dans sa volée" (297–98). However, as we discover in the very next lines, Charles has more or less hanged himself on those church bells; they ring the death-knell of time for him. At the age of twelve, through his education with the country priest, he begins to learn how to forget himself through an unrelenting series of missed experiences and lost moments:

A douze ans, sa mère obtint que l'on commençât ses études. On en chargea le curé. Mais les leçons étaient si courtes et si mal suivies, qu'elles ne pouvaient servir à grand'chose. C'était aux moments perdus qu'elles se donnaient, dans la sacristie, debout, à la hâte, entre un baptême et un enterrement; ou bien le curé envoyait chercher son élève après l'*Angelus*, quand il n'avait pas à sortir. On montait dans sa chambre, on s'installait; les moucherons et les papillons de nuit tournoyaient autour de la chandelle. Il faisait chaud, l'enfant s'endormait; et le bonhomme, s'assoupissant les mains sur son ventre, ne tardait pas à ronfler, la bouche ouverte. (298)

[When he was twelve years old his mother had her own way; he began his lessons. The curé took him in hand; but the lessons were so short and irregular that they could not be of much use. They were given at spare moments in the sacristy, standing up, hurriedly, between a baptism and a burial; or else the curé, if he had not to go out, sent for his pupil after the *Angelus*. They went up to his room and settled down; the flies and moths fluttered round the candle. It was close, the child fell asleep, and the good man, beginning to doze with his hands on his stomach, was soon snoring with his mouth wide open.]

The temporal units allocated for this education are designated as the "lost moments" between the various births and deaths in the parish. The obvious—and humorous—irony of such a designation stems, of course, from the fact that such "moments" between "birth" and "death" ought to constitute the very fabric of a lived life. But the importance of this description lies in the fact that there is something uncanny, and deadly serious, about Flaubert's meditation on the problem of "lost moments." Quite deliberately and with remarkable precision, Flaubert arrests the speedy tempo of his narrative and produces a textual "lost moment." The narcoleptic quality of this passage is quite striking. We are confronted with a scene in which the two main characters—priest and student alike—are shown asleep and unconscious. Flaubert attenuates some of the implicitly subversive and disturbing impact of this scene by calling our attention to the night moths circling around the candle. At the level of the narrative, those night moths compensate for the loss of consciousness, time, and experience that has befallen the human characters by serving as witnesses, albeit silent and inhuman ones, to moments that would otherwise appear as radically "lost" to the reader as they are to the characters who presumably live them. But the subsequent recurrence of the figure of the priest's open mouth works in the opposite way. Although this figure is not as brutally obscene as the open mouth we encountered in the classroom debacle with the casquette, it recalls, nonetheless, the same effects of deadened consciousness and lost memory that we first encountered there.

Although the figure of the open mouth always indicates the presence of a "lost moment," the very mention of any human face in *Madame Bovary* is usually associated with some form of temporal disorder. Quite frequently, when the image of the human face appears, it is projected onto inanimate representations of human figures who seem to bear witness to the loss of memory that afflicts their human counterparts. For example, during the ball at Vaubyessard, the shadows produced by the cracks on the varnished surface of the ancestors' portraits animate their visages into a petrified and petrifying stare:

Puis on distinguait à peine ceux qui suivaient, car la lumière des lampes, rabattue sur le tapis vert du billiard, laissait flotter une ombre dans l'appartement. Brunissant les toiles horizontales, elle se brisait contre elles en arêtes fines, selon les craquelures du vernis; et de tous ces grands carrés noirs bordés d'or sortaient, ça et là, quelque portion plus claire de la peinture, un front pâle, deux yeux qui vous regardaient, des perruques se déroulant sur l'épaule poudrée des habits rouges, ou bien la boucle d'une jarretière en haut d'un mollet rebondi. (334)

[One could hardly make out the next ones, for the light of the lamps lowered over the green cloth threw a dim shadow across the room. Burnishing the horizontal pictures, it broke up in delicate lines among the cracks in the varnish, and from all these great black squares framed in gold stood out here and there some lighter portion of the painting—a pale brow, two eyes that looked at you, wigs resting on the powdered shoulder of red coats, or the buckle of a garter above a well-rounded calf.]

This active gaze, produced by the shadows cast on the cracks of these paintings, provides us with one of the very few explicit references to historical memory in the entire text. Through these cracks, presumably produced by the passage of time, we perceive, however fleetingly, a ghostly trace of the petrified presence of the Ancien Régime. But this historical gaze seems relegated to the paintings rather than to their viewers. It is the inhuman portraits that have the eyes that look "vous regardaient," rather than the human spectators. The human characters rarely, if ever, "look" at one another.

But the most memorable instance of how the human face is transformed into a fetishistic, amnesic souvenir occurs when Rodolphe famously attempts to recall Emma's face in order to write her a letter informing her that he has decided to leave her. To Rodolphe's sudden discomfort (if not chagrin), a mere few moments after he decides consciously to forget Emma, he finds that she has quite suddenly dropped into a temporal abyss and has become relegated to a distant, irretrievable past: "Emma lui semblait être reculée dans un passé lointain, comme si la résolution qu'il avait prise venait de placer entre eux, tout à coup, un immense intervalle" [Emma seemed to him to have receded into a far-off past, as if the resolution he had taken had suddenly placed an immeasurable distance between them] (474–75). The premises and consequences of this moment are quite telling. In its own way, this passage announces an activity that can be read as a kind of proleptic, ironic reversal of the Proustian distinction between voluntary and involuntary memory. But here, in place of voluntary and involuntary memory, we are confronted with a complex mechanism of voluntary and involuntary forgetting. Rodolphe's conscious decision to forget Emma produces uncanny temporal effects. In a single instant, "tout à coup," Emma is blasted out of his present memory and becomes instantly frozen in and by time. The moment (on the preceding page) when he last looks at her produces a visceral shock and is depicted in an almost counterphotographic manner: "Au bout de quelques minutes, Rodolphe s'arrêta; et, quand il la vit avec son vêtement blanc peu à peu s'evanouir dans l'ombre comme un fantôme, il fut pris d'un tel battement de coeur, qu'il s'appuya contre un arbre pour ne pas tomber" [After a few moments Rodolphe stopped; and when he saw her with her white gown gradually fade away in the shade like a ghost, his heart beat so wildly that he had to support himself against a tree] (474). Her ghostlike image suddenly fades as if it were like a photograph in the process of undeveloping. It appears to be the shock of this perception (of her fading from his sight) that triggers the complete erasure of memory that follows. The shock seems to imply that Rodolphe's parting "perception" of Emma is, in fact, a hallucination produced by an impossible temporal split. He simultaneously perceives her in the present and as if, in the present, she were already no longer there. In other terms, Rodolphe attempts to compensate for her future absence by trying to perceive her—in the present—as absence.

As he sits down at his desk in order to write to her, Rodolphe discovers that he cannot even remember her clearly enough to execute his explicit plan to forget her. His supposedly "conscious" decision to forget is usurped by the sudden emergence of the very uncanny, insistent mechanism of involuntary (fetishistic) forgetting that permeates the temporal structure of the entire novel. Having unwittingly buried her in time, Rodolphe is then forced to attempt to resuscitate her (temporarily) so that he can ultimately rid himself of her more permanently. But because his active, living memory of her as a living creature has completely failed him, Rodolphe goes to his cabinet in order to retrieve the cookie box in which he stashes his keepsakes and souvenirs:

Afin de ressaisir quelque chose d'elle, il alla chercher dans l'armoire, au chevet de son lit, une vieille boîte de biscuits de Reims, où il enfermait d'habitude ses lettres de femmes, et il s'en échappa une odeur de poussière humide et de roses flétries. D'abord il aperçut un mouchoir de poche, couvert de gouttelettes pâles. C'était un mouchoir à elle, une fois qu'elle avait saigné du nez, en promenade; il ne s'en souvenait plus. (475)

[In order to recapture something of her presence, he fetched from the cupboard at the bedside an old Rheims cookie-box, in which he usually kept his love-letters. An odor of dry dust and withered roses emanated from it. First he saw a handkerchief stained with pale drops. It was a handkerchief of hers. Once when they were walking her nose had bled; he had forgotten it.]

When Rodolphe appeals to the contents of his cookie box in order to help him remember Emma, the cookie box first appears to belong, however ironically, to a set of classical representations of memory that use architectural, spatial figures (monuments, tombs, wells, etc.) as representations of the psyche in which things of the past are buried. As Paul de Man observes, "The emblem for interiorized memory, in Hegel, is that of the buried treasure or mine (*Schaft*), or, perhaps, a well."[34] But in this passage, we discover that Rodolphe's cookie box is not a figure for memory, nor does it stimulate remembrance. Instead, we find that Rodolphe's encounter with the cookie box rigorously and systematically undermines all potentially mnemonic systems. One by one, all possible means of remembering are reversed, disabled, and dismantled.

The passage begins by presenting the cookie box as a crypt or tomb. When Rodolphe opens the box, he is struck by the smell of damp dust and faded roses. But this sensuous evocation of memory and desire through smell produces no effects on him. After smell (normally conceived as the most potent trigger for involuntary memory) fails to help him, Rodolphe catches sight of Emma's stained handkerchief. This thing—a piece of clothing marked with her blood—has something of the status of a religious relic or erotic fetish. Like the smell that precedes it, it seemingly promises an absolutely unmediated trace of past experience; it ought to recall the past in its immediacy—without passing through any mediating system of representation. Emma's body is literally recorded on the handkerchief. The drops of blood on the handkerchief are like bits of her body that have been preserved in the box. But curiously, the sight of this relic, this body-thing, automatically provokes further forgetfulness: "C'était un mouchoir à elle, une fois qu'elle avait saigné du nez, en promenade; il ne s'en souvenait plus" (475).

After sensuous souvenirs (the smells and the handkerchief) fail to trigger either conscious or unconscious memories, Rodolphe's relationship to memory deteriorates even more radically. Now, even conscious, mimetic faculties begin to fail him. Rodolphe stumbles upon an actual representation of her—a small portrait of her face—and mistakenly assumes that by looking at her image he will be able to recall an image of her:

Il y avait auprès, se cognant à tous les angles, la minature donnée par Emma; sa toilette lui parut prétentieuse et son regard *en coulisse* du plus pitoyable effet; puis à force de considérer cette image et d'évoquer le souvenir du modèle, les traits d'Emma peu à peu se confondirent en sa mémoire, comme si la figure vivante et la figure peinte, se frottant l'une contre l'autre, se fussent réciproquement effacées. (475)

[Near it, almost too large for the box, was Emma's miniature: her dress seemed pretentious to him, and her languishing look in the worst possible taste. Then, from looking at this image and recalling the memory of the original, Emma's features little by little grew confused in his remembrance, as if the living and the painted face, rubbing one against the other, had erased each other.]

Here, we have moved into active forgetting. Rodolphe seemingly needs to use the painted image (the representation) in order to conjure up a mental picture of Emma's face that is presumably stored in his "memory." But there is no correlation between the two figures; the painted face does not correspond to the memory of its model. Although the disparity between the two "figures" is given a thematic explanation (Emma affects an artificial pose in the portrait that gives her a pathetic, staged "look"), Flaubert's text insinuates that these two figures are somehow even more primally at odds with one another. Paradoxically, the conflict between represented image and memory image is due to a kind of systemic collapse; the two images destroy one another because they are in an uncomfortable proximity to one another while, at the same time, at an unbreachable remove from anything remotely attached to their absent and forgotten referent—a lived perception of Emma's "living" face.

Flaubert's word choice in this passage is itself striking. On the one hand, this is one of the very few passages in the novel in which there is any explicit mention either of words associated with mnemonic functions such as "mémoire" or "souvenir," or of words associated with distinguishing facial features such as "figure" or "traits"—but all of these defining nouns are negated by the verbs to which they are attached: "se confondirent," "se frottant," "se fussent éffacées." In other words, the very (classical) system of mimetic representation announced by the nouns is in direct conflict with the action described by the verbs. The verbal actions (of confusing, rubbing, and effacing) counteract and cancel out any possibility of constructing (or sustaining) a system of representation that can distinguish between original and copy or that can maintain a correspondence between interior memories and external representations and, by extension, between present perceptions and past experiences.

The most subversive (and quasi-obscene) detail of the passage resides in Flaubert's use of the expression "se frottant l'une contre l'autre" in order to describe how the two images of Emma's face mutually efface one another because they "rub each" other off.[35] The problem with these representations is that they are depicted as concrete, physical bodies (rather than abstract mental pictures)—and perverse, feminine bodies at that. The external picture and the internal image are thus described as having been brought into physical, almost sexual contact with one another. Furthermore, if the physical contact between these two images has a sexual undertone, it would seem to point to the notion that imagined acts of "reciprocal rubbing" are viewed as being explicitly counter-reproductive. Here, the two representations erase one another (through reciprocal rubbing) because the contact between them destroys the specificity of both of them by removing their distinguishing marks.

It is important not to forget that this sexualized scene of "faces rubbing each other off" is itself nothing else than an elaborate metaphor designed to explain the mechanism of Rodolphe's forgetting. Thus, although one could argue that Rodolphe fails to remember Emma because (as we know well from earlier textual examples) he is incapable of distinguishing Emma from any other woman he has known and hence she has no specificity, one might also argue, more radically, that Rodolphe's failure to accord Emma any specificity is itself produced by the failure of a system of representation that is incapable of retaining memories of past experiences by reproducing those past experiences in mental pictures, memories, or words. This unsettling notion—that representation might become completely unhinged from any memory function whatsoever—is systematically borne out as Rodolphe continues to plunge deeper and deeper in the nether reaches of his cookie box. After her portrait fails to remind him of her, the next stage of Rodolphe's quest for any memory trace of Emma leads him to her letters:

Enfin, il lut de ses lettres; elles étaient pleines d'explications relatives à leur voyage, courtes, techniques et pressantes comme des billets d'affaires. (475)

[Finally, he read some of her letters; they were full of explanations relating to their journey, short, technical and urgent, like business notes.]

As it turns out, Emma's letters fail to function as linguistic signs. Since the more recent missives are "short and technical," these letters transform linguistic signs (language) into messages whose unique function is to convey usable information. But since these technical letters were written (probably in haste) in order to convey (time-sensitive) information pertaining to a future event that will never transpire (the aborted travel plans), they become completely meaningless when they are rendered useless. Furthermore, because they were written in technical, businesslike, goal-oriented language, they have become as useless in evoking the past as they are in planning the future: they evoke no sensations, feelings, or memories.

Rodolphe's next attempt to recall Emma places him in the absurd position of delving into an even more distant past—the era of Emma's earliest letters—in a vain attempt to find some material proof—some sign— that the past even exists:

Il voulut revoir les longues, celles d'autrefois; pour les trouver au fond de la boîte, Rodolphe dérangea toutes les autres; et machinalement il se mit à fouiller dans ce tas de papiers et de choses, y retrouvant pêle-mêle des bouquets, une jarretière, un masque noir, des épingles et des cheveux! De bruns, de blonds; quelques-uns, même, s'accrochant à la ferrure de la boîte, se cassaient quand on l'ouvrait. (475)

[He wanted to see the long ones again, those of old times. In order to find them at the bottom of the box, Rodolphe disturbed all the others, and mechanically began rummaging among this mass of papers and things, finding pell-mell bouquets, garters, a black mask, pins, and hair . . . lots of hair! Some dark, some fair, some, catching in the hinges of the box, even broke when he opened it.]

But Rodolphe finds no long love letters. Instead, this last foray into the cookie box culminates in a colossal collapse of all systems of representation by erasing all traces of differentiation. Now, Rodolphe "mechanically" stumbles into a realm where letters and things are indistinguishable ("ce tas de papiers et de choses") and where bits of women's bodies seem to multiply and proliferate. At this juncture, letters no longer signify, amorous keepsakes are relics of forgotten events, and all traces of Emma's memory are erased and displaced by the teeming mass of hair that overflows from the box. In collecting these locks of dead hair, Rodolphe erases, rather than preserves, the experience of the past. In "Central Park," Walter Benjamin observes that:

The souvenir (*Das Andenken*) is the relic secularized. The souvenir is the complement of the "experience" (*des "Erlebnisses"*). In it the increasing self-alienation of the person who inventories his past as dead possession is distilled. In the 19th century allegory left (*hat geräumt*) the surrounding world, in order to settle in the inner world. The relic derives from the corpse, the souvenir from deceased experience (*Erfahrung*) which calls itself euphemistically "*Erlebnis*."[36]

At the end of Rodolphe's cookie box memory quest, all distinctions between present and past, between language and thing, and between Emma and every other woman Rodolphe has ever known have been effaced. Instead of finding a discrete memory trace that might recall Emma's specificity, Rodolphe involuntarily (and unconsciously) integrates her into the seemingly infinite series of his previously forgotten women.

This cookie box contains no Proustian madeleine. It is a veritable forgetting machine, and as such it exposes the machinery of Flaubertian forgetting. Flaubert traces the mechanics of this forgetting through every possible system of representation. When all mnemonic representations (smells, relics, pictures, letters) break down, the only thing that remains are fetishistic amnesic souvenirs: letters reduced to material marks and locks of human hair that have erased their human faces.

Trauma, Addiction, and Temporal Bulimia
in *Madame Bovary*

> Lisez, et ne rêvez pas. Plongez-vous dans de longues études. Il n'y
> a de continuellement bon que l'habitude d'un travail entêté. Il s'en
> dégage un opium qui engourdit l'âme.
>
> [Read and do not dream. Immerse yourself in long studies. The only
> thing that is continually good is the habit of stubborn work. It emits
> an opium that numbs the soul.]
> —Gustave Flaubert to Louise Colet
>
> *Madame Bovary* I daresay is about bad drugs.
> —Avital Ronell, *Crack Wars*

If Flaubert's *Madame Bovary* remains so timely, it is because its heroine, Emma, suffers from the quintessential malady of modernity, the inability to incorporate time into experience. Emma's missed encounter with
her own life, her inability to "get a life," as we say now in America, renders
her our contemporary in the strangest sense of the word. She is our contemporary not because we live in the same time but because her failure to
live in time has come to define our own. Paradoxically, Emma Bovary has
been so well preserved (she is, in some sense, "more alive" now than ever)
because she incarnates and inaugurates a modernity that can be defined by
the erosion of the possibility of living in time. In Flaubert's minute and
meticulous descriptions of the particular temporal disorders that afflict
Emma (as we shall see, she can neither bear witness to an event nor remember one, she can neither live in the present nor project a future, she is
incessantly subject to bouts of involuntary forgetting even as she is preoc-

cupied by obsessive rites of recollection, she attempts simultaneously to conjure up time and to stop it), we can read the prophetic traces of a depiction of the temporal structure of the many forms of trauma and addiction that have come to define contemporary American culture.

But before turning to Flaubert's prescient and powerful analysis of how Emma Bovary suffers from a "temporal disorder," let us take a brief look at how the notions of trauma and addiction have been described in a contemporary analysis of modern culture. In a recent book *On Flirtation*, the British child psychoanalyst Adam Phillips redescribes ordinary neurosis as a traumatic response to an inability to live in time. He writes: "People come to psychoanalysis when there is something they cannot forget, something they cannot stop telling themselves, often by their actions, about their lives. And these dismaying repetitions—this unconscious limiting or coercion of the repertoire of life stories—create the illusion of time having stopped (or rather, people believe–behave as if—they have stopped time). In our repetitions we seem to be staying away from the future, keeping it at bay."[1] Phillips goes on to explain that: "For Freud these repetitions are the consequence of a failure to remember. . . . Whatever cannot be transformed, psychically processed, reiterates itself. A trauma is whatever there is in a person's experience that resists useful redescription. Traumas, like beliefs, are ways of stopping time."[2] Phillips's argument rings with a seductive simplicity: neurosis is defined as a temporal disorder and the contemporary psychoanalytic "cure" does nothing less than promise time. It presumably offers the subject a choice between accepting the contingencies of living in time over the pleasure and pain that attend the attempt to stop it.

Nonetheless, Phillips's claim—that contemporary neurosis can be expressed as an attempt to stop time—should, perhaps, make us pause. Stopping time, in the time of Balzac, Gautier, Baudelaire, and Flaubert, was once conceived of as part of the privileged domain reserved for art and the artist. We might have naively assumed that in the realm of the "real world," for "real people," time remains an implacable fact of life. The task of falling out of time, after all, would seem to necessitate either an accident of enormous magnitude (a trauma in the traditional sense) or the reliance upon an external substance—hashish, opium, alcohol, or cocaine—one of those mind-altering substances that so preoccupied the nineteenth-century advocates of "paradis artificiels." So what is surprising and particularly suggestive about Phillips's observations is not that the ordinary neurotic *fails* to stop time, but rather that he or she *succeeds* so well. This dubious "success" is incontestably well documented in the realm of American popular culture where, in television talk-shows, sitcoms, tabloids, self-help books, and twelve-step programs, as well as on the dwindling couches of analysts who have, for the most part, been replaced by millions of prescriptions for Prozac and Zoloft, trauma, along with its uncanny other, addiction, are visibly the most emblematic and paradoxically *popular* illnesses of our time.

Phillips's invocation of the notion of "trauma" in the context of everyday pathologies only further complicates the problem. When he writes, rather casually, that "traumas, like beliefs, are ways of stopping time," what has happened to our implicit understanding of what trauma is and how it occurs? Trauma is more or less classically understood as a response to an event so extraordinary that, in the language of the American Psychiatric Institute (cited by Cathy Caruth in her introduction to *Trauma: Explorations in Memory*) it is "outside the range of usual human experience."[3] Because the event is both so threatening (it often occurs in the case of near-death encounters) and because the experience cannot be assimilated, the event is mechanically reproduced as recollection bereft of memory. As Caruth writes, "The pathology consists, rather, solely in the *structure of experience* or reception: the event is not assimilated or experienced fully at the time, but only belatedly, in its repeated *possession* of the one who experiences it. To be traumatized is precisely to be possessed by an image or event."[4] Because this atemporal "possession" prevents the traumatized subject from experiencing (in the sense of assimilating) the precipitating event, that non-event comes to organize a systematic disruption of many, if not all, other life experiences. We could argue that in the uncontrollable and often unmanageable repetitions of the traumatic event, the subject's inability both to forget and remember the event is lived as if time itself had become a persecutory enemy, an overwhelming other.

But if the subject of "trauma" is, as we have said, "possessed" by time, what is the temporal status of the addicted subject? How and why can trauma and addiction be read as uncanny inversions of a similar temporal disorder? In both cases, certainly, the subject appears to be "possessed" and is apparently condemned to acts of compulsive repetition unto death in either literal or symbolic ways. But where the traumatic subject is seemingly dominated by an inability to forget, the addicted subject seems driven by a strange, compulsive *need* to forget. If trauma can be understood as the attempt to survive an inassimilable encounter with "near-death," the structure of addiction emerges as a strange kind of "near-life" experience.

Where the traumatized subject cannot get away from the voice of time, the addicted subject seemingly cannot find a place *in* it. Time, for the addict, is not figured as an anthropomorphized persecutory other—but rather appears almost like something that happens elsewhere, to other people. The time of addiction is a time, like trauma, "outside the range of usual human experience," but in the case of addiction, the subject appears to be exiled from time rather than possessed by it.

The temporal coincidence of the appearance of *Madame Bovary* with that of *Les Fleurs du mal* leads one to ask about the historical status of this failure of experience. The traumatized voice of a subject "possessed" by time echoes through many of Baudelaire's poems, but the most explicit example of traumatic paranoid possession can be found in "L'Horloge." In "L'Horloge," the poet conjures up a demonic figure of time in the opening first line, "Horloge, Dieu Sinistre," and immediately loses control over his own voice. The voice of the clock usurps that of the poet and then repeats the command "souviens-toi" again and again in increasingly mechanized tones until it condemns the poet to death in the last line. But where Baudelaire's work might be dominated by the figure of trauma (even though it is he and not Flaubert who put addiction at the center of his concerns), it is in Flaubert's novel that we find, in place of the druglike flowers of evil with their lure of opiate aroma, the full-blown structure of an addiction with no point of return. By insisting upon the effects of this addicted temporality, I hope to explain why, as any reader of *Madame Bovary* knows, Emma never had a life to lose.[5]

We can begin to appreciate the impact of finding oneself being shut out of time by turning to Flaubert's *Madame Bovary*, a text which is perhaps one of the most eloquent analyses of the temporal pathology of the language of everyday life available to us. Long before Marcel Proust dramatized the problem of time through the figures of *mémoire volontaire* and *involontaire*, Emma Bovary struggled against the demon of involuntary forgetting. If Proust must be seen as the indelible archivist of the telling of the modern subject's narration of his relationship to lost time, Flaubert can be read as the scribe, the copyist, of the modern subject's non-narratable relation to wasted time. But unlike Proust's narrator, Flaubert's Emma Bovary cannot quest for lost time; instead, as the novel explicitly demonstrates, she is in search for time itself, in the form of an event. Unable to isolate anything in her "daily life" that she can grasp in the form of an "event," she turns to fiction. While virtually all readers and critics of *Madame Bovary* (beginning, of course, with the legal, political, and cultural institutions that saw fit to put the book on trial) would agree with Michael Riffaterre's observation that "*Madame Bovary* is a fiction about the dangers of fiction,"[6] critics have widely divergent ways of interpreting the causes and consequences of Emma's reading habit.[7] Reading Emma's reading habits is a favorite activity of *Bovary's* critics, many of whom seem to be vaguely reassured by the notion that Emma's misfortunes and suffering can in large part be attributed to her unhealthy and ultimately misguided dependency on works of fiction. This tendency is exemplified by Victor Brombert's claim that "Emma's flaw is that she uses art to feed her dreams, instead of placing her dreams in the service of art."[8] Such a reading implies that Emma's suffering stems from the fact that she is a bad reader of the relationship between art and life.[9] By turning briefly to the first passage in the text that introduces *Madame Bovary's* reader to Emma as reader, I would like to suggest that if one too quickly concludes that Emma is simply a bad reader, Flaubert's reader risks glossing over the complexity of his idiomatic and highly disturbing articulation of how time and experience can become unhinged in both life and art. In the concluding paragraph of chapter 5, part 1, Flaubert writes:

Avant qu'elle se mariât, elle avait cru avoir de l'amour; mais le bonheur qui aurait dû résulter de cet amour n'étant pas venu, il fallut qu'elle se fût trompée, songeait-elle. Et Emma cherchait à savoir ce que l'on entendait au juste dans la vie par des mots de *félicité*, de *passion*, et *d'ivresse*, qui lui avaient paru si beaux dans les livres. (322)

[Before marriage she thought herself in love; but since the happiness that should have followed failed to come, she must, she thought, have been mistaken. And Emma tried to find out what one meant exactly in life by the words *bliss*, *passion*, *ecstasy*, that had seemed to her so beautiful in books.] (24)[10]

The obvious irony of this passage derives from the fact that Emma resolves the discrepancy between her lived experience of love and her reading knowledge of love by concluding that the error lies not in her books but in her life. Such a reading only confirms two common characterizations of Emma Bovary: at worst, she is a foolish, provincial woman who deludes herself with romantic fantasies, and at best she is a pathetic travesty of an artist because she tragically misrecognizes the proper hierarchy between "Art" and "Life." Both of these interpretations are certainly textually justified and are supported and seemingly solicited by Flaubert's explicitly contemptuous descriptions of Emma in the correspondence as well as his implicit critique of Emma throughout the text of *Madame Bovary*. Furthermore, in the passage itself Flaubert seemingly establishes a distance between the voice of narrative authority and Emma's faulty reasoning by adding the telltale attribution "songeait-elle" to Emma's conclusion that she has been mistaken about life: "il fallut qu'elle se fût trompée, songeait-elle." The phrase "songeait-elle" underscores the notion that even when engaging in the act of facing the barren reality of her life, Emma can do nothing other than dream.

Presumably bereft of any form of experience other than those received from books, Emma can only perceive that she has not yet had an event by comparing the lexicon of her life with that of the novels she has read. The word which trips her up is, not surprisingly, "amour." But what is surprising is that Emma's difficulty in reconciling the difference between book-love and her lived experience emerges not in relation to the word's meaning or definition, but rather in relation to its temporal effects and narrative function. Novel reading has taught Emma that "amour" ought to announce an inaugural event that propels a life into a durable and continued state of "bonheur" (happiness). Hence one only knows that one has "possessed love" (avoir de l'amour) when that love produces an event that guarantees temporal continuity in the form of "bonheur." The disappointing revelations occasioned by Emma's marriage are consequently multiple: in the first place, the marriage cannot function as an event in itself because it does not occur at the properly eventful hour of midnight: "Emma eût, au contraire, désiré se marier à minuit" (Emma would, on the contrary, have preferred to have a midnight wedding) (314/18, respectively). Next, the marriage fails to produce the anticipated state of happiness. And finally, and perhaps most important, these first two failures force her to acknowledge that she has been jilted by an "event" at the altar of time. The temporal finality and precision of the words "le bonheur qui aurait dû résulter de cet amour n'étant pas venu" almost anthropomorphizes "bonheur" into the missing bridegroom, whose absence at the wedding necessarily obliterates the meaning and the function of the event. Instead of enabling her to begin an eventful life by establishing a bridge between the world of fiction and the language of life, the word "love" opens up an irrevocable abyss between the formlessness of lived time and the experience of narrative meaning provided by fiction. The fissure between the fictional temporality of the word "love" and its seemingly absent corresponding referent in the real world functions rhetorically like a catachresis, a figural term that has no literal meaning. As we shall see in greater depth later on, the appearance of the word "amour" in *Madame Bovary* is always hyperinvested in strange ways and almost always signals the presence of a temporal disorder. In this passage, once Emma recognizes the disconnection between the word "amour" and its fictional referent, she learns that any and all words could potentially become meaningless in the language of life: "Et Emma cherchait à savoir ce que l'on entendait au juste *dans la vie* par des mots de *félicité*, de *passion* et *d'ivresse*" (italics mine).

When, however, this passage is read in the context of Flaubert's presentation of Emma's so-called life, it takes on additional resonances. Let us begin by recalling that according to the narrative structure of the novel, Emma, unlike Charles, never had any "real life experiences" onto which fantasy or fictional events were grafted. Whereas the narrative of *Madame Bovary* begins with the fabulous scene of Charles Bovary's primal traumatic schoolroom humiliation through "decapitation" (the loss of his beloved and monstrous "casquette") and traces the subsequent vicissitudes of his daily life (ranging from Charles's mediocre study habits to the events that culminate in his first marriage), the narrative of Emma's "life" prior to her encounter with Charles emerges only after it becomes clear in the above passage that her marriage has failed to constitute the inaugural event of her life. Immediately after this discovery, chapter 6 begins with the recitation of Emma's reading history ("Elle avait lu *Paul et Virginie* et elle avait rêvé la maisonette de bambous" [She had read *Paul and Virginia*, and she had dreamed of the little bamboo-house] (323/24), which introduces, supplements, and ultimately supplants the subsequent narration of her past lived life story: "lorsqu'elle eut treize ans, son père l'amena lui-même à la ville pour la mettre au couvent" [When she was thirteen, her father himself took her to the convent] (323/25). In other words, Emma's substitution of literature for life cannot merely be read as a character flaw since, at the level of the novel's narrative, Flaubert presents her life as if it were actually produced by her readings rather than as a series of lived experiences. Like Emma herself, who apparently has no access to her life that has not been mediated by a prior fictional referent, *Bovary*'s reader is given no access to Emma's "life" that has not already been presented as a fictional production. Paradoxically, however, in the very moment in the text when Emma the character discovers that her marriage has failed to inaugurate her life, at the level of the novel, Emma's disappointment in her marriage initiates the moment when the fictional life of the character known as Emma Bovary is truly born. Prior to this moment, as critics have often observed, the narrative voice displays Emma as a specular object of Charles's gaze, seen almost entirely through his eyes.[11] It is only after Emma literally becomes "Madame Bovary" and realizes that her newly acquired identity has nonetheless failed to provide her with a life that her thoughts and feelings begin to permeate the *style indirect libre* of the authorial voice.

Thus, from the outset of the novel, the subjective presence of the character "Madame Bovary" is animated by and depends upon her alienation from her experience of life. For this reason, rather than reading Emma's recourse to fiction as a cause of her future misfortunes, I prefer to read Emma's reading as the first significant manifestation of her temporal disorder—the fact that her life seemingly unfolds in a temporal void.[12] Therefore, while it is indisputable that Emma displays a naive belief that literature can be directly transformed into life, it is nonetheless quite possible that through her very inability to read her life, Emma provides Flaubert's reader with the novel's most rigorous and lucid embodiment of how time can be severed from experience in modern life. By starting from the assumption that Flaubert's oft-cited utterance "Madame Bovary, c'est moi" should be read quite literally, I hope to resist the temptation to read Emma's plight as either pathetic or tragic in order to uncover critical traces of the history of the modern subject.

Emma's gradual discovery that her life consists of a monotonous temporal vacuum motivates her growing dependency on fictional models of temporal structures. Her most significant early abuse of fiction occurs in the wake of her mother's death. Because the temporal void in which she exists prevents her from being able to sustain the experience in time or to secure its meaning by placing it within a meaningful temporal context, she attempts to compensate for the temporal insufficiency of the literal death by using literary devices to enhance and prolong the experience. Although the actual death fails to constitute a "natural" event for Emma, she welcomes the very idea of death as a potentially fortuitous cure for her timelessness. By applying the basic tenets of romantic aesthetic ideology onto the material fact of her mother's death, she fabricates the following fiction of the future: she anticipates an experience of durable, melancholic inconsolability that culminates in a productive projection of her own future death so that she might ultimately experience a dramatic, spiritual literary rebirth.

Quand sa mère mourut, elle pleura beaucoup les premiers jours. Elle se fit faire un
tableau funèbre avec les cheveux de la défunte, et, dans une lettre qu'elle envoyait
aux Bertaux, toute pleine de réflexions tristes sur la vie, elle demandait qu'on l'en-
sevelît plus tard dans le même tombeau. Le bonhomme la crut malade et vint la
voir. Emma fut intérieurement satisfaite de se sentir arrivée du premier coup à ce
rare idéal des existences pâles, ou ne parviennent jamais les coeurs médiocres. Elle
se laissa donc glisser dans les méandres lamartiniens, écouta les harpes sur les lacs,
tous les chants des cygnes mourants. . . . (326)

[When her mother died she cried much the first few days. She had a funeral picture made with hair of the deceased, and, in a letter sent to the Bertaux full of sad
reflections on life, she asked to be buried later in the same grave. The old man
thought she must be ill, and came to see her. Emma was secretly pleased that she
had reached at a first attempt the rare ideal of delicate lives, never attained by
mediocre hearts. She let herself meander along with Lamartine, listened to harps
on lakes, to all the songs of dying swans. . . .] (27–28)

However, as the conclusion of the passage demonstrates, Emma never
achieves the state of anticipated inconsolability that she had hoped would
serve as incontestable proof of an indelible memory. Despite all the excessive gestures that she performs in order to preserve it, her mother's memory quickly evaporates. And even Emma is disillusioned by how her
Romantic theories of death fail to endure the test of practical application
and hence cannot be considered particularly useful. Much to her dismay
and confusion, she discovers that Death offers no greater chance of a future
than life does. Her fantasy of a new life, a life renewed by literary tropes of
rebirth, is reduced to the vapidity of received ideas. Emma's factory of literary clichés not only fails to supply her with a durable experience of a lived
event, but also hastens its demise through empty repetition:

Elle s'en ennuya, n'en voulut point convenir, continua par habitude, ensuite par
vanité, et fut enfin surprise de se sentir apaisée, et sans plus de tristesse au coeur
que de rides sur son front. (326–27)

[She soon grew bored but wouldn't admit it, continued from habit first, then out
of vanity, and at last was surprised to feel herself consoled, and with no more sadness at heart than wrinkles on her brow.] (28, translation modified)

But in order to appreciate the gravity of this passage and to understand the
textual ramifications of its twisted logic, we must take a closer look at the
mother/daughter relationship depicted in it. In the first place, we are compelled to observe that this is virtually the only moment in *Madame Bovary*
where Emma makes any reference to her mother. Moreover, the missing

mother becomes the site of a disruption of moral, psychological, and temporal categories. It appears that this mother exists uniquely through her death and only by dying can she offer Emma a pretext for the activity of mourning and a promise of rebirth. In a perverse reversal of the natural tropes of maternity, when Emma asks to be buried with her mother in the same grave, the figure of the womb is replaced by that of the tomb in her fantasy of rebirth. But although Flaubert's transvaluation of the maternal function is announced through the substitution of figures of death for figures of life, what is at stake is not simply a confusion of life and death.

This dead mother appears as the first unmistakable annunciation of the activities of involuntary forgetting, mechanical repetition, and failed mourning that pervade the text of *Madame Bovary*. Unlike Charles's mother or Emma's father, the figure of Emma's mother never attains the status of a psychological character; she appears only to disappear and this disappearance becomes remarkable precisely because it leaves no mark. The only "surprise" that this terminal non-event can elicit is the surprise of nothingness itself. Flaubert circumscribes the surprising emptiness of this voided experience through an analogy between two unwritten texts: the absence of sadness in Emma's heart is strikingly compared to the absence of wrinkles on her forehead. The missing wrinkles prove that time remains unwritten there: "[Elle] fut enfin surprise de se sentir apaisée, et sans plus de tristesse au coeur que de rides sur son front." The ironic analogy between Emma's absent affect and her unmarked forehead reiterates that the mother's death fails as event because it cannot mark the passage of time. It comes as no surprise, therefore, that even in her death, Emma's mother cannot give her life because she cannot give her time.

Although she never reappears in the novel, Emma's dead mother is perhaps the most opaque and unreadable figure in the entire text of *Madame Bovary*.[13] This figure becomes unreadable in part because she is barely written—existing only as the void that serves as the apparent origin of all future non-events including, of course, Emma's warped nonmaternal relation to her own daughter, Berthe. But if one is tempted (as I am partially suggesting here) to read the failed mourning of the dead mother as the first and most extreme example of the many temporal dysfunctions that permeate this novel, it is no less important to insist that the textual meaning and function of this dead mother cannot simply be read through classical psychological or psychoanalytic paradigms. Flaubert hardly seems to be suggesting that Emma's problems can in any way be attributed to the lack of maternal care. He does, however, seem to place Emma, and the entire world of *Madame Bovary*, in a realm where mothers no longer guarantee the existence of a state of nature. Flaubert's maternal function connotes neither an inviolable, preverbal natural bond between mother and child nor a natural temporal frame in which birth and death constitute events and childbearing insures that generations progress forward naturally through time.

Emma's attempts to mourn the mother's death are doomed to repeat the very formlessness of this maternal non-event. Although she anticipates that the death will be accompanied by feelings of "sadness," Emma soon finds herself in a state of disconnected boredom ("elle s'ennuya"). In *Crack Wars*, Avital Ronell reminds us that nineteenth-century boredom, like melancholia, is mourning's dysfunctional evil twin. She goes on to argue that when failed mourning passes as boredom, the cultural site formerly assigned to death becomes occupied by addictive structures that often manifest themselves through drug dependency. Ronell writes:

As symptom, boredom is co-originary with melancholia. It pervades everything, and cannot be simply said to erupt. Nor does it desist of its own. It is prior to signification, yet it appears to be a commentary on life; it is, at least for Emma, the place of her deepest struggle. . . . Boredom, with its temporal slowdown and edge of anguish, is also an authentic mode of being-in-the-world. . . . Emma's boredom appears to exhaust a certain reserve before it has been tapped. It is a companion to loss, but raised on tranquilizers. In *Madame Bovary*, boredom opens up a listening to disappearance, fabricating a society's holding pattern over the death that traverses us. . . . This forms the threshold through which the existence of Emma Bovary is made to pass, a zone of experience that conspires with "nothing at all," the extenuation of the subject. Something like an ontology of boredom announces its necessity here. We are reminded that for Baudelaire and Gautier, Flaubert's contemporaries and acquaintances, this experience of nothing is at times laced with drugs.[14]

The link that Ronell suggests between boredom, failed mourning, and the structure of addiction is borne out by the conclusion of the passage: Emma's boredom transforms subjective mourning rituals into an empty habit ("habitude"). This alienated mechanical repetition ultimately degenerates into an eviscerated narcissism ("vanité") before fading away completely.

Although the legacy of the mother's death lies precisely in the fact that she passes away outside of the passage of time and without leaving a trace, the aftermath of this maternal disappearance seemingly produces a temporal void in Emma which she attempts to counteract by searching for an event. Having no access to the experience of an event in her life, she turns to fiction in order to learn how to manufacture one. Her readings dispense fictive highs which she confuses with lived events. The passions she feels when reading stimulate her desire to reproduce in life the excitations simulated by fiction. Because Emma's literary taste for the generic tropes of Romantic fiction teaches her that events (like the "coup de foudre" that heralds love) occur both instantaneously and by chance, she attempts to apply the laws of fiction to life by waiting for an eventful surprise in the form of love or adventure. But since the laws of fiction, unlike life, systematically guarantee the arrival of unanticipated events, Emma's readings place in her a peculiar historical and philosophical predicament: How can one anticipate the arrival of an event which must be, by definition, both surprising and instantaneous?

In the following passage, which comes from the last chapter of part I, as Emma waits impatiently for the arrival of a hypothetical event that presumably would transform her empty existence into the experience of a real life, she begins to realize, with increasing desperation, that she has not been invited to the dance of Life.

Au fond de son âme, cependant, elle attendait un événement . . . chaque matin, à son réveil, elle l'espérait pour la journée et elle écoutait tous les bruits, se levait en sursaut, s'étonnait qu'il ne vînt pas; puis, au coucher du soleil, toujours plus triste, désirait être au lendemain. . . . Dès le commencement de juillet, elle compta sur ses doigts combien de semaines lui restaient pour arriver au mois d'octobre, pensant que le marquis d'Andervilliers, peut-être, donnerait encore un bal à la Vaubyessard. Mais tout septembre s'écoula sans lettres ni visites. Après l'ennui de cette déception, son coeur, de nouveau, resta vide, et alors la série des mêmes journées recommença. Elles allaient donc maintenant se suivre ainsi à la file, toujours pareille, innombrables, et n'apportant rien! Les autres existences, si plates qu'elles fussent, avaient du moins la chance d'un événement. Une aventure amenait parfois des péripéties à l'infini, et le décor changaient. Mais pour elle, rien n'arrivait, Dieu l'avait voulu! L'avenir était un corridor tout noir, et qui avait au fond sa porte bien fermée. (348)

[All the while, however, she was waiting in her heart for an event. Each morning, as she awoke, she hoped it would come that day; she listened to every sound, sprang up with a start, was surprised that it did not come; then at sunset, always more saddened, she wished that it would already be tomorrow. . . . From the beginning of July she counted off on her fingers how many weeks there were to get to October, thinking that perhaps the Marquis d'Andervilliers would give another ball at Vaubyessard. But all September passed without letters or visits. After the shock of this disappointment her heart once again remained empty, and then the same series of identical days started all over again. So now they would keep following one another, always the same, innumerably, and bringing nothing. Other existences, however flat, had at least the chance of an event. One adventure sometimes brought with it infinite consequences and the scenery changed. But for her, nothing happened. God had willed it so! The future was a dark corridor, with its door at the end well locked up.] (44–45, translation modified)[15]

In the opening lines of this passage, it appears to Emma (and the reader) almost as if it is an "accident"—an event of some sort—that has interfered with the arrival of *her* anticipated event: "chaque matin, à son réveil, elle l'espérait pour la journée et elle écoutait tous les bruits, se levait en sursaut, s'étonnait qu'il ne vînt pas." The text begins by suggesting that it is the absence of an event that impedes Emma's ability to live life daily and concludes with the more disturbing notion that it is her inability to gain access to the temporal unit "day" that renders any potential future event impossible. For Emma, time cannot be measured; it flows away in smaller and smaller doses. Initially week by week, then day by day, and ultimately drop by drop, it becomes clear that the problem here is not with an event that has stopped time, but rather with a figure of time that cannot assimilate an event.

At first, Emma counts *on* time by attempting to count it, literally, in the weeks that she counts off on her fingers. But in order even to be able to count time—to represent time in meaningful units—Emma must be able to rely on the hope that the only event which has ever had any lasting meaning for her, the ball at the Vaubyessard, could be repeatable. The ironic futility of this hope is extremely complex and ultimately fatal; the event of the ball cannot be repeated as lived experience for Emma, in part because her presence at it was entirely determined by chance. The invitation to the ball depends on the convergence of an inimitable series of chance occurrences: the Marquis happened to develop an abscess in his mouth just prior to the ball, the cherries happened to be bad at the Vaubyessard and good at the Bovary's farm that year, and when the Marquis wants some cherries, he catches sight of Emma and whimsically decides to invite the couple to the ball. It is only by accident, therefore, that Emma goes to the ball in the first place, and once she gets there she is more an alienated and dizzied spectator to the event rather than a participant in it.

Perhaps because the ball at the Vaubyessard appears to correspond, almost uncannily, to the expectations she receives from fiction, it is virtually the only incident in the text of *Madame Bovary* that even remotely functions like a life event for Emma. Moreover, unlike the failed event of her mother's death, which loses all reality (it provides neither continuity nor consistency and evaporates from her memory without leaving a trace), the ball remains the only occurrence in her life that she doesn't inadvertently forget. Everything and everyone else, all other presences and absences, are subject to erosion and are effaced.

Functioning as the singular and traumatic temporal point of reference for Emma, the ball tantalizes her into temporary hopefulness by providing her with a powerful, if illusory, repository into which she tries to insert her own experiences. Upon leaving the ball, Emma seizes the viscount's lost cigar-case (that Charles had picked up) in order to sustain and preserve her memory of the event. Emma treats the cigar-case as if this thing could somehow objectify lost time—as if this object were uniquely endowed with the capacity to conserve time by giving it a physical form. As receptacle, this object seems to incarnate formally the very thing missing from her life: a temporal lost object, a representational container capable of incorporating time. From the scene at the ball until the end of part 1 of *Madame Bovary*, the cigar-case functions as a kind of sacred relic that promises that the life she witnessed at the ball will be hers in an imaginary afterlife. But in the pages directly preceding her discovery that she will never again be invited to the ball, the cigar-case no longer functions as a reliable container for memories of an imaginary future. Bereft of an external temporal object that could contain time for her, Emma now attempts to incorporate time with her body, by counting it on her fingers. But we understand that this attempt has failed when Flaubert writes, in the middle of the passage of "lost days" quoted above, that "tout septembre s'écoula sans lettres ni visites." The verb "s'écoula" reiterates the notion, everywhere present in the text of *Madame Bovary*, that time is made of fluids (water, sweat, blood, saliva) that flow away drop by drop. Thus, when the month of September "drips away," time dissolves and, like drops of rain, slips through Emma's fingers instead of being counted on them. After this line, time becomes irrevocably detached from both her experience and her body.

Emma's fall out of time is depicted as a fall from grace. When she is not invited to return to the ball, Emma's faith in the redemptive temporality of an event is shattered. And, as Flaubert rather rigorously demonstrates, to lose faith in time's capacity to contain an event is tantamount to losing faith in God, life, and the future. The future becomes lost and the past is unattainable. From the moment (which is not a moment) when days lose their numerability, Emma's days are effectively numbered. At first she encounters her days as if they are traumatic "shocks" ("elle écoutait tous les bruits, se levait en sursaut, s'étonnait qu'il ne vînt pas") and then falls out of them before they are over: "puis, au coucher du soleil, toujours plus triste, désirait être au lendemain." By the end of the passage, the unit of time normally called "day" has become entirely meaningless. In this context, the Alcoholics Anonymous refrain "one day at a time" rings like a perverse inverted echo of Emma's malady and reminds us, once again, how addiction can be read through its temporal disorders. For the alcoholic, the phrase "one day at a time" functions in a dual fashion—it both reminds the addict that time *exists* and attempts to allow him or her a way of breaking time down into meaningful units. But unlike the alcoholic, not only is there no twelve-step program to address Emma's predicament, but the fluid substance that she abuses is not alcohol, but time itself. Through the representations of time as well as the verbal time (tenses) of representation in the above passage, we can already read Emma's free-fall into the addictive temporality that leads inevitably to her death and dissolution.

Emma's exposure to the corrosive fluidity of time in the passage of "lost days" reminds us that Flaubert uses the rhythmic sound of water dripping "goutte par goutte" as the novel's temporal measure from the famous moment that melting snow first falls on Emma's umbrella during her early courtship with Charles: "L'ombrelle, de soie gorge-de-pigeon, que traversait le soleil, éclairait de reflets mobiles la peau blanche de sa figure. Elle souriait là-dessous à la chaleur tiède; et on entendait les gouttes d'eau, une à une, tomber sur la moire tendue" (The parasol, made of an iridescent silk that let the sunlight sift through, colored the white skin of her face with shifting reflections. Beneath it, she smiled at the gentle warmth; and one heard the drops of water, one by one, fall on the taut silk) (307/13, translation modified). But by the time we reach the passage of lost days, Emma's body is no longer granted the symbolic protection implied by the presence of a parasol. From this point on, when water falls, drop by drop, it gradually eats away at Emma's capacity either to conserve time or to be protected from its erosion.[16] Although I do not have the time to develop this point here, I would like to point out that this liquified time seeps into the very foundations of the novel. At every structural and metaphorical level, *Madame Bovary* relies heavily upon architectural figures. The novel's narrative is constructed on a foundation of literal or metaphorical edifices (from the bizarre "pièces montées" of Charles's hat and the infamous wedding cake to the elaborate structural blueprints that accompany most of the descriptions of houses, churches, statuettes, and factories) that become inundated by the increasingly corrosive presence of watery time.

But the beginning of Emma's ultimate dissolution can be traced in her inability to metabolize time through her body. In the verbal vertigos of the passage of lost days, we can already read the first unmistakable signs of what will later blossom into a full-blown addiction—an addiction that I am choosing to call "temporal bulimia." There is a direct correlation between Emma's anorectic refusal to eat and her numerous bulimic attempts to devour time. Unlike Charles, who consumes time as effectively as he eats dinner—"[Il] s'en allait, ruminant son bonheur, comme ceux qui mâchent encore, après dîner, le goût des truffes qu'ils digèrent" [He went on, rechewing his happiness, like those who after dinner taste again the truffles which they are digesting] (322/24)—Emma rejects food and tries to eat time instead. At the moment when she is planning to run away with Rodolphe, for example, Flaubert writes: "elle vivait comme perdue dans la dégustation anticipée de son bonheur prochain" [she was living as if lost in the anticipated taste of her future happiness] (469/my translation). But Emma never manages to digest the taste of the "future happiness" that tantalizes her. She vacillates between failed attempts to preserve time and bitter attempts to consume it, and falls into despairing acts of abjecting it.

In the context of this discussion, one might even go so far as to say that Emma is as unable to digest her own death as she is to swallow her future happiness or to assimilate her experiences into the corpus of a "life."[17] As *Bovary*'s readers know well, Emma tries to kill herself by literally stuffing her face with poison: "[Elle] saisit le bocal bleu, en arracha le bouchon, y fourra sa main, et, la retirant pleine d'une poudre blanche, elle se mit à manger à même" [She seized the blue jar, tore out the cork, plunged in her hand, and withdrawing it full of white powder, she ate it greedily] (578–79/229). As several critics have observed, Emma's attempt to swallow her own death constitutes the final term in a long series of attempted auto-ingestions and self-incorporations.[18] Philippe Bonnefis has pointed out that while the curious expression "elle se mit à manger à même" is almost grammatically meaningless, the words "à même" function as homophonic reversal of Emma's name and thus indicate that in the act of eating the poison, she effectively eats her own name.[19] As such, Emma feeds herself with herself in a final attempt to provide herself with a body capable of containing and retaining her experience. It is not clear whether to read this ultimate auto-cannibalistic act as Emma's attempt to feed her death with her life or as an attempt to feed her life with her death. The terrible irony of the gesture is, of course, that both acts are indistinguishable and that they both fail. Emma's death is not more containable than her life was; the suicide scene (if it actually deserves the name) is flooded with vomit. Although Emma's agony consists of constant vomiting, she manages to retain just enough poison in order to live and not quite enough in order to die convincingly.

Let us recall that Emma's vomit continues to flow even after she is dead. Although Emma presumably "dies" at the end of part 3, chapter 8, the most infamous instance of her suicidal vomit occurs posthumously. In chapter 9, Emma's body spews streams of black liquid: "il fallut soulever un peu la tête, et alors un flot de liquides noirs sortit, comme un vomissement, de sa bouche" (They had to raise the head a little, and a rush of black liquid poured from her mouth, as if she were vomiting) (594/242). This powerful and strange image raises several questions concerning the fate of Emma Bovary and the text in which she is written. In the first place, it would seem that Emma's body refuses to acknowledge the moment of her own death; paradoxically, her body vomits her death instead of "living" it. The temporal disjunction between the fact of her subjective death and her body's sustained mechanical expulsive activity only repeats in death the many prior instances of failed events Emma experiences in her life. Furthermore, the black liquid which oozes out of Emma's lifeless body seems to transform the death scene into a parodic inversion of a birth scene. But instead of the formless "afterbirth" that accompanies the birth of a child, Emma's posthumous peristalsis appears almost as a figure of a kind of "afterdeath." Here, if we recall Emma's attempts to give herself a life by confusing her own rebirth with her mother's death, we discover that Emma has no greater access to her own death than she did to her own life.

Although critics have interpreted the black liquid which flows from Emma's mouth as a figure for a writer's ink, the association between posthumous vomit and ink renders the figure even more difficult to read.[20] In other words, who is writing this scene and whose failure to live, die, or write is being expressed in it? If we follow the path indicated by feminist readings by Naomi Schor and Janet Beizer, we might conclude that Flaubert needs to abject his feminine identification with Emma by perversely transforming the formless, ineffectual vomit of her lifeless body into the formal ink of his style.[21] And although such a reading is both possible and plausible, I would like to suggest that in this monstrous moment, which couples a disgusting image of lifeless bodily expulsion with a distorted image of literary production, the corrosive liquid temporality of Emma Bovary's "life" seeps into Flaubert's narrative voice through his *style indirect libre*.

For in much the same way as Emma Bovary fails to transform her life or death into an event, the narrative voice of *Madame Bovary* displays the same strange temporal uncertainty about whether a life can be lived, whether a death constitutes an event, and whether the act of writing is an addictive response to a temporal disorder that manifests itself through failed mourning. Throughout the corpus of *Madame Bovary*, we find that the bodies that cannot digest time end up by being consumed by it. As we have seen, although Emma's life was eaten by the time she couldn't contain, her body suffers an even more horrifying fate. It vomits its own death, and corrodes the lives of the surviving characters. Emma's death leaks into Charles's life; he attempts to contain her death by ordaining that she be buried in three coffins; he attempts to mourn Emma by liquidating his remaining funds in order to adorn his own body with the clothes that might have pleased her. In short, as the narrative voice makes clear, "elle le corrompait par delà le tombeau" [She corrupted him from beyond the grave] (604/250). But Charles's memory, in spite of his all-consuming efforts to commemorate Emma, is ultimately subjected to the corrosive force of involuntary forgetting: "une chose étrange, c'est que Bovary, tout en pensant à Emma continuellement, l'oubliait; et il se désespérait à sentir cette image lui échapper de la mémoire au milieu des efforts qu'il faisait pour la retenir" [A strange thing was happening to Bovary; while continually thinking of Emma, he was nevertheless forgetting her. He grew desperate as he felt this image fading from his memory in spite of all efforts to retain it] (607/252). Thus, Emma's posthumous existence produces in Charles the same strange combination of simultaneous preservation and erosion that permeated her living existence. Flaubert describes this uncanny temporal dysfunction in one of the most significant, and signatory, abject images in the entire novel. In part 2, chapter 1, Flaubert's narrative voice shifts abruptly to the present tense and he writes:

Depuis les événements que l'on va raconter, rien, en effet, n'a changé à Yonville . . . les foetus du pharmacien, comme des paquets d'amadou blanc, se pourrissent de plus en plus dans leur alcool bourbeux, et, au-dessus de la grande porte de l'auberge, le vieux lion d'or, déteint pas les pluies, montre toujours aux passants sa frisure de caniche. (357)

[Since the events about to be narrated, nothing in fact has changed at Yonville . . . the spongy white lumps, the pharmacist's foetuses, rot more and more in their cloudy alcohol, and above the big door of the inn the old golden lion, faded by rain, still shows passers-by its poodle mane.] (51–52)

This is one of the rare moments (perhaps unique) in *Madame Bovary* where Flaubert links a future tense ("que l'on va raconter") to a past tense ("n'a changé") through a present tense ("se pourrissent"). But the temporal perversity of this passage undermines the apparent normality of its verbal structure: all of these verb tenses depict actions that take place outside of time and that refer to the monstrous nonactivities of aborted nonsubjects. Paradoxically, the very action described is one of a stasis (preservation) that is nonetheless engaged in a nonending process of erosion and decomposition. Moreover, this description of the impact of time on the fetuses in the bottle encapsulates, in miniature, the temporal structure of Emma Bovary's "life." Emma's access to "life" is as stillborn and continuously eroded as that of the bottled babies. And, as Homais's fetuses go on marinating in their bottles long after the events recounted in the text of *Madame Bovary* have occurred, Emma's body floats in that fluid, bitter, and viscous narrative substance that has been aptly called Flaubert's *free indirect style*. But that name is far too proper, too antiseptic, for the phenomenon which it purports to describe. One must not forget that when Flaubert describes Homais's fetuses in their bizarre state of suspended petrification and erosion, he addresses us—his readers—directly in the narrative voice of our own time. In the strange reflexive present of the verb "se pourrissent," Flaubert announces a temporal structure of addiction that exceeds the confines of the literature of the nineteenth century and seeps into the experience of modern life. Like Emma Bovary, and Homais's fetuses, addicted culture is fermented by a corrosive past that is strangely preserved without being remembered. Whether or not Flaubert ever actually said "Madame Bovary, c'est moi," we should recall that from the novel's enigmatic first word, "nous," it is certain that Flaubert was always already writing to and about us.

Madame Bovary's Perversion of Death

For people as they are today there is only one radical novelty, and
that is always the same: Death.
—Walter Benjamin

In the analysis of two young men I learned that each—one when he
was two years old and the other when he was ten—had failed to take
cognizance of the death of his beloved father—had "scotomized" it—
and yet neither of them had developed a psychosis. Thus a piece of
reality which was undoubtedly important had been disavowed by the
ego, just as the unwelcome fact of women's castration is disavowed in
fetishists.
—Freud

As everyone knows, *Madame Bovary* was a perverse project from the
get-go. Despite Flaubert's notorious éloge to the formal purity of Art in the
oft-cited letter to Louise Colet: "je voudrais écrire un livre sur rien, un livre
sans attache extérieure, qui se tiendrait de lui-même par la force interne de
son style, comme la terre sans être soutenue se tient en l'air . . . les oeuvres
les plus belles sont celles où il y a le moins de matière" [I should like to
write a book about nothing, a book with no external attachment, which
would hold itself up by the internal force of its style, like the earth which
holds itself in the air without being supported . . . the most beautiful works
are those in which there is the least matter],[1] virtually every Flaubertian text
exhibits a kind of gleeful wallowing in the most excessive, grotesque, and
abject descriptions of the physical and material world. According to his version of things, Flaubert decided to chain himself to the desk writing a book

about everything he hated most in the universe—the small-minded customs and impoverished language of middle-class provincial life, deformed legacies of Romanticism, the misguided appropriation of Enlightenment values with its fantasies of historical "progress," the blindness of the medical profession, the cancerous impact of capitalism on the bourgeoisie, and last but not least, the spectacle of excessive feminine desire run amok. But if one really takes him at his word, all of these specific "subjects" have no valid specificity—they are merely empty placeholders that provide a material support for his real subject, which is "nothing."[2] He derived perverse pleasure from the thought that the ethereal style that he craved was to be created out of the most vile matter. But it seems that this quasi-Baudelaireian alchemy depends not on transcending the distance between subject and style, but on maintaining it resolutely at every turn.[3] The libidinal charge of Flaubert's texts is not characterized by sublimation, but by perversion.[4] Thus, although Flaubert inflicted intense suffering upon himself in the act of writing the novel, he evidently gained immense satisfaction from the notion that the pain of writing was itself evidence of a sustained abyss and tension between its ostensible aim (purified style) and its object (debased content). Flaubert's reader cannot avoid negotiating with the impossibly charged and volatile nature of this perverse dualism: Flaubert's "style" cannot be read as a negation or sublimation of the thematic content; the thematic content cannot simply be read as the subject of the book. In short, although recent critics have been increasingly drawn to the perverse elements *in* the Flaubertian text, these thematic perversions themselves partake of a perverse strategy present at every level of the text's construction.[5] An inevitable consequence of this unsettling duality is that many of the critics who display extraordinary sensitivity to the complexities of Flaubert's "style" tend to stabilize the meanings of the novel's thematic subject matter, whereas those critics who focus on the novel's signatory thematic excesses are often less well equipped to read those textual details in relation to the novel's formal concerns.

I have insisted upon retelling this well-worn narrative of the tension between style and subject matter in order to challenge a particular assumption made by the vast majority of *Madame Bovary*'s readers. Throughout 140 years of rich and persuasive readings of the novel, there is an almost universal consensus that Emma Bovary's desire is the primary theme of the novel. The nature and meaning of this desire has been exhaustively debated and analyzed. Critics have variously described the heroine's desire as thwarted, transgressive, hysterical, perverse, deluded, masculine, feminine, and small-minded. Some readers stress the importance of the socio-historical forces that transform her adulterous passions into a futile transgressive critique of provincial middle-class morality. Other readers insist that Emma's desire is debased by its consumerism and materialism—she pursues money and material goods in place of true love. There are readers who place the emphasis on a kind of diagnostic pathology of desire: Emma is hysterical or fetishistic. And there are others who insist that her desire is aroused by her dependency on the clichés of romantic fiction. While it would be ludicrous (and just plain wrong) to dispute the validity of these readings or to deny that Emma's desire propels the plot forward like a textual libido that drives the novel through a charade of "actions" that take place under the psychological cast of a desiring subject, I would nonetheless like to suggest that the ubiquitous insistence upon "desire" in the novel obscures the primary importance of another, equally powerful thematic textual drive. In the following pages, I would like to claim that insomuch as it is "about" anything, this novel is "about" death. More specifically, the novel investigates a changed relationship to death—how the experience of death has, in the modern world, been turned into "nothing." It asks how death is perceived, how it is understood, and how the modern subject fails to recognize it, symbolize it, or mourn it. Furthermore, to say that the novel is "about" death is not to say that it is not about desire. The perverse tension that Flaubert establishes between "style" and "subject"—between the two structural drives of the novel—is itself replayed through the tension between death and desire in the novel. By looking at what happens to death in and through the novel, one comes to a different understanding of the question of Emma's desire.

But since I will argue that the very specificity of Flaubert's meditation on death entails a rigorous and systematic disfiguration of it, one cannot perceive what Flaubert has done to the face of death by gazing at the subject head-on. Representations of death are no longer contained by familiar signs and symbols. Death no longer occupies its traditional place and function at the level of narrative development. Although Emma's suicide would seem to indicate that death is a major theme of the novel, it is not primarily at the thematic level that Flaubert's most radical rewriting of death takes place. Therefore, I propose a kind of anamorphic reading of death in the text. By looking at the question obliquely both from the perspective of the novel's most marginal details and characters and from the central vanishing point of the plot—Emma's death—I hope to retrace Flaubert's insidious and insistent unwriting of death. It goes without saying that this trajectory can only be taken by paying strict attention to matters of style. Flaubert's treatment of death is everywhere present in his inimitable and hallucinatory stylistic blanks and erasures. Death is not figured in Flaubert as merely or simply "unsayable," but rather as "unsaid" in the strictest and most active sense of the word, as if every detail and every character were engaged in a verbal undoing of the signifying links between language and death. Or, to put it another way, it is as if Flaubert set out to challenge and refute Freud's famous meditation on the subject's response to death in "Mourning and Melancholia." Where Freud proposes that mourning is a complicated form of psychic work that takes place over time and functions according to an economic model of accommodating and compensating for loss, Flaubert's novel almost takes as its founding premise the notion that death itself might stop working, become lazy, forgetful, unreal. And when death fails to work, time becomes unhinged, memory evaporates, and speech devolves into cliché or becomes utterly impossible.

The Grave-Digger

Although I would argue that this dramatic undoing of death touches almost every element in the novel, the character who incarnates this dynamic most absolutely, whose textual function is reduced to this activity, is the grave-digger Lestiboudois. Curiously, Lestiboudois has received less critical attention than almost any other figure in the text. While Bovary's readers have scrupulously scrutinized other cameo characters like La Guérine, Binet, Dr. Larivière, the organ grinder, and the Blind Beggar, Lestiboudois remains the most significant and significantly underread presence in the novel. This liminal character makes his appearance at a pivotal moment in this text: although he will be defined by his incapacity to distinguish between the living and the dead, between human and non-human organic forms, he is the first "living" character that we encounter directly in the narrator's celebrated description of Yonville that opens part 2 of the novel.

Before turning to the grave-digger himself, we must first take a detour back to the end of part 1 in order to clarify the narrative significance of the timing of Lestiboudois's appearance at the beginning of part 2. Let us recall that the concluding sentence of part 1, "Quand on partit de Tostes, au mois de mars, Madame Bovary était enceinte" [When they left Tostes in the month of March, Madame Bovary was pregnant] (353/49), announces the fact that the Bovarys' life at Tostes has come to an end. The reference to Madame Bovary's pregnancy, which ought to signify the hope that a future birth will inaugurate a future life, works in precisely the opposite fashion. As we saw earlier, by the end of the last chapter of part 1 Emma has finally reached the unhappy conclusion that she has no future, that "L'avenir était un corridor tout noir, et qui avait au fond sa porte bien fermée" [The future was a dark corridor, with its door at the end shut tight] (348/45). More specifically, in the concluding pages of part 1, we learn that Emma is quite literally at death's door. She is pale and has heart palpitations: "Elle pâlissait et avait des battements de coeur" [She grew pale and suffered from palpitations of the heart] (352/48). On some days, she is feverish and babbles incoherently: "En de certains jours, elle bavardait avec une abondance fébrile" [On certain days she chattered with feverish profusion] (352/48). At other moments, she is paralyzed and can only move when "reanimated" by eau de cologne. Finally, in an explosive binge of what I have described earlier as "temporal bulimia," Emma wastes herself away by drinking vinegar until she completely loses her appetite and develops a dry cough: "Dès lors, elle but du vinaigre pour se faire maigrir, contracta une petite toux sèche et perdit complètement l'appetit" [From that moment she drank vinegar to lose weight, contracted a sharp little cough, and lost all appetite] (352/48). If we read these passages according to the accepted temporal structures of traditional literary paradigms, we might conclude that Emma's violent, self-inflicted illness is a *figurative* suicide that foreshadows her actual, literal death at the end of the book. This interpretation is more or less valid at the crudest level of the novel's plot. However, the assumption that this novel unfolds through the narration of events that simply move forward in time, even at the level of plot, does not do justice to the temporal leaps, discontinuities, repetitions, and disruptions that contaminate every temporal narration and every narrative of time in the novel. But if we read this passage according to a different kind of temporal paradigm altogether, one which I will argue is implicitly suggested by Flaubert, despite its wildly "unrealistic" and even psychotic aspect, we might go so far as to say that by the time we discover she is pregnant, the narration of Emma Bovary's "real" life is already over, all of the "events"—and they are the major ones in the novel—take place in a temporal vacuum that I will later define as "dead time." The fetishistic reliance upon temporally unlivable alternatives which express the belief that one is *simultaneously* not yet living and not quite dead is suggested by Emma herself: "Elle avait envie de faire des voyages ou de retourner vivre à son couvent. Elle souhaitait à la fois mourir et habiter Paris" [She longed to travel or to go back to live in her convent. She wanted both to die and to live in Paris] (346/43, translation modified). I would argue that Emma has already begun to die at the end of part 1—she just fails to recognize it. And, paradoxically and perversely, among the many omens of this unacknowledged death is the curious combination of pregnancy, vinegar, and eau de cologne. The fact that Emma prepares her body for pregnancy with a ritual more suited to the preparation of a mummy is only part of the story.[6] Her demented ingestion of a fermented and preserving liquid substance links the announcement of Emma's pregnancy in part 1 to the image of Homais's eternally fermenting undead fetuses in the beginning of part 2. Although we have not yet prepared the ground enough to turn to Lestiboudois, I would point out that the description of Homais's preserved babies immediately follows the textual introduction and discussion of the grave-digger.

For the time being, let us pursue the problematic textual and temporal thread of Emma's pregnancy. Throughout *Madame Bovary*, every relation between mothers and daughters is fraught with a precise mixture of ephemeral inconsistency and accidental annihilation. All mother-daughter encounters are missed encounters that are always accompanied by evidence of searing discontinuities and abrupt, if intangible, ruptures. There is no sustainable bond, thread, or tie between mothers and daughters. Furthermore, the absence of this connection always takes the form of a temporal problem—a sudden and unaccountable failure of both memory and continuity. The narration of Emma's inconclusive suicide supplants the missing narrative of the child's conception; the signs that she finds her life literally distasteful taint the coincidental revelation that she is, as we like to say, "expecting." But although Emma may or may not be capable of expecting anything from life, the one thing she most certainly fails to expect is her baby. Thus, later, in part 2, when Emma's pregnancy is discussed, it is Charles, and not Emma, who "carries" the baby through the gestating time. Only Charles, and not Emma, retains a continuous "memory" of the existence of the baby. Charles waits for the baby, prepares for the baby, and reaps a sense of continuity from the baby: "Un souci meilleur vint le distraire, à savoir la grossesse de sa femme. A mesure que le terme en approchait, il la chérissait davantage. C'était un autre lien de la chair s'établissant, et *comme le senti-ment continu* d'une union plus complexe" [A more positive worry came to distract him, namely, the pregnancy of his wife. As the time of birth approached he cherished her more. It was another bond of the flesh between them, and, *as it were, a continued sentiment* of a more complex union] (371 /62, italics mine). Emma, on the other hand, has a negative, troubled, and intermittent awareness of the child she is carrying: "Elle ne s'amusa donc pas à ces préparatifs où la tendresse des mères se met en appétit, et son affection, dès l'origine, en fut peut-être atténuée de quelque chose. Cependant, comme Charles, à tous les repas, parlait du marmot, *bientôt elle y songea d'une façon plus continue*" [Thus she did not amuse herself with those preparations that stimulate the tenderness of mothers, and so her affection was perhaps impaired from the start. As Charles, however, spoke of the baby at every meal, *she soon began to muse about it more continually*] (371/63, italics mine, translation modified). Emma's missing tenderness is described as maternal anorexia; she lacks the requisite "appetite" to antici-pate the birth of her child. Charles compensates for her missing "appetite" by spending every mealtime speaking about the child. He feeds her words at regimented intervals; she consumes his words like food. It is a further irony that Charles's words manage to stimulate the maternal appetite since they are, by definition, empty. We are given no indication of what he says, only that he speaks at precisely those specifically designated times that Emma has already identified as being the most unbearable moments of her marriage: "Mais c'était surtout aux heures de repas qu'elle n'en pouvait plus" [But it was above all the mealtimes that she couldn't bear] (351/47, translation modified). Flaubert concludes this unsavory division of labor with a final sinister twist: "bientôt elle y songea d'une façon plus continue." Every word in this clause is problematic, beginning, of course, with "bien-tôt." The temporal marker "soon" that ought to serve as a point of reference through the creation of a sequential temporality—a presumed "before" in relation to a possible "later"—is here set adrift. The very sentence whose ex-plicit stated function is to say that Emma has found a way of sustaining the knowledge that she is pregnant enacts its own denial through its abuse of the word "bientôt." But even this denial is denied. The future baby (and we shall see later on that this continues to be the case in relations between Emma and Berthe) is reduced to a pronoun of place, "y," and becomes real by becoming an object of dreams, "songea." Finally, the end of the sentence undercuts the whole operation. By attributing a comparative term, "plus," to the impression of "continuity," Flaubert has subjected an essentially qualitative state (an ongoing sense of continuity) to an impossibly quantitative analysis. The conclusion to this temporal quandary rings like the punchline of a bad joke: it is as impossible to have a greater or lesser sense of continuity as it is to be "more or less" pregnant. But there it is; instead of her pregnancy providing her with a missing sense of continuity, her lack of continuity undermines the reality of her pregnancy.

In similar fashion, after Emma has died and been buried, her daughter Berthe is simply informed that her mother is absent: "Elle demanda sa maman. On lui répondit qu'elle était absente, qu'elle lui rapporterait des joujoux. Berthe en reparla plusieurs fois; puis à la longue, elle n'y pensa plus. La gaité de cette enfant navrait Bovary, et il avait à subir les intolérables consolations du pharmacien" [She asked for her mamma. They told her she was away; that she would bring her back some toys. Berthe mentioned her again several times, then finally thought no more about it. The child's gaiety pained Bovary, and he had to endure the intolerable consolations of the pharmacist] (603/249, translation modified). Although there is certainly nothing particularly surprising about employing the euphemism "absent" in talking to a child about death, this passage nonetheless indicates the remarkable irreality that attends this and all mention of death in the novel. But the most troubling detail in this passage is the reference to the toys. As is often the case in *Madame Bovary*, the denial of death is marked and rewarded by some kind of promise of pecuniary gain. We see it here in the excessive and doubly phantasmatic promise made to the child that her mother will come back and that her return will be accompanied by toys. Next, the text stipulates that the child "en reparla." But what, exactly, does she speak about—the mother?—or the toys? One does not know. The lost object does not even have the status of a direct object—but becomes "en." Finally, in the gesture most characteristic of the novel's temporal logic, we find that the mother's disappearance is marked by involuntary forgetting: "Elle n'y pensa plus." Berthe's unlocatable experience of her mother's death vanishes somewhere in the vague attributions of the pronouns "en" and "y." But although Berthe does not think any more about it, we must continue to think through the causes and consequences of this mother/daughter temporal disjunction.[7]

What do we make of all of this? The word "enceinte" is, as we have said, the final word of part 1. As the verbal link between part 1 and part 2, the pregnancy ought to constitute the temporal bridge that links the

Bovarys' past existence in Tostes to their future life in Yonville. But as we have seen, Emma's sense of continuity is destabilized rather than reinforced by her pregnancy. The compromised sense of continuity that Emma experiences in relation to her pregnancy must itself be read in relation to the problem of continuity in the larger narrative structure in which it is imbedded. In other words, just as Emma's pregnancy fails to provide her with a sense of continuity at the level of character and plot, at the level of the novel's narration, the word "enceinte" signals discontinuity in place of the continuous temporal thread promised by the word's purported "meaning." At the textual level, the word "enceinte" announces the curious hiatus that takes place in the narrative descriptive pause between parts 1 and 2 of the novel.

And, sure enough, although the ostensible subject of the opening pages of part 2 is the geographical move from Tostes to Yonville, this narrative of spatial relocation ultimately serves as an alibi for the increasingly unsettling rewriting of temporal paradigms that begin to accumulate in these pages. The bizarre nature of this entire section, comprised roughly of fourteen paragraphs, cannot be overstated.[8] From the opening pages of part 2, Flaubert situates Yonville l'Abbaye in a kind of paradoxical temporal framework. On the one hand, Yonville is depicted as an allegorical junk heap of historical periods and references piled on top of one another in a fashion quite similar to what has become familiarly recognizable as postmodern bric-a-brac. On the other, it is in Yonville, and not in Tostes (with the possible exception of the Vaubeyessard chapter) that Flaubert explicitly, albeit slyly, uses dates and references to actual historical events in order to create a recognizable, if problematic, "historical context" for the novel. The town is initially defined through its capacity for total and complete erasure of any material legacy of the source of its own name: "Yonville l'Abbaye (ainsi nommé à cause d'une ancienne abbaye de Capucins dont les ruines n'existent même plus)" [Yonville l'Abbaye (named after an old Capucin abbey of which not even the ruins remain)] (354/49). But although this place has managed to eradicate all traces of its own historical ruins, contemporary Yonville continually produces ruins out of history. Like an active construction site, the town manufactures ruins out of events that purport to bear the fruits of historical, technological, or economic "progress." This temporal logic is at work throughout the remainder of the novel—we see it in the cotton factory that is rusted before it is finished and in Hippolyte's gangrenous leg that must be amputated after his ill-advised clubfoot oper-

ation. The unifying thread of all these "events" is that they are eroded before they are completed. Thus, the most emblematic architectural detail of
Yonville is the already-rusted-or-rotten-but-not-yet-finished edifice. The
description of the reconstruction of the church during the Restoration is a
case in point: "L'église a été rebâtie à neuf dans les dernières années du
regne de Charles X. La voûte commence à pourrir par le haut et, de place
en place, a des enfonçures noires dans sa couleur bleue. . . . Les stalles du
choeur, en bois de sapin, sont restées sans être peintes" [The church was re-
built during the last years of the reign of Charles X. The wooden roof is beginning to rot from the top, and here and there black hollows appear in the
blue paint. . . . The choir stalls, of pine wood, have been left unpainted]
(356/50). Most often, however, the purported "historical" references are deployed in ways that subvert a simple or direct historical reading of them.

As the narrative voice takes us on our inaugural tour of the monuments of Yonville, we are informed via an extremely rare explicit mention
of a yearly "date" that "jusqu'en 1835, il n'y avait point de route praticable
pour arriver à Yonville; mais on a établi vers cette époque un chemin de
grande vicinalité qui relie la route d'Abbeville à celle d'Amiens, et sert
quelquefois aux rouliers allant de Rouen dans les Flandres. Cependant,
Yonville l'Abbaye est demeuré stationnaire, malgré ses *débouchés nouveaux*"
[Up to 1835 no practicable road for getting to Yonville existed, but about
this time a crossroad was cut, joining the Abbeville to the Amiens highway;
it is occasionally used by the Rouen teamsters on their way to Flanders.
Nevertheless, Yonville l'Abbaye has remained stationary, in spite of its "new
outlet"] (355/49, translation modified). The mention of the date 1835 situates the narrative in historical time just about as effectively as the newly
built highway connects the inhabitants of Yonville to the rest of the world.
Let us be clear about this: this highway of historical information is a one-
way road that leads to a hellish nowhere-land. The new highway does not
lead us into the time of "history," but into an allegorical, mythical place
that is haunted by its inability to retain a living memory of its own history.
Put in other terms, "historical" references proliferate in inverse proportion
to their ability to communicate a sense of historical meaning. But in a way
at least partly reminiscent of Walter Benjamin's analysis of the role of allegory in Baudelaire, Flaubert analyzes the ever increasing abyss between the
experience of historical "events" and a "continued" sense of history by su-
perimposing allegorical emblems of Greek mythology onto the increasing
presence of contemporary referential information. Thus, in the description

of the "mairie," we find that the building's attempt to "bring the town up
to date" devolves into a misshapen hodgepodge of historical and cultural
references. The monument's failure to incarnate the present moment—
even through its banal aspiration to cosmopolitan trendiness—becomes
visible in the untenable juxtaposition between its Classical Greek foundation and its allegorical history of France from Gallic ancestry to postrevolutionary Charter:

La mairie, construite *sur les dessins d'un architecte de Paris*, est une manière de temple grec qui fait l'angle, à côté de la maison du pharmacien. Elle a, au rez-de-
chaussée, trois colonnes ioniques et, au premier étage, une galerie en plein cintre,
tandis que le tympan qui la termine est remplie par un coq gaulois, appuyé d'une
patte sur la Charte et tenant de l'autre les balances de la justice. (356)

[The town hall, constructed "after the designs of a Paris architect," is a sort of
Greek temple that forms the corner next to the pharmacy. On the ground-floor are
three Ionic columns and on the first floor a gallery with arched windows, while the
crowning frieze is occupied by a Gallic cock, resting one foot upon the Charter
and holding in the other the scales of Justice.] (51)

Although one could argue that this description of the "mairie" conforms
to the familiar Flaubertian descriptive technique of the "pièce montée,"
unlike the two most famous examples from part 1, Charles's hat and the
wedding cake, this architectural joke is explicitly constructed out of cultural and historical signifiers that are severed from their signifying context.
The most striking difference between this description and the earlier ones
is the insistence upon the figures of classicism through the specific invocation of the formal properties of the Greek temple. I insist upon this detail because I believe that readers of *Madame Bovary* have too often been
seduced by the lure of Flaubert's so-called realism (or, for that matter, by
the Oriental excesses of his so-called lyricism) and therefore have not ac-
corded sufficient weight to Flaubert's difficult, and perverse, use of classical tropes and motifs.[9] For the moment, I would like to suggest that the
references to classical Greek tropes and figures that are introduced in part
2 and that culminate in Emma Bovary's explicit invocation of *Phèdre* as she
begins her quest for death in part 3, function, like the liminal word "enceinte," in order to mark a disruption in a continued sense of time rather
than as a purveyor of cultural or historical continuity. In other words,
Flaubert uses Classical emblems and references in order to express a peculiarly contemporary sense of lost time rather than as stable markers of eternal timelessness.[10]

At this juncture, following the road that has taken us into Yonville, when we finally reach our final destination we discover that it is quite literally a dead end. The road through the town leads right up to the cemetery and stops there. But this literal dead end leads to the novel's clearest allegorical figure of a historical end to the experience of death. Despite the narrator's coy declaration that there is "nothing more to see in Yonville," we are invited into the cemetery where we meet its semi-idiotic demigod of the undead, Lestiboudois:

Il n'y a plus ensuite rien à voir dans Yonville. La rue (la seule) longue d'une portée de fusil et bordée de quelque boutiques, s'arrête court au tournant de la route. Si on la laisse sur la droite et que l'on suive le bas de la côte Saint-Jean, bientôt on arrive au cimetière.

Lors du choléra, pour l'agrandir, on a abattu un pan de mur et acheté trois acres de terre à côté; mais toute cette portion nouvelle est presque inhabitée, les tombes, comme autrefois, continuant à s'entasser vers la porte. Le gardien, qui est en même temps fossoyeur et bedeau à l'église (tirant ainsi des cadavres de la paroisse un double bénéfice), a profité du terrain vide pour y semer des pommes de terre. D'année en année, cependant, son petit champ se rétrécit, et, lorsqu'il survient une épidémie, il ne sait pas s'il doit se réjouir des décès ou s'affliger des sépultures.

—Vous vous nourrissez des morts, Lestiboudois! lui dit enfin, un jour, M. Le curé.

Cette parole sombre le fit réfléchir; elle l'arrêta pour quelque temps; mais, aujourd'hui encore, il continue la culture de ses tubercules, et même soutient avec aplomb qu'ils poussent naturellement. (357)

[Beyond this there is nothing more to see at Yonville. The street (the only one) a gunshot long and flanked by a few shops on either side stops short at the turn of the high road. Turning right and following the foot of the Saint-Jean hills one soon reaches the graveyard.

At the time of the cholera epidemic, a piece of wall was pulled down and three acres of land purchased in order to make more room, but the new area is almost uninhabited; the tombs, as before, continuing to crowd together towards the gate. The keeper, who is at once gravedigger and church sexton (thus making a double profit out of the parish corpses), has taken advantage of the unused plot of ground to plant potatoes. From year to year, however, his small field grows smaller, and when there is an epidemic, he does not know whether to rejoice at the deaths or regret the added graves.

"You feed on the dead, Lestiboudois!" the curé finally told him one day.

This grim remark made him reflect; it stopped him for some time; but, still today, he continues the cultivation of his little tubers, and even maintains stoutly that they grow naturally.] (51, translation modified)

As I have previously mentioned, Lestiboudois here appears as the first active, "living" inhabitant of Yonville that we see directly in the light of day. But just prior to the invocation of Lestiboudois, the narrator gives us a brief, nocturnal glimpse of Homais's shadow illuminated from inside his window frame:

Le soir, principalement, quand son quinquet est allumé et que les bocaux rouges et verts qui embellissent sa devanture allongent au loin, sur le sol, leurs deux clartés de couleur, alors, à travers elles, comme dans les feux de Bengale, *s'entrevoit l'ombre du pharmacien* accoudé sur son pupitre. (356, italics mine)

[In the evening especially its lamp is lit up and the red and green jars that embellish his shop-front cast their colored reflection far across the street; beyond them, as in a Bengal light, *the shadow of the pharmacist can be espied* leaning over his desk.] (51, translation modified)

So why, we might ask, does this narrative prologue relegate a character as important as Homais to the shadows while it designates Lestiboudois as the town's first representative citizen? In fact, these two characters seem to change narrative places and functions in the opening section of part 2: the novel's central everyman of everyday life is first seen working furiously away in the dark while the novel's marginal grave-digger takes center stage as he happily plants his potatoes in the sunny narrative spotlight. Furthermore, not only does Homais work in the dark, but the fact that he is explicitly depicted as "*l'ombre du pharmacien*" makes him appear more like a ghostly "shade" in the red and green hellish light than like a simple "shadow" of a living person. It is certainly no accident that in the textual space allocated to Lestiboudois we find reversals of textual hierarchies (between center and margin), inversions of representational systems (light and shadow, surface and depth), and confusions of essential differences (living and dead). By focusing on Flaubert's explicit rendition of the prologue as a microscopic representation of Yonville through a glass darkly, we see that by examining the figure of Lestiboudois we can catch a glimpse of the tubercular underside of the narrative's plot.

Lestiboudois is *Madame Bovary's* quintessential untermensch. He occupies the lowest stratum of existence in the novel. Although he is a modern allegorical figure for death—or what has happened to it—Lestiboudois does not inhabit an "underworld" but a subworld. If Homais can justly be called the "spokesman" of the dominant culture in Yonville, Lestiboudois must be seen as Yonville's "unspokesman." Although he receives and processes information, he himself is incapable of producing speech. He is, almost quite literally, beneath words. Not even human enough to have access to the clichés of Flaubertian "bêtise," Lestiboudois underwrites the entire temporal, historic, and linguistic economy of the novel.

Like the misbegotten "mairie," the invocation to Lestiboudois is framed by an explicit historical reference: the appearance of cholera in France. In fact, in an earlier version of *Madame Bovary*, Flaubert had situated the cemetery scene in relation to a precise, dated event: "Pour l'agrandir, lors du choléra de 1832, on a abattu un pan de mur" [To make more room, during the 1832 cholera epidemic, a piece of wall was pulled down] (*MBNV* 242). But this historical event produces decidedly ahistoric effects. The acquisition of "new terrain" does not make more space for the dead, but rather reduces the specificity of the dead. As Flaubert explains, "mais toute cette portion nouvelle est presque inhabitée, les tombes, comme autrefois, continuant à s'entasser vers la porte" [the new area is almost uninhabited; the tombs, as before, continuing to crowd together towards the gate]. The first sign of significant trouble appears through the use of the word "inhabitée" deployed in reference to the dead: the unseen "living" inhabitants of the town are implicitly displaced by the conjured presence of the unnamed and unburied dead in their "uninhabited" graves. The figure of the cholera epidemic introduces a figure for death that contaminates water and earth and that spreads imperceptibly. But the defining duplicitous characteristic of Lestiboudois—who himself fills a double function—"en même temps fossoyeur et bedeau à l'église"—is to reap a double profit from the dead by refusing to recognize the difference between the space of the living and the space reserved for the dead: "(tirant ainsi des cadavres de la paroisse un double bénéfice), a profité du terrain vide pour y semer des pommes de terre." Lestiboudois introduces and incarnates a particular fetishistic relationship to death that pervades the entire remaining text of *Madame Bovary*. This attitude toward death almost always expresses itself through a precise double gesture—first the symbolic meaning of death is denied and then that very denial is affirmed by subsequent attempts to convert symbolic loss into financial or material gain. This gesture depends upon a mechanism that confuses and interweaves economic, linguistic, and temporal registers. Lestiboudois clearly has no understanding or respect for the laws of property. He embodies a principle of deformed capitalism—his abuse of Church property is made possible by the fact that he appears to have no capacity for differentiating between the living and the dead, between inanimate forms that were once conscious (cadavers) and organic forms that will never be conscious (potatoes). Although he cannot recognize the value of "life," he does recognize a principle of productive and paradoxically overproductive labor. By fertilizing human food with the remains of human dead, Lestiboudois overturns the foundations of Western culture and mindlessly confuses "Culture" with "cultivation." Thus, although he cannot understand the pun that Bournisien addresses to him— "Vous vous nourrissez des morts, Lestiboudois!"—his embodiment of a total collapse in levels of meaning resembles something like the verbal structure of a joke. And of course, we must read Lestiboudois as a joke, albeit a deadly serious and significant one.

Despite his comical cast (or perhaps because of it), the figure of Lestiboudois produces temporal textual effects and highlights an important aspect of the theory and function of language in *Madame Bovary*. At the temporal level, we discover that Lestiboudois introduces a new verb tense into the textual world of *Madame Bovary*. Although his entry into the narrative coincides with a historical event of epidemic death, he himself exists in an unchanging "present" and he is incapable of dying. When the priest accuses him of feeding off the dead, Lestiboudois appears to take his words literally. And in the very sentence in which he tries to assimilate the fact that he may be eating the dead, he appears to engulf the time of the narrative itself. In a single sentence, Flaubert removes him from sequential narrative time and deposits him into a strange new present tense in which both life and death lose all meaning:

Cette parole sombre le fit réfléchir; elle l'arrêta pour quelque temps; mais, aujourd'hui encore, il continue la culture de ses tubercules, et même soutient avec aplomb qu'ils poussent naturellement.

[This grim remark made him reflect; it stopped him for some time; but, still today, he continues the cultivation of his little tubers, and even maintains stoutly that they grow naturally.]

The most shocking words in this passage are "aujourd'hui encore." Flaubert could not have underscored his point more strongly nor made it more clearly. The violent introjection of this explicit "present" makes Lestiboudois the symbolic survivor of the narrative. He is *Madame Bovary*'s first and last man. He literally "prepares the ground" for Homais's triumphant appropriation of the hellish present that takes over the final sentences of the novel: "Il fait une clièntele d'enfer; l'autorité le ménage et l'opinion publique le protège. Il vient de recevoir la croix d'honneur." The eternal present tense that Lestiboudois inaugurates is infernal; it does not transcend the passage of time, but rather denies it. By putting death to end-less work—transforming graveyards into potato fields—Lestiboudois pre-empts the work of death. In his little field, there is no time for death, no space for death. If everything is unendingly subjected to the law of profit, which does not even stop for death, then there is no end to work and work can never come to an end.[11] Furthermore, although this present tense is predicated upon a denial of all differences that destroys the ability to read historically, Flaubert gives it an implicitly historical name: "today." By spec-ifying that Lestiboudois continues to cultivate his potatoes "today," Flaubert establishes Lestiboudois as the explicit emissary between the tem-porality of the text and the temporality of the world. The invocation of the word "today" can only disrupt the sense of narrative continuity for the reader: today in the novel never coincides with the "today" of the reader. But Flaubert's insistence upon Lestiboudois's continued activity into the present—today—asks us to consider how Lestiboudois, who cannot speak, might be read as the expression of something that continues to speak to us today about "today."

The Paternal Dysfunction

Before leaving Lestiboudois suspended in the "dead time" of "today," we are compelled to recall a curious fact about this figure which has gone entirely unremarked by the critical literature on *Madame Bovary*. In the first ten "scénarios, esquisses et plans" presented in *Madame Bovary: La Nouvelle Version*, we discover that Flaubert had originally designated "Lestiboudois" as Emma's maiden name and hence as the name of her fa-ther. An early scenario describes Emma as "Emma Lestiboudois, grande, mince, et noire—admirables yeux" [Emma Lestiboudois, tall, slim, and dark—admirable eyes]—and introduces the father as follows: "son père type carré du Cauchois, a été depuis la mort de sa femme se ruinant petit à petit, en cafés et en mauvaises récoltes—a voulu spéculer et s'est achevé" [her father square type from the pays de Caux, has been little by little going to ruin since the death of his wife, in cafés and failed harvests—wanted to speculate and did himself in] (*MBNV* 23). Then, in the later scénarios, the name "Lestiboudois" is given to the priest (*MBNV* 62). But strangely, in

the first written version of the text—the version that is scrupulously reconstructed by Pommier et Leleu—the entire passage about Lestiboudois in
the graveyard that we have just examined appears fairly similar to the one
in the definitive version—except for the fact that in the earlier version the
figure of grave-digger is explicitly left unnamed and there is no mention of
the words "aujourd'hui encore." Thus, the early version reads as follows:

Le gardien du cimetière, qui est en même temps fossoyeur et bedeau à l'église a
profité du terrain vide pour y semer des pommes de terre.[. . .]Chaque année
pourtant le petit champ se rétrécit, quand il vient des épidemies, il ne sait s'il doit
se réjouir des enterrements ou s'affliger des tombeaux.
—Vous vous nourrissez des morts, lui dit un jour M. Le curé.
Cette parole l'impressionna, le fit rêver et le soir il n'en mangea pas; mais il
continue malgré les représentations et prétend même qu'elles poussent toutes
seules. (*MBNV* 242)

[The keeper, who is at once gravedigger and church sexton, has taken advantage of
the unused plot of ground to plant potatoes.[. . .]Each year, however, the small
field grows smaller, and when epidemics happen, he does not know whether to rejoice at the burials or regret the tombs.
"You feed on the dead, Lestiboudois!" the curé told him one day.
This remark made an impression on him, sent him into a reverie and that
evening he could not eat because of it; but he continues in spite of all representations and even claims that they grow all by themselves.]

Despite the fact that the grave-digger is not given a proper name in this version of the passage, this unnamed figure is paradoxically more "human"
than the one who will ultimately receive the iterant proper name
"Lestiboudois." For although this grave-digger has no name for himself, he
does have a limited capacity to recognize that things have names. In this
version, the grave-digger is not merely "stopped" by the priest's joke, he is
"impressed" by it. Furthermore, although he cannot name either death or
the dead, the priest's words compel him to produce representations in the
form of dreams: "le fit rêver." He even provides a generic category for the
very linguistic function that he lacks. He calls the disturbing sense of
malaise produced by the image of eating the dead "les représentations."
However, like his counterpart "Lestiboudois," he continues to function by
refusing to accord any significance to these "representations." In the later
version, Flaubert perversely gives this character a proper name while removing him completely from the field of "representations." But by reading

these two versions together, we get a clearer sense that the proper name "Lestiboudois" is in fact a very improper name for the unnaming of the world through a disavowal of death. And, in turn, it is precisely this unnaming of death that enables "Lestiboudois" to become synonymous with subsistence in the dead time of "today."

The fact that Flaubert ultimately resuscitates the name he had initially chosen for Emma's father and gives this discarded paternal name to the grave-digger establishes a kind of textual "parenté" between "père Rouault" and the grave-digger. It is no accident that these two figures become linked through the erasure of the name "Lestiboudois" as a name for an explicitly paternal function. The ghostly rapport that will be established between these two characters emerges as an effect of the role that father figures play in the representation of death and in a crisis of "representation." Although the connection between Emma's father and the grave-digger may not be immediately apparent, these two characters share a common textual function in *Madame Bovary*. The actions and significance of both characters are defined through their respective relationship to, and representation of, death. Just as Lestiboudois is defined and introduced through his radical denial of death, Emma's father is virtually the only character in the novel who recognizes the existence of death, experiences death as loss and, most important, attempts to represent and communicate this experience through spoken language. Furthermore, Emma's father is the character most radically "transformed" by the events in the novel. We shall see later that as the novel moves progressively more and more into the dead time that swallows up the event of Emma's death, Emma's father becomes afflicted and affected by the undead culture of Yonville and ultimately loses his defining capacity to assimilate the experience of death by naming it.

I insist upon the implicit paternal connection between Lestiboudois and Rouault because the character who is universally recognized as incarnating paternal authority in the novel is Dr. Larivière. And although the character of Lestiboudois has received virtually no critical attention, Dr. Larivière, who occupies an equally minimal space in the plot, has often been elevated to the status of the text's stabilizing moral mouthpiece.[12] The most symptomatic celebration of Dr. Larivière's function appears in Harry Levin's "*Madame Bovary*: Cathedral and Hospital." In the final paragraph of his essay, Levin substantiates his claim that Flaubert is an ethical "moraliste" by pointing to the "affirmative" presence of Dr. Larivière:

Flaubert's ideal, though more honored in the breach than in the observance, fortifies him against those negative values which triumph in his book, and rises to an unwonted pitch of affirmation with the character sketch of Dr. Larivière: his disinterested skill, his paternal majesty, his kindness to the poor, his scorn for all decorations, his ability to see through falsehood. His most revealing epithet is hospitalier, since it connotes not only hospitality but Flaubert's birthplace, his father's hospital at Rouen, and also the stained-glass figure of Saint Julian the Hospitaler, whom the verger of the cathedral pointed out in an earlier draft, and who would later be Flaubert's knightly hero. The hospital and the cathedral: such, in retrospect, are the substance and the form of *Madame Bovary*.[13]

While I would not entirely dispute the validity of Levin's reading of the good doctor, I would argue that this humanistic, moralist reading of Flaubert's text reveals an almost desperate investment in providing the novel with a figure of "paternal majesty" while at the same time it betrays a latent desire to contain and neutralize the disturbing force of the "negativity" that pervades the text. Ironically, that negativity resurfaces in Levin's subliminal reference to Lestiboudois, the self-same "verger of the cathedral," who hardly affirms the sacred function of the "knightly hero." Levin's reading asks us to reinterrogate the figure of Dr. Larivière in order to understand more precisely why he is so profoundly reassuring. Or, to put it another way, what would happen to our understanding of the text if the figure of Lestiboudois were to displace Larivière's privileged position as the final repository of the paternal function in *Madame Bovary*?

Reading Lestiboudois's Improper Name

If Dr. Larivière commands such a significant place in the critical literature, it is most probably because he is the only clearly "meaningful" character in the entire novel.[14] As Levin's interpretation makes abundantly clear, the figure of Dr. Larivière tempts critics to reward this rare apparition of meaning in a Flaubertian character (the doctor's dignity, profundity, intelligence, memory, and sense of history are all conjured up in a single paragraph) by attempting to reap the text's meaning from him. But Dr. Larivière's overwhelmingly unique "meaningfulness" only increases the textual impact of the meaninglessness of everyone else around him. In a chapter of *Adultery in the Novel* called "Dr. Larivière Makes a Joke," Tony Tanner extensively and brilliantly explores how the problem of meaning in the text can be read through the unnoticed pun—"Oh! Ce n'est pas le *sens* qui le gêne" [Oh, it isn't his blood I'd call too thick] (586/236)—that the doctor makes upon leaving the scene of Emma's deathbed. Although we will return to a more detailed discussion of Dr. Larivière later, Tanner's treatment of the significance of the doctor's pun provides another startling example of how Lestiboudois's latent presence insistently subverts and subtends the production of meaning in the novel. In uncanny ways, Tanner's reading follows an invisible thread that retraces a paternal lineage connecting the witty and verbal father figures Larivière and Rouault to the mute grave-digger Lestiboudois.

In order to explain the importance of the fact that the doctor's joke goes unnoticed, Tanner contrasts Dr. Larivière's "calembour inarpeçu" to a "noticed pun" made by another character in the book. Although Tanner astutely recognizes the important distinction between "noticed" and "unnoticed" puns, he substitutes the name of the grave-digger for that of the priest Bournisien and thus mistakenly identifies Lestiboudois as the author of the "noticed" pun. If I believed that this mistake could be explained as a simple "error," I would not call attention to it. All readers, no matter how meticulous, are subject to occasional mistakes. But Tanner's "error" is no mere error—it obeys the precise and implacable logic of a Freudian slip. By violating the "proper" name "Bournisien" with the improper name "Lestiboudois," Tanner has effectively re-created the very phenomenon at work in his analysis of "Lestiboudois's (Bournisien's)" empty pun since the very pun in question consists of nothing other than a deformation of a proper name:

Et moi, quelquefois, par plaisanterie, je l'appelle donc Riboudet (comme la côte que l'on prend pour aller à Maromme), et je dis même: Mon Riboudet. Ah! Ah! Mont Riboudet! L'autre jour j'ai rapporté ce mot-là à Monseigneur, qui en a ri . . . il a daigné en rire. (393; qtd. in Tanner 323)

[And so sometimes for a joke I call him *Ri*boudet (like the hill on the way to Maromme), and I even say "*Mon* Riboudet." Ha! ha! "*Mont* Riboudet." The other day I repeated this little joke to the bishop, and he laughed . . . he deigned to laugh.] (80, translation modified)

But the uncanny and hallucinatory effects of Tanner's "slip" are most tellingly revealed in the language of his own interpretation of the meaning of this "noticed" pun. Although Tanner employs the name "Lestiboudois" in place of "Bournisien," the language of his argument pertains more appropriately to the real character "Lestiboudois" than it does to the actual author of the pun, Bournisien. Here is what Tanner writes about Lestiboudois-Bournisien:

We can note straight away that *Lestiboudois's* pun is entirely pointless. . . . In some puns two apparently disparate meanings, or realms of significance, are suddenly brought together (or condensed) in surprising and sometimes embarrassing propinquity. (Why do we laugh at puns? They are not in themselves funny—are we responding to a sudden recognition of two meanings being in one place where before we had never considered that they had any possible connection? Thus punning can be seen as a kind of *verbal adultery*. I will come to Freud's comments on this subject later.) *Lestiboudois's* pun is simply an empty echo, and there is a curious kind of *linguistic desolation* engendered by the totally empty pun that doesn't have in it the slightest trace of semantic shock. It is a *debasement* and devaluation of language into mere noise and must necessarily be something of a *depressant* to any would-be meaning maker or meaning seeker, whether it is Emma Bovary in her quest or us in our readings. We all know how purely empty, pointless puns such as *Lestiboudois's* can suddenly introduce a *dead patch* into a conversation, as though language has suddenly gone deaf to its obligations and forgotten its purposes. (324, italics mine)

In Tanner's own text, each mention of the improper proper name (Lestiboudois) produces the very effect of "linguistic desolation" that he describes because the real "Lestiboudois" could never even have made this "empty" pun. The real "Lestiboudois" not only does not speak, he *cannot* speak by definition; in order to speak one must have, as we have seen, a capacity for "representations," which entails the ability to tell the difference between potatoes and cadavers. But the source of the real "Lestiboudois's" inability to speak subtends the "linguistic desolation" that motivates Tanner's response. As we have seen, the name "Lestiboudois" is *Madame Bovary's* improper name for the "dead patch" in "language gone deaf to its obligations and forgotten its purposes." In Tanner's own text, the improper name "Lestiboudois" functions like a return of the repressed of the real "Lestiboudois," who cannot speak but whose unspeaking presence infiltrates the priest's empty words.

To make matters even more compellingly complicated, Tanner's analysis contains a latent explanation for how and why his own theoretical paradigm compels him to make this "mistake" in the first place. In this passage, Tanner defines puns as "a kind of verbal adultery." But because he relies too extensively on the category of "adultery" as the organizing figure for language in *Madame Bovary*, Tanner's text represses an interrogation of a death drive that returns, hauntingly, in the uncanny substitution of the name of the idiotic grave-digger in place of the name of the priest who fails to treat Emma for her adulterous desire. In other words, Tanner's investment in the problem of adultery blinds him to the problem of death. But since he is an impeccable reader, his own text "remembers" the very figure that his critical paradigm invites him to "forget." To his credit, Tanner attempts to compensate for the limitations of his paradigm by using *Madame Bovary* in order to rearticulate our understanding of "adultery." He comes to redefine "adultery" as a linguistic denial of difference: "It seems as if Flaubert is constantly making words of apparent difference turn and recognize their shared similarities . . . a procedure that suggests the general tendency to merging and loss of difference that I have described as permeating the book. It enacts a loss of category distinction, thus a loss of meaning, that in experiential terms reaches its climax when Emma discovers that adultery and marriage are effectively the same thing" (326). Toward the end of his book, in the last chapter on *Madame Bovary*, "Adultery Triumphant," Tanner concludes that "the triumph of adultery is the destruction of difference" (367). But what kind of difference is destroyed here? Despite Tanner's attempt to expand the limits of the term, adultery, whether in the language of puns or in the language of bodies, is based on an exchange that is made possible by a substitution of one element for another in its own category: one word is substituted for another word or one man is substituted for another man. In this sense, and we will return to this later, adultery, like puns, is structured like a metaphor. Adultery can alter or displace particular "meanings," but it alone does not threaten the very foundation of the production of "meaning."[15] The exchange of one word for another word, or one man for another man, is not the same exchange as the failure to recognize the difference between a potato and a cadaver. Thus, paradoxically, although Tanner explicitly seeks to explore the radical transgression of the social contract that *Madame Bovary* performs, by insisting upon naming this transgression "adultery," he ultimately reinscribes the text's perverse negativity into a familiar, knowable, and recognizable historical, social, and cultural context. While I can well imagine that this approach has certain immediate political benefits (in the context particularly of Marxism and feminism), I would like to explore the hypothesis that by resisting the familiarity of the available category of "adultery," we might come to a different appreciation of why this novel was perceived as so threatening in its day and why it continues to haunt our understanding of contemporary culture.[16]

Death on Trial

At this point, it is startling to remark that the first reader to express deep concern about the moral and political force of *Madame Bovary's* bizarre depiction of death was the very reader who was most zealously committed to censuring the novel in 1857: M. Ernest Pinard, attorney for the prosecution in the trial against Flaubert. As Dominick LaCapra points out in his important study of the trial, Pinard was a more sensitive reader of the novel's unsettling novelty than was the defense lawyer, M. Sénard. LaCapra observes that:

Sénard's interpretation . . . made the novel out to be altogether conventional in nature. Pinard, on the contrary, experienced its insinuations and unsettling potential despite his effort to construe it in terms of simple deviance from established norms. Indeed, at times he did broach issues of a broader nature. At the very least, Pinard may have been "poisoned" or contaminated by the "painting of passion" in the novel and, himself facing temptation, may have set out in a self-preservative quest to find a legal antidote to Flaubert's writing.[17]

LaCapra ingeniously interprets Pinard's virulence against the novel as an attempt to use the legal institution in order to inoculate himself against his own unhealthy attraction to the seductive power of Flaubert's prose. By describing the novel's effect on Pinard as "poisonous," LaCapra accentuates the potentially "lethal" nature of the text's adulterous sexuality. Throughout his analysis of the trial, LaCapra aptly and astutely reminds us that Pinard's predominant objection to Flaubert's work resides in the *way* in which the adulterous sexuality is depicted rather than in the simple fact of adultery. In the course of his argument pertaining to the "poisonous" status of the text, LaCapra calls our attention to Pinard's repeated gloss of one particularly "poisonous" line of the novel. LaCapra writes:

In developing his argument, Pinard interrupts a quotation to interject a parenthetical expression of scandalized dismay. The phrase over which he stumbles and whose peculiar nature he senses is: "*les souillures du mariage et les désillusions de l'adultère*" [the defilements of marriage and the disillusions of adultery]. He notices the telling reversal of ordinary expectations that Flaubert effects with this phrase. "There are those who would have said: 'The disillusions of marriage and the defilements of adultery.'" And shortly thereafter, he repeats this complaint and adds: "Often when one is married, instead of the unclouded happiness one expected, one encounters sacrifices and bitterness. The word disillusion might be justified; that of defilement could never be."

The effect of the novel on the reader—and perhaps the intention of the author—is for Pinard one of demoralization and corruption. The novel is literally poison. (*MBOT* 37–38)

But although LaCapra is certainly correct to point out that Pinard believes that the novel is poison, LaCapra's reading overemphasizes the categorical importance of the figure of poison (Pinard actually invokes the word only once—and only in the specific context of the dangers to the *feminine* readers of the novel) while at the same time he underplays the critical importance of the underlying rationale for Pinard's insistent complaint against the phrase "les souillures du mariage et les désillusions de l'adultère." Although LaCapra locates the scandalous nature of this sentence in its "telling reversal of ordinary expectations," I would argue that the source of Pinard's evident discomfort with this Flaubertian locution is actually more complicated and less easily described. For Pinard, the scandal of Flaubert's prose does not merely entail a "reversal of ordinary expectations" but a radical confusion of all moral, historical, political, linguistic, aesthetic, religious, and philosophical categories.

Throughout the trial, again and again, Pinard attempts to describe the uncanny effect created by the perverse confusion of the stability of *all* of his meaningful categories. His first major stumbling block occurs on the (for him) impossible conjunction of a debased subject (adultery) described through an exalted literary form (poetry). He writes: "Ainsi, dès cette première faute, dès cette première chute, elle fait glorification de l'adultère, elle *chante le cantique de l'adultère, sa poésie, ses voluptés*. Voilà, messieurs, qui pour moi est bien plus dangereux, bien plus immoral que la chute elle-même!" [Thus, from this first fault, from this first fall, she glorifies adultery, *she sings the song of songs of adultery, its poetry and its carnal delights*. This, gentlemen, to me is much more dangerous, much more immoral than the fall itself!] (*OC* 1:623, italics mine). Having introduced the confusion between the sacred and the profane through the use of the word "cantique," Pinard goes on to assert that Emma's temporal inconsistencies, coupled with her inability to distinguish the difference between sacred and profane *language*, render her uniquely sacrilegious:

Voluptueuse un jour, religieuse le lendemain, nulle femme, même dans d'autres régions, même sous le ciel d'Espagne ou d'Italie, ne murmure à Dieu les caresses d'adultères qu'elle donnait à l'amant. Vous apprécierez ce langage, messieurs, et vous n'excuserez pas ces paroles de l'adultère introduites, en quelque sorte, dans le sanctuaire de la divinité! (*OC* 1:625)

[Voluptuous one day, religious the next, there is no woman, even in other countries, under the sky of Spain or Italy, who murmurs to God the adulterous caresses which she gives to her lover. You can appreciate this language, gentlemen, and you will not excuse adulterous words penetrating in any way into the sanctuary of the Divinity!"]

Furthermore, Pinard's objections are not limited to the descriptions of Emma's ecstasies. He pauses at an important point to be scandalized by the sexually charged spectacle of the bas-relief made by her corpse under her funeral shroud:

Et puis ensuite, lorsque le corps est froid, la chose qu'il faut respecter par-dessus tout, c'est le cadavre que l'âme a quitté. Quand le mari est là, à genoux, pleurant sa femme, quand il a étendu sur elle le linceul, tout autre se serait arrêté, et c'est le moment où M. Flaubert donna le dernier coup de pinceau.
      "Le drap se creusait depuis ses seins jusqu'à ses genoux, se relevant ensuite à la pointe des orteils."
      Voilà la scène de la mort. Je l'ai abrégée, je l'ai groupée en quelque sorte. C'est à vous de juger et d'apprécier si c'est là le mélange du sacré au profane, ou si ce ne serait pas plutôt le mélange du sacré au voluptueux. (*OC* 1:630)

[And then later, when the body is cold, the thing that must be respected above all is the cadaver that the soul has just left. When the husband is there on his knees, weeping for his wife, when he draws the shroud over her, anyone else would have stopped, but this is the moment where Mr. Flaubert offers his final brush stroke:
      "The sheet sunk in from her breast to her knees, and then rose at the tip of her big toes."
      This is the death scene. I have abridged it and reclassified it after a fashion. It is now for you to judge and determine whether there is a mixture of the sacred and the profane in it, or rather, a mixture of the sacred and the voluptuous.]

As all of these examples make clear, in the very act of enumerating the alleged indecencies of Flaubert's text, Pinard appears to be ambivalently torn between the need to describe Flaubert's violation of nameable categories and the desire to give a precise name for the nature of the infraction. Thus he feels compelled to note that his abridged rendition of the death scene is less damaging than the Flaubertian version because he, Pinard, has already subjected it to the necessary and rightful laws of reclassification.

      But the most curious moment in Pinard's entire text occurs at the very end. After he has paraphrased the novel and offered numerous exemplary citations of Flaubert's indecency, Pinard begins his conclusion by as-

sessing why the novel ought to be condemned from a "philosophical" perspective. He links the philosophical immorality of the book directly to the
narrative form that will later be known as "style indirect libre" and to the
central absence of the authorial voice that will later be described by critics
as Flaubert's "impersonality." Pinard argues that the book should be condemned because there is not one single incarnation of a stable moral voice
in the novel. After listing all of the paternal male characters who *ought*
to provide such a moral center but fail to do so—Charles, Homais,
Bournisien—he looks for the inscription of what he calls "the author's
conscience." Surprisingly, Pinard isolates one unique sentence in which he
purports to find a ghostly inscription of the "author's conscience."
Shockingly—and it certainly shocks Pinard—this single sentence is nothing
other than a commentary on the radical deniability of death. Here is how
Pinard presents the scene:

> Le condamnerez-vous au nom de la conscience de l'auteur? Je ne sais pas ce que
> pense la conscience de l'auteur; mais, dans son chapitre X, le seul philosophique de
> l'oeuvre (livr. Du 15 déc.), je lis la phrase suivante:
>> "Il y a toujours après la mort de quelqu'un comme une stupéfaction qui se
>> dégage, tant il est difficile de comprendre cette survenue du néant et de se résigner
>> à y croire."
> Ce n'est pas un cri d'incrédulité, mais c'est du moins un cri du scepticisme.
> Sans doute il est difficile de comprendre et d'y croire; mais, enfin, *pourquoi* cette
> *stupéfaction qui se manifeste à la mort? Pourquoi?* (OC 1:633, italics mine)

> [Will you condemn it in the name of the author's conscience? I know not what the
> author thinks, but in his chapter X, the only philosophical one of his book, I read
> the following:
>> "There is always after the death of someone something like a stupefaction
>> which emanates from it, so difficult is it to comprehend this advent of nothingness
>> and to resign oneself to believe in it."
> This is not a cry of incredulity, but it is at the very least a cry of skepti-
> cism. Without a doubt it is difficult to comprehend and believe it, but why this
> stupefaction which manifests itself at death? Why?]

There is something stupefying about the affective urgency in Pinard's repeated demand to know "Why?, Why?" the author only appears in this
book in order to question the believability of death. Pinard's own argument
stutters, falters, and comes to a close on this point. This quotation is the
final citation in his text. Everything he has argued up to this point about
religion, about poetry, about history, about morality, even about adultery

brings him inexorably to this final unrestful place. Implicit in the structure of Pinard's argument—which moves from point to point to this strange conclusion—is the notion that Flaubert's perverse and innovative treatment of death is inextricably bound up in a threat to the symbolic power of paternal authority and the legal, political institutions of the time.

Curiously, LaCapra analyzes the entire conclusion of Pinard's argument except for his remarks about Flaubert's treatment of death. LaCapra interrupts Pinard in mid-sentence and without indicating that the sentence continues: "'Would you condemn her [*sic*] in the name of the author's conscience? I do not know what the author's conscience thinks'" (quoted *MBOT* 39). LaCapra, like Tanner, glosses over this bizarre invocation of death in Pinard's conclusion because he, like Tanner, is convinced that the conceptual model for *Madame Bovary*'s "poison" is adultery. Thus, LaCapra's reading of Pinard's text cannot fully account for the uncanny and prescient power of Pinard's first "institutional" reading of Flaubert's text. Perhaps Pinard was the first reader to respond, albeit reactively and negatively, to that elusive element in Flaubert's style that continues to render the text of *Madame Bovary* so strangely "new" and so uncannily "present." And perhaps this text's subsequent and resolutely undying appeal is due, in part, to its perversely contemporary disfiguration of symbolic representations of death.

In his essay "A propos du 'style' de Flaubert," Marcel Proust offers some fascinating observations about Flaubert's style that might help us to begin to understand why *Madame Bovary* continues to be so resonant today. Proust opens his essay with an expression of stupefied outrage about the necessity of defending Flaubert against a critic who dares to accuse him of bad writing:

Je lis seulement à l'instant (ce qui m'empêche d'entreprendre une étude approfondie) l'article du distingué critique de *La Nouvelle Revue française* sur "le Style de Flaubert". J'ai été stupéfait, je l'avoue, de voir traiter de peu doué pour écrire, un homme qui par *l'usage entièrement nouveau* et personnel qu'il a fait du passé défini, du passé indéfini, du participe présent, de certains pronoms et de certaines prépositions, *a renouvelé* presque autant notre vision des choses que Kant, avec ses Catégories, les théories de la Connaissance et de la Réalité du monde extérieur.[18] (italics mine)

[I have only just now read (which prevents me from undertaking a detailed study) the article by the distinguished critic of the *Nouvelle Revue française* on "Flaubert's Style." I was stupefied, I confess, to see described as an ungifted writer a man who, by the *entirely new and personal use* he made of the definite past, the indefinite past, the present participle, and certain pronouns and certain prepositions, has renewed our vision of things almost as much as Kant, with his categories, his theories of knowledge and of the reality of the external world.]

In the very next sentence, however, Proust goes on to launch his own personal attack on Flaubert's style:

Ce n'est pas que j'aime entre tous les livres de Flaubert, ni même le style de Flaubert. Pour des raisons qui seraient trop longues à développer ici, je crois que *la métaphore seule* peut donner une sorte *d'éternité* au style, et il n'y a peut-être pas dans tout Flaubert une seule belle métaphore.[19] (italics mine)

[It is not that I love Flaubert's books above all, nor even Flaubert's style. For reasons that would be too long to develop here, I believe that *metaphor alone* can give a sort of *eternity* to style, and there is perhaps in the whole of Flaubert not a single beautiful metaphor.]

If we read these two sentences through Proust's explicit invocation to the temporal dimension of Flaubert's writing, we understand that there is absolutely no contradiction between his vigorous defense and his scathing critique of Flaubert's style. The stylistic quality that Proust celebrates—and deems necessary to defend against the blindness of bad readers—is the "newness" of Flaubert's writing. He argues that the entire French language is renewed and that the world appears recast by a "new vision" because of Flaubert's idiosyncratic and personal usage of French verb tenses, personal pronouns, and prepositions. But there appears to be something inherently excessive about this very celebrated "newness" that prevents Flaubert from being able to write the beautiful metaphor that would, for Proust, render his style "eternal." Paradoxically, Proust's argument suggests that the very thing that is uniquely new about Flaubert's "newness" is the absence of a temporal link between the new and the eternal. One might imagine that Proust is thinking here of Baudelaire's argument in *The Painter of Modern Life*, that beauty must combine *both* a modern (changing) element and an eternal (unchanging) element. But Proust's explicit complaint centers on the necessary connection between Flaubert's failure to produce a beautiful metaphor and the absence of an "eternal" quality to his style. I would like to suggest, somewhat tentatively, that Flaubert's apparent inability to produce a beautiful metaphor can be linked to the perverse denial of death that we have seen at work throughout the text of *Madame Bovary*. As numerous theorists, philosophers, and writers have observed, the structure of metaphor requires an inscription of some form of absence through symbolic representation. And, as we have seen through our reading of the function of Lestiboudois in *Madame Bovary*, the grave-digger's denial of death leads directly to a failure to produce or comprehend "representations," to a perceived threat to patriarchal institutions, and to a particular form of undead survival that continues to reverberate in the surprising ways in which *Madame Bovary* remains peculiarly relevant to the culture of today.

Madame Bovary, Today

In order to understand how *Madame Bovary* has survived its canonical inscription into literary history and contemporary culture, we shall take a brief look at the way in which this text continues to renew itself in the workings of contemporary culture.

The *Petit Robert* defines Bovarysme as follows: "Insatisfaction romanesque; pouvoir qu'a l'homme de se concevoir autre qu'il n'est" [Novelistic lack of satisfaction; man's power to conceive of himself as other than he is]. This word, which was adopted by the French language a few years after the publication of *Madame Bovary*, highlights the curious fact that because the most memorable, and most singular, heroine of the nineteenth century defined herself and her own experiences through common clichés, Emma Bovary has become a paradigmatic pseudonym for a rather peculiar set of common experiences. From the nineteenth century onward, the name Emma Bovary has become synonymous with bored housewife syndrome, adultery, hysteria, rampant consumerism, romantic delusions, sexual ambiguity, narcissism, and masochism. In each case, Emma Bovary is invoked in order to represent classes of experiences which are paradoxically defined as being simultaneously *generic* and *pathological*. These classes of experiences are generic in that they seem to describe aspects of existence that often come to occupy the habitual lives of ordinary people; but they are pathological because they invariably reveal how often these common people suffer extraordinary failures to live their ordinary lives.

Thus, while it may not appear particularly shocking that Emma Bovary has been asked to represent almost all of the paradigmatic cultural pathologies of the nineteenth century—she is, after all, presumably a product of her time—it is nonetheless rather surprising to remark that, in the very last decade or so, Emma Bovary has made a spectacular paraliterary comeback as a privileged representative and spokesperson for some of the *new* pathologies that have come to fascinate the late twentieth century: addiction and female perversion. In 1992, for example, Avital Ronell based her investigation of the relationship between addiction and contemporary culture on a reading of *Madame Bovary.* Similarly, in Emily Apter's 1993 collection *Fetishism as Cultural Discourse*,[20] Naomi Schor invokes Flaubert as the patron saint of the ironic fetishisms of postmodernism.

Madame Bovary as Contemporary Case History: Female Perversions

Most recently, the psychoanalyst Louise Kaplan has written a book on *Female Perversions*, which is subtitled *The Temptations of Emma Bovary*, and which goes so far as to use the text of *Madame Bovary* as a vehicle through which she communicates the cases of her contemporary analysands while protecting their anonymity. Toward the middle of *Female Perversions*, Kaplan explains her reliance upon the text of *Madame Bovary* as follows:

> I will be using Madame Bovary as the template for developing some of my ideas about the nature of the female perversions. Not by chance, as I was beginning to think about writing this book, I chose to reread Madame Bovary and discovered there in one form or another, directly or indirectly, in every character and every turn of the plot the personal and social factors that facilitate the perverse strategy and also some proto-types of the female perversions that I had already discovered through my clinical practice and research. Since I would not use my patients to illustrate what I was discovering about the female perversions, I was happy to discover Flaubert's penchant for creating perverse scenarios. (202–3)

Kaplan's use of Madame Bovary implies not only that Flaubert's nineteenth-century *literary* narrative *can* be read as a viable substitute for the *lived* experiences of Kaplan's twentieth-century patients, but also, conversely, and more radically, that the lived experiences of these patients are, in a sense, better expressed by Flaubert's fictional narrative than they would have been by more contemporary fictional narratives, or even, paradoxically, by their own personal life stories.

For the sake of argument, we are not only going to accept Kaplan's premise that Flaubert's novel can be read as a privileged description and analysis of her patient's maladies, but we are also going to use Kaplan's articulation of the perverse strategy in order to reexamine why this text is so peculiarly resonant today. Very schematically, Kaplan's theory of the perverse strategy is largely dedicated to a detailed discussion of how perversions *conserve* the social order by making use of clichés of gender stereotypes in order to mask and regulate primal anxieties and traumas. Kaplan writes: "What makes a perversion a perversion is a mental strategy that uses one or another social stereotype of masculinity and femininity in a way that deceives the onlooker about the unconscious meanings of the behaviors she or he is observing" (9). "Central to my thesis about the sexual perversions, is the idea that they are pathologies of gender stereotyping" (196). For Kaplan, like Freud before her, perversions always entail a peculiar sort of disavowal of sexual difference, which is exemplified by the structure of fetishism. Although Kaplan ultimately diverges from the classical Freudian understanding of fetishism, she does concur with Freud that fetishistic disavowal does not entail the repression of sexual difference, but the radical denial of it. Thus, although the fetishist can consciously admit, for example, that his mother does not have a penis, the fetish that he chooses—say a feminine high-heeled shoe—sustains a belief in the presence of the maternal phallus in order to maintain the belief that sexual difference does not exist. But because Kaplan expands her definition of perversion to include all kinds of unconscious denials of sexual difference through gender stereotyping, she encourages us to pay strict attention to the underlying motors of the perverse strategy. Thus, by following closely precise mechanisms involved in Kaplan's exposition, we discover that the gender stereotypes that Kaplan identifies as fetishistic disavowals of sexual difference actually function as generic, empty placeholders—psychic clichés—that disavow a difference of another kind altogether. The psychic clichés that the perverse strategy seizes hold of and reproduces function as desperate unconscious attempts to manage and contain a horrific, traumatic, and ultimately unspeakable dysfunction of the death drive. Thus, if we read the subtext of her book carefully, we find the following kinds of arguments: "Perversions are an instance of the erotic passions frantically trying to restrain impulses toward destruction and death" (27). "In perversions, the compulsion to repeat a trauma is decisively more powerful than the seeking of pleasure and the avoidance of pain. Those who offer comfort or concern or understanding watch helplessly as an entire life gets used up, bit by bit, in an attempt to maintain these cycles of castration and restitution, abandonment and reunion, death and resurrection, until sometimes the dread punishments are meted out. It is as though the slave of love is seeking castration, abandonment, and death through the medium of love and pleasure" (218).

But what, you may ask, does this have to with Flaubert's *Madame Bovary*? Time permitting, I would like to argue that although Kaplan's intuition and intelligence correctly encourage her to ground her investigation of female perversions in Flaubert's text, she does not ultimately read Flaubert closely enough in order fully to recognize how his articulation of the "case of Emma Bovary" anticipates her arguments, analyzes them, and radically subverts them. But by reading Flaubert through Kaplan—by reading Flaubert's reading *of* Kaplan—we may be better able to see how his novel provides an unprecedented articulation and diagnosis of a cultural and historical disavowal of death itself. Thus, the particular sorts of contemporary perversions that fascinate cultural critics of the twentieth century are but the belated responses and symptoms—to a phenomenon that was already implicitly theorized by Flaubert in *Madame Bovary*.

Dr. Larivière's Tear

Since Kaplan's analytic and therapeutic investment in the question of female perversions motivates her reading of *Madame Bovary*, it is not surprising that she introduces the project of her own book with a discussion of the various representations of doctors and the medical profession depicted in the novel. Her medical interest in the text invariably leads her to open up her examination of female perversions through Dr. Larivière's medical examination of Emma Bovary's dying body. But because Kaplan wants to pattern her analytic reading through an explicit identification with the doctor, she fails to recognize the highly perverse textual function that Dr. Larivière performs at one of the most enigmatic and critical junctures of the novel. Here is what Kaplan writes:

Then there is Dr. Larivière, who was different from all the others. A tear fell on his shirt as he regarded Emma's cadaverous face. He was conjuring the beautiful flesh that once adorned it, knowing he must admit that there was nothing he could do to arrest the processes of death. Larivière belonged to the line of surgeons that sprang from Marie-François-Xavier Bichat. . . . When Bichat lectured that life is only "the sum of the functions that oppose death," he wanted to impress on his students the narrow border between health and disease. He would say that the physical properties of flesh and organs, which tend by their very functioning to lead toward death, are held back from that inevitable fate by the vital properties that also inhabit the cells of the body. But, alas, the vital properties too use them-selves up and become exhausted: "Time wears them away." As a follower of Bichat, Larivière might have wondered if perhaps perversion was less about sexual abnor-mality than about the failure of the erotic properties to regulate and contain the processes of death—and he would have been right about that. . . . Larivière, the Bichat disciple, would also have understood that the manifest or topmost layer of perversion could tell almost nothing about its meaning. . . . Larivière's glance, "as sharp as his lancet, plunged deep into your soul, through all pretense and reserve, and laid bare any lies hidden there." . . . Like Dr. Larivière, we are about to scru-tinize the world of perversion, penetrate the surface, and lay bare the deceptions that are hidden beneath. (4–5)

On one level, Kaplan's focus on this precise textual moment is remarkably insightful. Very simply, she asks us to focus on the place given to the figuration of death in *Madame Bovary*. By reading the novel through the figure of Dr. Larivière, she implicitly asks us to look at the entire book through the eyes of a doctor who is looking into a dying face.[21] But al-though she correctly points out that Dr. Larivière's medical gaze most cer-tainly reflects Bichat's changing perceptions of the rearticulation between life and death, she symptomatically assumes, far too quickly, both that she can know what Dr. Larivière sees and that what he sees can be known. By paraphrasing the scene and by overestimating the penetrating prowess of the doctor's gaze, she actively refuses to see what is happening in it. Here is the scene as Flaubert actually wrote it:

Il fronça les sourcils dès la porte, en apercevant la face cadavéreuse d'Emma éten-due sur le dos, la bouche ouverte. Puis, tout en ayant l'air d'écouter Canivet, il se passait l'index sous les narines et répétait:
—C'est bien, c'est bien.
    Mais il fit un geste lente des épaules. Bovary l'observa: ils se regardèrent; et cet homme, si habitué pourtant à l'aspect des douleurs, ne put retenir une larme qui tomba sur son jabot. Il voulut emmener Canivet dans la pièce voisine. Charles le suivit.
—Elle est bien mal, n'est-ce pas? Si l'on posait des sinapsismes? Je ne sais quoi! Trouvez donc quelque chose, vous qui avez tant sauvé!
    Charles lui entourait le corps de ses deux bras, et il contemplait d'une manière effarée, suppliante, à demi pâmé contre sa poitrine.
—Allons, mon pauvre garçon, du courage! Il n'y a plus rien à faire.
    Et le docteur Larivière se détourna. (584)

[He frowned as soon as he had passed the door when he saw the cadaverous face of Emma stretched out on her back with her mouth open. Then, while apparently listening to Canivet, he rubbed his fingers up and down beneath his nostrils, repeating;

"Fine, fine . . ."

But he slowly shrugged his shoulders. Bovary watched him; they looked at one another; and this man, accustomed as he was to the sight of pain, could not keep back a tear that fell on his shirt front.

He tried to take Canivet into the next room. Charles followed him.

"She's sinking, isn't she? If we put on poultices? Anything! Oh, think of something, you who have saved so many!"

Charles put both arms around him, and looked at him in anxious supplication, half-fainting against his breast.

"Come, my poor boy, courage! There is nothing more to be done."

And Doctor Larivière turned away.] (234)

Kaplan's rendition of this scene subtracts a significant detail and adds an unwarranted interpretation. Remember that she began her discussion of Dr. Larivière by observing that: "A tear fell on his shirt as he regarded Emma's cadaverous face. He was conjuring the beautiful flesh that once adorned it, knowing he must admit that there was nothing he could do to arrest the processes of death." But nothing in Flaubert's text allows us to conjecture that when he looks at Emma's cadaverous face he is conjuring up her "beautiful flesh." What he sees, in place of the "beautiful flesh" that Kaplan hallucinates, is the terrifying spectacle of a body that is no longer living and not yet dead. What he actually sees, when he enters the room, and Flaubert makes it clear that the sight causes him to contract his gaze in a frown, is Emma's face disfigured by her open mouth. I would argue that Kaplan's direct substitution of a conjured figure of "beautiful flesh" in place of the disturbing figure of Emma's open mouth is not accidental. The knowing, clinical gaze through which she wants to read this scene cannot read the unknowability of that mouth and must, at all costs, attempt to close it by putting comforting and familiar words like "beautiful flesh" into it.

But although Louise Kaplan identifies with the penetrating power of the doctor's gaze, Flaubert's Dr. Larivière performs a rhetorical, not medical, operation on this patient. In response to Emma's open mouth, he makes a curious repetitive gesture of rubbing his index figure, again and again, in the place over his own mouth and under his nostrils while repeating the empty words "C'est bien, c'est bien." But although he makes empty gestures and speaks empty words, Dr. Larivière does something in this scene that no one else in the novel can do. He sheds a single, involuntary tear. The very singularity of this tear (as opposed to the undifferentiated torrents that flow throughout the text) points to the singularity of the moment. Through this one tear, Dr. Larivière expresses, literally and symbolically, both that he has assimilated the reality and inevitability of Emma's death and that he is therefore capable of acknowledging the fact of this death by mourning it. As we have seen, however, in the textual logic of this book, the experience of death is rigorously and fetishistically disavowed at every turn and therefore does not exist as such. Dr. Larivière's tear functions as a catachresis, a figure for something that has no literal referent. Although Dr. Larivière arrives too late to save Emma and leaves before she actually dies, his tear is the only textual evidence (with one exception) that the difference between life and death itself constitutes a difference in the lived experience of its characters. And so by looking at the singularity of this exceptional moment, through this exceptional figure, we are able to recognize its critical difference from every other expression of death in the novel.

To complicate matters even further, Flaubert makes it overwhelmingly clear that Dr. Larivière doesn't even belong in this book. As many critics have pointed out, Dr. Larivière beams into the intrigue of *Madame Bovary* like an alien from another world or another novel. Flaubert literally compares his arrival to the appearance of a God: "L'apparition d'un dieu n'eût pas causé plus d'émoi. Bovary leva les mains, Canivet s'arrêta tout court, et Homais retira son bonnet grec avant que le docteur fût entré./Il appartenait . . . à cette génération, maintenant disparue" [The apparition of a god would not have caused more commotion. Bovary raised his hands; Canivet stopped short; and Homais pulled off his cap long before the doctor had come in./He belonged . . . to that generation, now extinct] (584/ 233). Tony Tanner's description of the impact of his arrival is particularly apt:

> He arrives from another level of reality—he is ontogenetically discontinuous with the world he enters. . . . In a world of copies, duplicates, and triplicates, he is an "original," singular, inimitable. Which is why Flaubert describes him in such a way as to make us register him as *entering* this world (book) but not being *of* it. He might pass for a "saint" or "demon" but not, in the terms of this book, for a man. Homais is the measure of an *homme* in this world. Larivière is only a hasty, disdainful visitor. (320–21)

Although I am fully convinced by Tanner's beautiful reading of the textual alterity that the doctor's arrival produces, I am far less persuaded by his conclusions concerning the doctor's textual function. He claims that "Dr.

Larivière is that father-god whom Emma never had and cannot name or define." Given the context of this reading, I would argue that Dr. Larivière's status as "father-god" stems directly from the fact that he remains the sole surviving witness of a "now defunct generation of doctors" whose mediation of death serves to underwrite and guarantee the progression of historical time. But even if we assume that the doctor's rhetorical intervention makes Emma's death momentarily real by bearing witness to it through his tear, that single tear does not repair the empty and absent representation of death that is located in the gaping hole of her open mouth.

An Open Mouth and a Lock of Hair

Before, during, and after her physical death, the process of Emma's dying is simultaneously enunciated and effaced through the various activities that take place in and around this open mouth. Her attempted suicide, as you recall, begins in the mouth. As we saw earlier, she stuffs her face with poison and, as Philippe Bonnefis has pointed out, although Flaubert's description of this gesture, "elle se mit à manger à même," is almost grammatically meaningless, the words "à même" are a homophonic reversal of Emma's name and thus indicate that her act of eating the poison can be read as an attempt to swallow her own name. In the context of this discussion, we might say that Emma tries to represent her own death by attempting to fill her open mouth with the sounds of her name. But Emma's mouth cannot be closed. She vomits continuously during her death and after it. The description of her final death agony focuses on the obscene detail that her tongue protrudes, in its entirety, from her open mouth: "La langue toute entière lui sortit hors la bouche" [Her whole tongue came protruding out of her mouth] (588/237, translation modified). Although Emma's mouth remains open after her death, Flaubert does inscribe one indication that her death has made a difference: the open mouth is now described as a black hole that disfigures her face. "Emma avait la tête penchée sur l'épaule droite. Le coin de sa bouche, qui se tenait ouverte, faisait comme un trou noir au bas de son visage" [Emma's head was drooping onto her right shoulder. The corner of her mouth, which was gaping open, made like a black hole at the bottom of her face] (593/241, translation modified). But the move from a speechless open mouth to that of a black hole in speech does not resolve the disturbing unreadability and indeterminacy of this disfiguring figure. In the image of this black hole, we find that an obscene erotic cliché, a woman's black hole, has become indistinguishable from an inadequate articulation of death. Quite simply, we might say that this mouth is left open because it is missing a meaningful word for death itself. The perversity of this image, which is itself an image of perversion, is the ultimate fetishistic figure through which the division between life and death is radically disavowed in the novel. Whether open in speech or open in death, the word that these mouths cannot utter, form, or comprehend is, in fact, the word "death." Thus, in some sense, Emma cannot die, does not die, because in the world in which she is condemned to exist, the word "death" has no referent, no meaning, no relation to her reality. Although her body ceases to perform its vital functions, no one named in the novel acknowledges her death as a radical removal from the realm of the living.

There is, however, one fleeting moment in which a member of the Yonville community momentarily acknowledges the fact of Emma's death. Significantly, however, not only is the word "death" never named, but the figure who sobs inconsolably at her grave becomes curiously unnamed in the very act of mourning her:

Il y en avait un autre qui, à cette heure-là, ne dormait pas.
   Sur la fosse, entre les sapins, un enfant pleurait agenouillé, et sa poitrine, brisée par les sanglots, haletait dans l'ombre, sous la pression d'un regret immense, plus doux que la lune et plus insondable que la nuit. (602)

[There was another who at that hour was not asleep.
   On the grave, between the pine-trees, a child was on his knees weeping, and his heart, rent by sobs, was panting in the dark, under the weight of an immense sorrow, more tender than the moon and more unfathomable than the night.] (248, translation modified)

This fleeting textual interlude—whose romantic lyricism charmed Sainte-Beuve, recalls Chateaubriand, and anticipates Duras—is abruptly interrupted and savagely rewritten by the arrival of Lestiboudois:

La grille tout à coup craqua. C'était Lestiboudois; il venait chercher sa bêche qu'il avait oubliée tantôt. Il reconnut Justin escaladant le mur, et sut alors à quoi s'en tenir sur le malfaiteur qui lui dérobait ses pommes de terre. (603)

[The gate suddenly grated. It was Lestiboudois coming to fetch the spade he had forgotten earlier. He recognized Justin climbing over the wall, and knew at least who had been stealing his potatoes.] (248–49, translation modified)

Lestiboudois's reappropriation of his claim on the cemetery as garden co-incides with his reinscription of the unnamed "child" Justin into the Yonville community. In the act of using the cemetery as a site of mourning, Justin momentarily loses his proper name. Lestiboudois can only "recognize" Justin as "Justin" by explaining his presence in the cemetery as potato thief. Thus, all of the "mourners" in the novel—Père Rouault, Dr. Larivière, and Justin—are systematically exiled from the linguistic community of Yonville through the very act of mourning.

In a world where death is not symbolized, mourning is impossible. Charles does not actually mourn Emma, he becomes her by encrypting her. He indiscriminately appropriates her animate and inanimate characteristics. At this juncture, in this twilight world of the undead where the failure to die undoes the very principle of life, we are compelled to recall that Emma is not the only Bovary to expire with an open mouth. On the final page of the novel, we find that Charles's death remains even more unspeakable than Emma's:

Il avait la tête renversée contre le mur, les yeux clos, la bouche ouverte, et tenait dans ses mains une longue mèche de cheveux noirs.

"Papa, viens donc!" dit-elle.

Et, croyant qu'il voulait jouer, elle le poussa doucement. Il tomba par terre. Il etait mort.

Trente-six heures après, sur la demande de l'apothicaire, M. Canivet accourut. Il l'ouvrit et ne trouva rien. (611)

[His head was leaning against the wall, with closed eyes and open mouth, and in his hand was a long tress of black hair.

"Papa, come!" she said.

And thinking he wanted to play, she gave him a gentle push. He fell to the ground. He was dead.

Thirty-six hours later, at the pharmacist's request, Monsieur Canivet came running. He opened him up and found nothing.] (255, translation modified)

This time, not even Dr. Larivière is called in to shed a tear. This time, literally no one knows when Charles dies, how he dies, or even that he dies. His own daughter interprets his immobility as a form of play and does not recognize his death when she sees it. Like a perverse parody of Saint Thomas, she does not know that he is dead until he falls over at her touch. The medical gaze also does not recognize his death. This man who dies with an open mouth is opened up by a doctor's autopsy that reveals nothing at all. Finally, in strict accordance with the perverse logic of this book,

Charles dies holding on to locks of Emma's hair. And this hair, which is of course one of the quintessential emblems of *sexual* fetishism, here appears as a fetish of death. Like the perverse strategy to which it belongs, this hair compromises the distinction between animate and inanimate matter. Like the person to whom it was once attached and like the person who dies desperately clutching it, this hair, neither living nor dead, is the final token of *Madame Bovary's* unspeakable death.

Post-Scriptum

In a volume of *L'Arc* devoted to Flaubert, Marthe Robert speculates about why Kafka should have been so fascinated by Flaubert. She writes: "Ce que l'on peut dire, c'est que les deux écrivains ont en commun la conviction qu'écrire empêche de vivre, tout au moins de vivre comme un homme normal, installé, qui a un métier, une femme et des enfants. Il faut choisir: ou tu écris ou tu te maries,—ou tu écris ou tu vis" [What we can say is that both writers hold in common the conviction that writing prevents living, or at least living the life of a normal man, set up with a job, a wife, and children. You must choose: either you write or you get married; either you write or you live].[22] She goes on to suggest that Flaubert, for the first time, defined literature as the space radically opposed to life, and more important than life. But I want to turn this idea around. I want to suggest that if Flaubert chooses literature over life—if he radically defines literature as the rigorous articulation of the choice *not to live* life as life—it is not, as she suggests, merely because he believes that literature is more important or exalted than life, but because he sensed that something about life itself had become suspect: unrecognizable, unknown, unnameable, and ultimately unlivable.

Notes

Introduction

1. Benjamin, *Charles Baudelaire* (hereafter cited as *CB*), 110.

2. In *The Politics of Prose*, Denis Hollier describes Sartre's description of Baudelaire's relationship to his time as follows:

> Every century must be content with its intention or discovery. The sixteenth had America, the eighteenth, the present. In the *Baudelaire* study, the nineteenth is called "the era which had just discovered the future," that future on which, now that it existed, the author of *Les Fleurs du mal* was to be accused of turning his back. (88)

3. Lyotard, *The Inhuman*, 25.

4. Jameson, *The Seeds of Time*, 84. In the following passage, Jameson distinguishes "modernity" from "modernism" and shows how the two are related through the works of both Baudelaire and Flaubert. He writes:

> What happens in the West to the existential . . . can most instructively be observed in the realm of time, which on the one hand is seized upon its measureability (the working day, that struggle within the factory for possession of the chronometer or timepiece itself . . .) and on the other becomes the deep bottomless vegetative time of Being itself, no longer draped and covered with myth or inherited religion. It is this new and unadorned experience of time that will generate the first expressions of the modern in the West—in the crucial year 1857, the year of the poems of Baudelaire and of Flaubert's first published novel. Modernization, by stripping away the traditional representations with which human temporality was disguised and domesticated, revealed for one long stark moment the rift in existence through which the unjustifiability of the passing of time could not but be glimpsed, by Baudelaire, who called it *ennui*, the ticking of the meter still running, the look downward into the meaninglessness of the organic, which does not set you any tasks but only condemns you to go on existing like a plant. (84–85)

5. See Blanchot, *La Part du feu*, 133–52, and Bataille, *La Littérature et le mal*, 37–68.

6. I am thinking here of Janet Wolff's essay, "The Invisible Flâneuse," in *Feminine Sentences*, 34–50. Wolff concludes her discussion of women, modernity, and misogyny as follows:

> It is not at all clear what a feminist sociology of modernity would look like. There is no question of inventing the *flâneuse*: the essential point is that such a character was rendered impossible by the sexual divisions of the nineteenth century. Nor is it appropriate to reject totally the existing literature on modernity, for the experiences it describes certainly defined a good deal of the lives of men, and were also (but far less centrally) a part of the experience of women. What is missing in this literature is any account of life outside the public realm, of the experience of "the modern" in its private manifestations, and also of the very different nature of the experience of those women who *did* appear in the public arena: a poem written by "la femme passante" about her encounter with Baudelaire, perhaps. (47)

Wolff's essay has been widely read by other feminists, who have responded to it in various ways. Anne Friedberg builds upon Wolff's essay in *Window Shopping*, where she writes:

> The impossibility of the flâneuse has been forcefully argued by Janet Wolff. Wolff describes a modernity that was predominantly identified with the public sphere of work, politics and urban life—realms that were exclusively male. In her account, the literature of modernity accepts the confinement of women to the private sphere, and hence fails to delineate women's experience. Certainly the literature that Wolff surveys—Simmel, Baudelaire, Benjamin—describes the experience of men in the public sphere from which women are invisible. Wolff wants to produce a feminist sociology that would supply the experiences of women, but it seems important also to turn to some literary texts by female "modernists." (37)

Wolff, however, does not seem to make any distinction between the "literary" depictions of men and women in Baudelaire's poetry and the actual lives of men and women in the nineteenth century. When she says that "the existing literature on modernity . . . defined a good deal of the lives of men," she both "elevates" literature to the status of an "unmediated" (and hence "accurate" historical document) while "reducing" other aspects of literature's powers of expression. Perhaps closer attention to the "literary" aspect of Baudelaire's work would reveal that the status of women, in Baudelaire, cannot be read according to the public/private schema she invokes. Chapter 1 of this book, "Women Tell Time: Traumatic and Addictive Temporality in *Les Fleurs du mal*," is my extended response to Wolff's stated wish to hear how a "flâneuse" might have addressed Baudelaire. I'm fairly sure, as I point out, that he, for his part, would be doing his darndest to shut her up. I would like to add, however, that both Wolff's and Friedberg's work have been very productive for feminist scholarship; that scholarship need not be slavishly devoted to following Baudelaire in order to produce its own forms of truth.

7. By thinking about fetishism through close readings of Flaubert (and Baudelaire), we are led to examine why so many pivotal male "modernist" writers—like Baudelaire and Flaubert (and perhaps even Kakfa)—so often inscribed fetishistic forms of male sexuality (often accompanied by blatant admissions of misogyny) into their expressions of the temporal disorders of modernity. Although feminist critics have been extremely attentive to the misogynistic aspects of "modernism" for some time now, perhaps it is time to return to those "modernist" texts in order to ask them to help us reexamine how sexuality and temporality become bound up together in modern experience.

8. Schor, *Bad Objects*, xv.

9. Perhaps we could consider Richard Klein's book, *Cigarettes Are Sublime*, as another incarnation of a theory of "loiterature."

10. Chambers, *Loiterature*, 215.

11. Lyotard, *The Inhuman*, 30–31.

Chapter 1

This chapter is dedicated to the memory of Mary Quaintance. The echo of her voice can be heard throughout these pages.

1. Baudelaire, *Les Fleurs du mal*, in *Oeuvres complètes*, 1:45. All subsequent citations are to this edition and will be noted by the abbreviation *OC* with volume and page number. I have consulted numerous English translations of *Les Fleurs du mal* and have found that none of them is entirely satisfactory. I have retranslated, with Geoffrey Bennington, all passages from Baudelaire's poems.

2. Benjamin, *Das Passagen-Werk*, J.57.9. All references to the *Passegen-Werk* come from *Gesammelte Schriften*, vol. 5, *tome* 1. In "Central Park," Benjamin expands this idea and credits it to a woman: "Another comment of Adrienne Monnier: Baudelaire's readers are men. Women are not fond of him. To the men he represents the depiction and transcendence of the lewd side (*cote* [sic] *ordurier*) of their libidinal life (*Triebleben*). If one goes further Baudelaire's Passion reveals itself in this light as being for many of his readers a *rachat* (repurchasing, redemption, e.g. of annuity, atonement) of certain elements of their libidinal life" (43–44).

3. See Sartre, *Baudelaire*.

4. Agamben, *Stanzas*, 43.

5. Bersani, *Baudelaire and Freud*, 38.

6. Benjamin, "Central Park," 43.

7. I should here add that there are important exceptions to this claim. Not surprisingly, the status of the speaking woman has been interrogated by Baudelaire's feminist readers. Most recently, see Françoise Lionnet's "Reframing Baudelaire," in which Lionnet listens to the site-specific cadences of Creole in Baudelaire's "Indian

Ocean" poems. She writes: "The word 'Cafrine' in the prose poem actually gives us the sound of the black woman herself, a voice Baudelaire knew, had heard, and that he lets us hear in the reported speech or indirect discourse . . ." (73). Lionnet concludes her essay as follows: "Perhaps the time has come to reconsider Baudelaire's poetry as one of the first places of emergence of the native Creole woman's voice, a ventriloquized voice to be sure, but the only one we have from the first half of the nineteenth century" (84). By uncovering the traces of the "real" historical woman who speaks through Baudelaire's poetry, Lionnet enables us to hear different voices in the poems. However, this revelation of a "ventriloquized" voice of a "real woman" heard through the poetry does not exhaust the problems raised by the *poetic* figuration and allegorical function of the speaking woman in Baudelaire's poetry. Furthermore, although Lionnet successfully shows how Baudelaire "speaks to Mauritians of realities that *historians* have failed to record" she does not seem to be as interested in exploring how this (muted) inscription of those historical realities is both changed by and changes our reading of his *poems*. In other words, the poetry is treated as a "cultural object"—a historical document—rather than as a poem. Although I do think that works of literature can and should be asked to perform this sort of cultural labor, I believe that the value of such functions is limited when not accompanied by a commitment to formal concerns as well.

8. Examples of Baudelaire's (self-consciously) blatant misogyny abound. I will cite here one of his more notorious remarks from "Mon Coeur mis à nu":

> La femme est le contraire du Dandy.
> Donc elle doit faire horreur.
> La femme a faim et elle veut manger. Soif, et elle veut boire.
> Elle est en rut et elle veut être foutue.
> Le beau mérite!
> La femme est *naturelle*, c'est-à-dire abominable.
> Aussi est-elle toujours vulgaire, c'est-à-dire le contraire du Dandy.
> (*OC* 1:677)
> [Woman is the opposite of the Dandy.
> So she must inspire horror.
> Woman is hungry and wants to eat. Thirsty, and she wants to drink.
> She is in heat and wants to be fucked.
> Some achievement!
> Woman is *natural*, i.e., abominable.
> So she is always vulgar, i.e., the opposite of the Dandy.]

9. Benjamin, *CB*, 143. All subsequent English quotations from "Some Motifs in Baudelaire" come from this edition; where necessary, I have inserted the corresponding German words from the *Gesammelte Schriften*.

10. The "irritated" heart is a mark of Spleen. It is echoed in use of the same verb in the opening lines of Spleen (I): "Pluviôse, irrité contre la ville entière."

11. In *Das Passagen-Werk*, J.67.5, Benjamin expands on this theme as follows:

"Die Prostitution kann in dem Augenblick des Anspruch erheben, als 'Arbeit' zu gelten, in dem die Arbeit Prostitution wird. In der Tat ist die Lorette die erste, die auf die Verkleidung als Liebhaberin radikal Verzicht leistet. Sie lässt sich schon ihre Zeit bezahlen; von da ist es kein sehr weiter Weg mehr zu denen, die auf 'Arbeitslohn' Anspruch machen."

["Prostitution can claim to be considered as 'work' from the instant that work becomes prostitution. In fact the *lorette* was the first to have renounced radically disguising herself as a beloved. She already lets her time be paid for; henceforth there is no great distance between her and those who demand a 'salary.'"]

See also Ross Chambers's subtle and fascinating discussion of prostitution, labor, and parasitism in Baudelaire's "Tableaux parisiens." In a reading of "Le Crépuscule du soir," he writes:

> Prostitution, which in the "process" reading emblematized complicity, desire, mediation, here stands out as exceptional. . . . It is unlike the other daytime and nighttime activities mentioned in the poem in that it is not a form of work, being described, instead, as parasitic. . . . Misogynistically, the work that women do is singled out, then—I will say scapegoated—as (in thematic terms) not work at all, but a tapeworm of desire that secretly saps the energy and undermines the substance of daytime and nighttime work alike. (*Loiterature* 232–33)

12. See Rainer Nägele's essay, "The Poetic Ground Laid Bare (Benjamin Reading Baudelaire)," for a suggestive reading of the economic rhetoric of Benjamin's description of the gaze and the aura:

> It is striking that Benjamin presents the exchange of the gaze in terms of two precapitalist economies: first, via a "primitive" economy of gift exchange in which the expectation rests on a gaze that gives itself as a gift (*dem er sich schenkt*), the gift produces the expectation of a corresponding gift, and where the exchange works, the plenitude of a gift is given (*fällt . . . in ihrer Fülle zu*); then, via the word *belehnen*, which does refer to capital investment, but means to invest someone with a fief, in which a feudal economy is evoked. (130)

13. Nietzsche, *Untimely Meditations*, 62.

14. In "Central Park," Benjamin writes:

> The structure of the *Fleurs du mal* . . . lies in the ruthless exclusion of every lyrical theme which did not bear the imprint of Baudelaire's own sorrowful (*leidvollen*) experience. And exactly because Baudelaire knew that his affliction (Leiden), *spleen*, and *taedium vitae* was an age-old one, he was in a position to bring into relief the imprint of his own experience with utmost precision. (32)

15. Cadava, *Words of Light*, 139 n. 29.

16. A word of caution is needed here. The historical articulation of the "decline of the aura" and the articulation of history in the notion of the "decline of the aura" are very complex matters indeed. See the chapter "Art, Aura and Media in the Work of Walter Benjamin" in Samuel Weber's *Mass Mediauras* for a careful reconsideration of the notion of the "decline of the aura." Part of Weber's argument consists in rethinking the "decline" itself. He writes:

> In this sense, the "decline" or "fall"—*der Verfall*—of the aura would not be something that simply befalls it, as it were, from without. The aura would from the start be marked by an irreducible element of *taking-leave*, of departure, of separation. Were this to be this case, however, then the narrative, sequential, "historical" aspect of the aura, expressed in a movement of decline and fall might well turn out to be part and parcel of its mode of being. . . . This can also help us to explain something that Benjamin himself at times seems to have had difficulties coming to terms with: the fact that the aura, despite all its withering away, dilapidation, and decline, never fully disappears. Far from it, since it returns with a vengeance, one might say, in those forms of representation that would, according to Benjamin's account, seem most hostile to it: film, for instance, and we can now add, television as well. . . . The aura would then be something like an enabling limit, the *emanation* of an object from which it removes itself, a *frame* falling away from a picture and in its fall, in its *Verfall*, becoming light: a *bright shadow*. (87–88)

17. In his discussion of "le jeu" in the "Motifs" essay, Benjamin makes an explicit distinction between the gamblers who succumb to the narcotic impulse and the poet who bears lonely witness to it. He writes: "The poet does not participate in the game. He stands in his corner, no happier than those who are playing. He too has been cheated out of his experience—a modern man. The only difference is that he rejects the narcotics with which the gamblers seek to submerge the consciousness that has delivered them to the march of the second-hand" (*CB* 137). From this passage, we understand that Benjamin emphasizes the "heroic" quality of the poet who watches others do drugs but doesn't do them himself. This "abstention" does not hold if one examines the relationship between Baudelaire and the women in his "love" poems. Love is the drug the poet cannot resist. However, Benjamin was planning on addressing the question of fetishism and dysfunctional male sexuality in his unfinished sequel to the "Motifs" essay. In "Central Park" he writes:

> Impotence is the fundament of the Way to Calvary (*Passionsweg*) trodden by masculine sexuality. Historical index of this impotence. From this impotence emanates equally his involvement in the angelic image of women and his fetishism. Reference should be made to the determinacy and precision of the apparition of women (*Frauenerscheinung*) in Baudelaire. (36)

18. By "demoting" the figure of the fencer/poet from central stage, I realize that

I risk offending some serious Benjamin scholars. I would defend this by remind-
ing the reader that although this gesture may do some damage to Benjamin's
thought, my specific project in this chapter is to read Benjamin through Baudelaire
rather than Baudelaire through Benjamin. Furthermore, many devoted readers
have already produced numerous rigorous readings of the importance of the
fencer/poet to Benjamin's conception of language and history. See, for example,
Hans-Jost Frey, "On Presentation in Benjamin," and Rainer Nägele's "The Poetic
Ground Laid Bare (Benjamin Reading Baudelaire)." See also Kevin Newmark's
eloquent discussion of shock and trauma, "Traumatic Poetry: Charles Baudelaire
and the Shock of Laughter."

19. E. S. Burt writes about the double figurations of the woman in her illuminating and remarkable reading of "Les Bijoux," "'An Immoderate Taste for Truth.'"

20. In "Notes Nouvelles sur Edgar Poe," Baudelaire writes about "literary history" through the allegory of the setting sun:

Le mot *littérature de décadence* implique qu'il y une échelle de littératures. . . .
Ce soleil qui, il y a quelques heures, écrasait toutes choses de sa lumière droite
et blanche va bientôt inonder l'horizon occidentale de couleurs variées. Dans
les jeux de ce soleil agonisant, certains poètes trouveront des délices nouvelles:
ils y découvriront des colonnades éblouissantes, des cascades de métal fondu,
des paradis de feu, une splendeur triste, la volupté du regret, toutes les ma-
gies du rêve, tous les souvenirs de l'opium. Et le coucher du soleil leur appa-
raîtra en effet comme la merveilleuse allégorie d'une âme chargée de vie, qui
descend derrière l'horizon avec une magnifique provision de pensées et de
rêves. (*OC* 2:320)

[The phrase 'literature of the decadence' implies a scale of literatures. . . .
The sun which, some hours ago, was shattering everything with its harsh
white light will soon be flooding the western horizon with multifarious
colours. In the restless sport of this dying sun certain poetic spirits will discover new delights—dazzling colonnades, cascades of molten metal, fiery
Elysiums, melancholy splendours, the sensuous pleasures of regret, all the
magic of dreams, all the memories of opium. And the sunset will in fact
seem to them like a wonderful allegory of some life-charged soul dipping
below the horizon with a magnificent profusion of thought and dreams.
(from *The Painter of Modern Life*, trans. and ed. Jonathan Mayne, 93–94)]

21. Proust, *Contre Sainte-Beuve*, 628–29.

22. Bersani, *Baudelaire and Freud*, 37.

23. Freud, "Fetishism," 21:155.

24. See Eliane DalMolin's discussion of fetishism and the composed/decom-
posed female body in "'Tout entière': A Mystifying Totality." DalMolin writes:

When woman's body falls into Baudelaire's lyric hands, it is certain to be examined in its minutest details, to be decomposed the better to be exposed.

In fact, Baudelaire's punctilious passion for woman's body has led his poetry on a fetishistic course, a celebration of woman's body parts in a poetic frenzy that the poem itself allows us to call diabolical. (87)

25. Giorgio Agamben associates synecdoche with fetishism and modern art in his essay "Freud; or, The Absent Object":

It is interesting to observe how a mental process of fetishistic type is implicit in one of the most common tropes of poetic language: synecdoche (and in its close relative, metonymy). The substitution, in synecdoche, of part for whole (or of a contiguous object for another) corresponds, in fetishism, to the substitution of one part of the body (or an object annexed to it) for the whole sexual partner. That we are not dealing with a superficial analogy is proved by the fact that the metonymic substitution is not exhausted in the pure and simple substitution of one term for another: the substituted term is, rather, at once negated and evoked by the substitution through a process whose ambiguity closely recalls the Freudian *Verleugnung*, and it is precisely from this kind of "negative reference" that the particular poetic character that invests the word arises. The fetishistic character of the phenomenon . . . has become one of the essential stylistic instruments of modern art: the nonfinished. (*Stanzas* 32)

26. If, for a Freudian, these are the qualities that make hair the chosen object of fetishism, for Walter Benjamin, these same characteristics make hair the emblem of baroque allegory. In *The Origin of German Tragic Drama*, Benjamin writes:

It is no accident that precisely nails and hair, which are cut away as dead matter from the living body, continue to grow on the corpse. There is in the physis, in the memory itself, a *memento mori*. (218)

I thank Eduardo Cadava for having provided me with this reference. Also, although I have not presented this idea in rigorous fashion, I am suggesting that there is a connection between the *structure* of the Freudian fetish and Benjamin's notion of modern allegory.

27. "Happy" is Bersani's word. He writes:

There is a happy psychic mobility in Baudelaire. The cradling rhythms of desire and the metamorphoses which accompany them are, in poems such as "La Chevelure ". . . sources of a luxuriant serenity. (*Baudelaire and Freud* 48)

28. Johnson, *Défigurations du langage poétique*, 52–53.

29. Avital Ronell offers this evocative gloss on the mnemic function of alcohol:

It was by working on Edgar Allan Poe that Baudelaire recognized the logic of the tomb, to which he attached the stomach. The stomach *became* the tomb. At one point Baudelaire seems to ask: whom are you preserving in alcohol? This logic called for a resurrectionist memory, the supreme lucidity of intoxication, which arises when you have something that must be encrypted. Hence the ambivalent structure stimulant/tranquilizer. (*Crack Wars* 5)

30. See Jonathan Culler's chapter entitled "Apostrophe" in his *The Pursuit of Signs*. I relied on many of Culler's observations in formulating my analysis of how apostrophe functions in "La Chevelure." The following passages are particularly resonant for the purposes of this discussion:

> To apostrophize is to will a state of affairs, to attempt to call it into being by asking inanimate objects to bend themselves to your desire. In these terms the function of the apostrophe would be to make the objects of the universe potentially responsive forces: forces which can be asked to act or refrain from acting, or even to continue behaving as they usually behave. (139)
>
> The vocative of apostrophe is a device which the poetic voice uses to establish with an object a relationship which helps to constitute him. (142)
>
> To read apostrophe as sign of a fiction which knows its own fictive nature is to stress its optative character, its impossible imperatives: commands which in their explicit impossibility figure events in and of fiction. (146)
>
> Apostrophe resists narrative because its *now* is not a moment in a temporal sequence but a *now* of discourse, of writing. (152)

31. Benjamin, *CB*, 125.
32. Benjamin, "Central Park," 42.
33. Something similar occurs in "Les Petites vieilles":

> Ces monstres disloqués furent jadis des femmes . . .
> Ils trottent, tout pareils à des marionettes . . .
> Ou dansent, sans vouloir danser, pauvres sonnettes
>
> [These dislocated monsters were once women . . .
> They trot along, just like marionettes . . .
> Or dance, without meaning to dance, poor little bells . . .]

Proust expresses a particular love for the "atonal" musicality of this poem:

> L'étrangeté qui fait pour moi le charme enivrant de ces derniers quatuors, les rend à certaines personnes qui en chérissent pourtant le divin mystère, iné-coutables, sans qu'elles grincent des dents, autrement que transposés au piano. C'est à nous de dégager ce que contiennent de douleur ces petites vieilles, *débris d'humanité pour l'éternité mûrs*. Cette douleur, le poète nous en torture, plutôt qu'il ne l'exprime. . . . Ce poème des *Petites Vieilles* est un de ceux où Baudelaire montre sa connaissance de l'Antiquité. (*Contre Sainte-Beuve* 626)
>
> [The strangeness that produces for me the intoxicating charm of these last quartets, makes them, for certain people who nonetheless cherish their divine mystery, something they cannot listen to without grinding their teeth,

unless transposed for the piano. It is up to us to bring out the pain these little old women have in them, *debris of humanity ripe for eternity.* The poet tortures us with this pain, rather than expressing it. . . . This poem, "The Little Old Women," is one of those in which Baudelaire shows his knowledge of Antiquity.]

34. In "L'Idéal," for example, we find that even Michelangelo's statue of Night is deprived of sleep. The poet speaks to her thus: "Ou bien toi, grande Nuit . . . / Qui tords paisiblement dans une pose étrange" [Or else you, great Night . . . / Writhing peacefully in a strange pose"].

35. Benjamin, *CB*, 83.

Chapter 2

1. The other pivotal poem in the "Motifs" essay is, of course, "Le Soleil." For a powerful recent reading of "Le Soleil" in relationship to the problem of experience, trauma, and modernity in Benjamin and Baudelaire, see Kevin Newmark's "Traumatic Poetry: Charles Baudelaire and the Shock of Laughter."

2. Benjamin, *CB*, 122.

3. In *Das Passagen-Werk*, for example, he notes that "Just as in 'A une passante,' the crowd was neither named nor described, in 'le jeu,' the instruments of the gambling don't come up" (J.87a.6), and "In relation to the 'la rue assourdissante' and related formulations, one should not forget that the road surface at that time was, most frequently, cobblestones" (J.82a.8).

4. Benjamin, *CB*, 120.

5. Ibid., 124.

6. Ibid., 125.

7. The phrase "sa jambe de statue," read along with the phrase "fugitive beauté," clearly evokes a relationship between the "fleeting beauty" in "A une passante" and the allegorical figure of Beauty in the poem "La Beauté": "Je suis belle, ô mortels, comme un rêve de pierre." For the purposes of this essay, however, I propose to demonstrate that Benjamin has a very precise stake in choosing not to acknowledge the relationship between these two poems.

8. Jauss, "Reflections on the Chapter 'Modernity' in Benjamin's Baudelaire Fragments," 176.

9. Benjamin, *CB*, 82.

10. Ibid., 83–84.

11. Ibid., 170.

12. Letter to Horkheimer, 16 April 1938, in Benjamin, *Correspondence*, 555–56.

13. Benjamin, *Das Passagen-Werk*, J.61.3.

14. I am glossing some of the issues that Susan Buck-Morss discusses in her chapter "Historical Nature: Ruin," in *The Dialectics of Seeing* (159–201). Although I certainly agree with her statement that "in the Arcades project Benjamin himself practiced allegory against myth," I am not entirely convinced by her conclusion that

"he was aware of its 'regressive tendency'" (201). Or, to be more precise, I am not sure that Buck-Morss and I would agree about how to read the status of the "regression" to which she alludes. In any case, the passages she cites about the relationship between allegory and ruins, as well as her own discussion of the status of the ruins in "Le Cygne" are both useful and illuminating. Among the important fragments that she translates in this chapter is fragment J.22.5, in which Benjamin writes: "If Baudelaire did not fall into the abyss of myth that constantly accompanied his path, it was thanks to the genius of allegory" (182). Henceforth, I will occasionally use Buck-Morss's translations of fragments from *Das Passagen-Werk*; when I do so, they will be cited as "trans. by Buck-Morss in *The Dialectics of Seeing*."

15. Benjamin, *Das Passagen-Werk*, J.67.4.

16. Ibid., J.82a.4.

17. Benjamin, *CB*, 45.

18. Ibid., 125.

19. Ibid., 46.

20. As in the following fragment (J.21a.4): "Baudelaire introduces the figure of sexual perversion, which looks for its objects in the street, into the lyric. But what is characteristic, is that he does so in a line like 'crispé comme un extravagant' from one of his most successful love poems, 'A une passante'" (J.21a.4). It might be useful to remember, however, that the enormous importance that Benjamin accords to the figure of the lesbian in Baudelaire does *not* fall under the rubric of "sexual perversion," but rather the lesbian incarnates the figure of the "heroine of modernism" (*CB* 90). For Benjamin's discussion of the lesbian in Baudelaire, see *CB*, 90–94.

21. One might want to read the poetic "source" ("ce petit fleuve") depicted in "Le Cygne" in relation to Samuel Weber's discussion of the "source" ("*Quellpunkt*") of poetry in his essay "Art, Aura, and the Media in the Work of Walter Benjamin." Weber writes: "Benjamin . . . speculates that the auratic projection of the reciprocated glance constitutes one of the origins of poetry itself. Once again, this conjecture is hidden away in a footnote. In that note, Benjamin asserts that it is precisely the 'endowing' (*Belehnung*) of others—whether human, animal or inanimate—with the 'power of looking up (*den Blick aufzuschlagen*)' that is the major source (*Quellpunkt*) of poetry" (*Mass Mediauras* 104).

22. Benjamin, *Das Passagen-Werk*, J.66a.2.

23. Ibid., J.59a.5.

24. Benjamin, *CB*, 170.

25. See the infamous letter dated 10 November 1938, which is reprinted in *Aesthetics and Politics* (New York: Verso, 1977) 126–33.

26. Benjamin, *CB*, 123.

27. Ibid., 154.

28. Ibid., 152.

29. The fragment N.15a.1 is particularly evocative: "The past has left images of itself in literary texts that are comparable to those which light imprints on a pho-

tosensitive plate. Only the future possesses developers active enough to bring these plates out perfectly" (trans. by Buck-Morss in *The Dialectics of Seeing*, 250).

30. In the "Fusées," Baudelaire writes: "créer un poncif, c'est le génie. Je dois créer un poncif" (*OC* 1:662).

31. The *Petit Robert* defines the word "poncif" as a "feuille de papier à dessin piqué . . . pour reproduire le contour du dessin" [a piece of drawing paper perforated . . . for the purposes of reproducing the contours of the design].

32. The implications of Benjamin's claim that Baudelaire "went so far as to proclaim his goal 'the creation of a cliché' " are further complicated by a look at this passage in the German text. The German text reads: "Unbeirrbar war Baudelaire im Bewusstsein seiner *Aufgabe*. Das geht so weit, dass er als sein Ziel 'eine *Schablone* zu kreieren' bezeichnet hat" (in *GS* 1:651). There are two remarks to be made here. It is interesting that the word that Benjamin uses to express mission is "*Aufgabe*"—"*Aufgabe*" immediately invokes the "Task of the Translator." And, more important, for this analysis, is Benjamin's use of the word "Schablone" as a translation for "poncif." In the letter dated 2 August 1935, Adorno writes: "Incidentally, the idea of an early history of the feuilleton, about which so much is contained in your essay on Kraus, is most fascinating. . . . In this connection an old journalistic term occurs to me: (*Schablonstil*) [cliché style], whose origin ought to be investigated" (*Aesthetics and Politics* 116).

33. The original meaning of the word "cliché" related to the mechanical reproduction of letters on a page. The *Robert* gives its definition as a "plaque portant en relief la reproduction d'une page de composition, d'une image, et permettant le tirage de nombreux exemplaires." To simplify matters, I have translated all subsequent French definitions from the *Robert* into English.

34. Benjamin, *CB*, 132.

35. Ibid., 111; *GS* 1:609.

36. For a reading of the question of "feminine presence" in Baudelaire, in relation to "A une passante" and "La Beauté," see Peggy Kamuf's "Baudelaire's Modern Woman."

37. In *Camera Lucida*, Barthes writes: "In short, the referent adheres. And this singular adherence makes it very difficult to focus on Photography" (6).

38. Benjamin, *CB*, 45.

39. Barthes, *Camera Lucida*, 90.

40. My thinking in this essay was initially motivated by an attempt to understand what the word "history" means in Paul de Man's writings. Although I cannot address that problem here, this essay is haunted, in particular, by the concluding lines of "Anthropomorphism and Trope in the Lyric" in *The Rhetoric of Romanticism* (see p. 262). For a careful and powerful reading of this essay, see Newmark, "Paul de Man's History."

41. Barthes, *Camera Lucida*, 3.

42. Ibid., 93.

43. Ibid., 92.

44. Ibid.

Chapter 3

1. Freud, "Mourning and Melancholia," 14:246.

2. For a different reading of realism, see Roland Barthes's "L'Effet de réel."

3. For a cogent and useful, albeit cranky, reminder that the term "realism" was used in a rather loose and slippery fashion in the 1850s, see Pierre Bourdieu's discussion of the political use of the term. Bourdieu claims that "the word 'realism', no doubt more or less as vaguely characterized in the taxonomies of the time as any of its equivalents today (like 'gauchiste' or radical), allowed it to encompass in the same condemnation not only Courbet, the initial target, and his defenders, with Champfleury at their head, but also Baudelaire and Flaubert—in short, all those who, in form or substance, seemed to threaten the moral order and thereby the very foundations of the established order" (*The Rules of Art* 75). This entire chapter makes interesting claims about the specificity of Flaubert and Baudelaire's form of resistance to their historical and economic context.

4. Brombert, *The Novels of Flaubert*, 5.

5. Benjamin, *CB*, 117.

6. Ibid., 132.

7. Barthes, *La Chambre claire*, 142–43; translation from Barthes, *Camera Lucida*, 91.

8. Flaubert, *Madame Bovary*, in *Oeuvres*, 293. All further citations are from this edition. Translations are taken from Paul de Man's revision of Eleanor Marx Aveling's version (New York: Norton, 1965).

9. Culler, *Flaubert*, 92.

10. Ibid., 93.

11. Ibid.

12. Flaubert, *L'Education sentimentale*, 131.

13. Brombert, *The Novels of Flaubert*, 41.

14. Chambers, *The Writing of Melancholy*, 17.

15. As readers of Lacan will note, *jouissance* is associated with a feminine position in relation to language.

16. One can, of course, read this "new genre" as the novel itself. Pierre Bourdieu describes the status of the novel in Flaubert's time as follows:

> In choosing to write novels, Flaubert laid himself open to the inferior status associated with belonging to a minor genre. In fact, the novel was perceived as an inferior genre, or rather, to use Baudelaire's words, a 'routine genre', a 'bastard genre', despite the acknowledged prestige of Balzac, who, by the way, himself scarcely liked to define his books as novels. . . . The Académie Française, which held the novel in suspicion, waits until 1863 to crown a

novelist. . . . But, through what he invests in his choice—that is, a transformed definition of the novel involving a denial of the rank it has been assigned in the hierarchy of genres—Flaubert contributes to transforming the novel and transforming the social representation of the genre. (*The Rules of Art* 89)

17. Porter, "*Madame Bovary* and the Question of Pleasure," 120–21.

18. Ross Chambers and Tony Tanner have both provided fertile and subtle interpretations of the classroom scene. They both show, albeit in different ways, that the scene dramatizes the assimilation of the "nouveau" into a dominant ideological regime and social class. See Chambers, *The Writing of Melancholy*, and Tanner, *Adultery in the Novel*, 236–54.

19. As Philippe Bonnefis and Bruno Chaouat have both pointed out to me, this is not strictly true. We find the flaccid penis in the form of the classical statue. Perhaps it is the erect, stonelike quality of a statue itself that gives it a phallic underpinning, and therefore mitigates the threat of the flaccid penis.

20. Depussé, "Les Innocents," 77–78.

21. Flaubert, *Madame Bovary: Nouvelle version*, 134. All subsequent references to manuscripts and early drafts refer to this edition.

22. As Janet Beizer puts it: "The myth of hysteria here feeds into and fuses with the larger story the nineteenth century was telling itself about sexual difference; it provided one means of neutralizing the threat of female alterity" (*Ventriloquized Bodies* 53). Similarly, Jann Matlock writes: "Hysteria was the collective fantasy of the medical profession of the nineteenth century" (*Scenes of Seduction* 128).

23. See Marc Redfield for a subtle, intelligent, and thought-provoking reading of the fetish. He writes:

> What, then, is a fetish? A dazzlingly overdetermined locus of speculation, knotting questions of language, religion, commerce, and desire. The word returns etymologically to artifice or representation (facticius) by way of the Portuguese *feitiço*. . . . This densely linguistic dimension of the fetish grants it great theoretical power. Though the Freudian and the Marxist appropriations of this term to some extent move in opposite directions—the former conceiving it as a palliative for loss, and the latter as an occlusion of labor—both draw on the fetish as a figure for illusory authority, and both elaborate this figure into a story of the production of a subject of desire. (*Phantom Formations* 181)

24. For example, Beizer writes:

> Flaubert can indulge in society's clichés of hysteria and mock them too, if he takes a rhetorical stance that suggests to the reader a knowing distance from a discourse that is inherent in, yet alien to, the text. But irony is often an alibi for hypocrisy; . . . Flaubert allows himself to subscribe to the *doxa* because he avoids acknowledging it as truth. . . . But I am also pointing out a

similarity, thoroughly exploited by Flaubert, between such structures of ambivalence as irony and the fetish, and the construction of hysteria. Like irony, like the fetish, hysteria is a compromise formation. It is a means of retaining belief in a difference that knowledge rejects. (*Ventriloquized Bodies* 163–64)

In a similar vein, Naomi Schor argues: "Fetishism defines the limits of realist description, for the fetishist cannot describe that which he would deny: women's genitals and the threat they represent" ("Fetishism and Its Ironies" 97).

25. For a discussion of fetishism and borderline states, see Green, *On Private Madness*, 254–76. See also papers by Radó, Glover, and Wurmser for links between fetishism and addiction, in Yalisove, *The Essential Papers on Addiction*.

26. Loewald, *Papers on Psychoanalysis*, 403.

27. Bass, "The Problem of 'Concreteness,'" 646.

28. Ibid., 661–62.

29. Freud, "Fetishism," 21:155.

30. See Marc Redfield for a reading of the rhetorical and epistemological ramifications of the structure of fetishism. Redfield writes:

The fetish may be understood as the occlusion not of lack but uncertainty. It requires an act of interpretation, after all, to see a lack, particularly a lack taken as the antonym—and the potential destiny, or deeper reality—of a penis's presence. The maternal phallus would thus be a fiction erected not over a void but over illegibility. Freud registered this dimension of the fetish in epistemological terms as the mechanism of disavowal whereby the mother's "castration" is at once accepted and denied: the child believes and disbelieves, and the ego splits around this double bind. . . . Thus, despite its overwhelmingly visual aetiology in Freud, the fetish must in some sense be understood as prior to and productive of sight rather than the product of it. The terrifying "sight of something" has to be *read* as "something" to see before it can be "seen." One may thus speak of a fetishism at the origin of perception itself. (*Phantom Formations* 183–84)

31. Stoller, *Perversion*.

32. Bernheimer, *Flaubert and Kafka*, 160.

33. As psychoanalyst Louise Kaplan observes, "On nearly every page of *Madame Bovary* there is a fetish of one sort or another: not only the false beliefs and deceptive ideologies of social progress that were infiltrating the modern world, but a whole assortment of fetishistic icons from everyday life, the banalities that are always fetched up into something other than what they actually are—napkins in the shape of bishop's hats, country stews with Parisian names, green silk cigar cases, cradles in the form of boats, clocks inlaid with tortoiseshell, demascened rifles" (*Female Perversions* 203).

34. De Man makes these comments about memory in Hegel in the context of

a discussion of Baudelaire's "Spleen [II]." The figures in the cookie box recall the figures in Baudelaire's poem. One would have to work much harder to see how memory functions in that poem in relation to Flaubert's text. Furthermore, this is as good a time as any to acknowledge that Paul de Man's writings on Baudelaire are a "hidden figure" throughout this book. This particular reference comes from *The Resistance to Theory*, 69.

35. I am implying that there is a *soupçon* of lesbian resonance here. In the mid-nineteenth century, the word for lesbian was "tribade," which comes from "tribein," the Greek word for "frotter." Thus, in French, the meaning of the word lesbian is "frotter."

36. Benjamin, "Central Park," 48.

Chapter 4

1. Phillips, *On Flirtation*, 153.

2. Ibid., 153–54.

3. Caruth, Introduction to *Trauma: Explorations in Memory*, 3.

4. Ibid., 4–5.

5. The problem of drugs and addiction in *Madame Bovary* was of course first raised by Avital Ronell in *Crack Wars*. My analysis supports most of her conclusions but is more focused on the relationship between time and addiction.

6. Riffaterre, "Flaubert's Presuppositions," 183.

7. Riffaterre's actual argument is, of course, far more complicated. He shows that the act of reading functions as a metaphorical hinge between Romantic definitions of women and the overdetermined presuppositions of the word "adultery." He writes: "Nothing could be clearer: one word's ultimate presupposition, its etymology, entails the whole fictional text. . . . The adulteress either commits suicide or sinks into prostitution. As for the first metaphorical step, I might call it fictional without any play on words, since the errant wife is stepping out of bounds when she secretly indulges in the reading of scandalous novels and in a daydreaming identification with the women who slink about the never-neverland of wish-fulfillment" ("Flaubert's Presuppositions" 182–83).

8. Brombert, "Flaubert and the Status of the Subject," 113.

9. The implication of this claim would be that Emma is Flaubert's mirror image—where he understands that Life should be put in the service of Art, she, by contrast, is unable to convert her life into Art. It is interesting to observe that in this context, feminist critics such as Naomi Schor and Janet Beizer establish a dichotomy between Flaubert and Emma Bovary similar to that espoused by more traditional critics like Victor Brombert. Of course, the feminist critics diverge with traditional readings about the *cause* of the inverted identification between Emma and Flaubert. I am deeply indebted to Naomi Schor's chapter entitled "For a Restricted Thematics: Writing, Speech, and Difference in Madame Bovary," which appears in her work *Breaking the Chain*, and to Janet Beizer's chapters on Flaubert

and Louise Colet in her *Ventriloquized Bodies*. Beizer offers a brilliant and persuasive account of how Flaubert hysterizes Emma Bovary in an attempt to purge himself and his text of femininity.

10. De Man, ed. and trans., *Madame Bovary*.

11. See Rousset's chapter on "Madame Bovary ou le livre sur rien" in *Forme et signification*. And, more recently, Peter Brooks discusses how Emma Bovary's body is systematically inserted into a visual field (*Body Work* 88–122).

12. Here, I diverge from Jonathan Culler's oft-cited remark in *Flaubert*: "If there is anything that justifies our finding the novel limited and tendentious it is the seriousness with which Emma's corruption is attributed to novels and romances" (146).

13. Curiously, the absence of this figure has rarely been addressed in the critical literature. One notable exception is Dominick LaCapra's suggestive remarks in *Madame Bovary on Trial*. LaCapra observes that "equally significant for the rupture of the generational cycle is the fact that Emma's mother is dead as the story opens, and she does not seem to play a significant part in Emma's life" (181). It is surprising to note in this context that although Avital Ronell brilliantly identifies the presence of a "toxic maternal" in *Madame Bovary*, she focuses more on Emma's toxic effect on her daughter than on the toxic effect of her own mother's absence (see *Crack Wars*). Likewise, Janet Beizer stresses the importance of the repression of motherhood in the novel from the perspective of Emma as mother rather than as daughter. I think LaCapra is correct in seeing the mother's death as a temporal, generational rupture. As he puts it, "Economically as well as socially, Emma has no productive or reproductive function" (181).

14. Ronell, *Crack Wars*, 119–20.

15. I am fascinated by the fact that there are several glaring mistranslations of this particular passage in Paul de Man's otherwise remarkable translation of *Madame Bovary*. For example, he translates "l'ennui" as "shock" and "innombrables" as "immovable." These "mistranslations" seem to be the result of an interpretative move rather than simple "errors." More precisely, it seems plausible that if de Man were reading Flaubert through Walter Benjamin's writings on Baudelaire, he might have been compelled to stress the paralytic, traumatic nature of time reflected in his translation. Of course, it could also have been a simple mistake. For the entire passage, see pp. 44–45.

16. For extremely useful discussions of the importance of fluids in *Madame Bovary*, see Richard, *Littérature et sensation* and Beizer, *Ventriloquized Bodies*. I particularly admire Beizer's conclusion to her chapter "Writing with a Vengeance": "He chose his poison: it was water. Playing with madness like Mithridates with poison, he volatized the water, the emotional effusion, the rush of ink, the romantic flow. Poisoning himself gently in measured doses, he turned liquid to vapor and cured his style; he vaporized hysteria and hysterized the text" (166).

17. As Jean-Pierre Richard puts it: "C'est l'un des aspects de la maladie bo-

varyste que ce manque fondementale de *retenue*. . . . Emma se jette goulûment sur toutes les proies: en voulant tout immédiatement consommer, elle ne peut rien retenir. Tout l'abandonne, et ses expériences l'apprauvrissent au lieu de l'enrichir" [The fundamental lack of *reserve* is one of the traits of the Bovary illness. . . . Emma pounces greedily on any and every prey: but by wanting to consume everything immediately, she can retain nothing. Everything abandons her, and her experiences impoverish her instead of enriching her.] (*Littérature et sensation* 142, my translation).

18. See Tanner, *Adultery in the Novel*; Richard, *Littérature et sensation*; and Ronell, *Crack Wars*. See also Dennis Porter, who reads this "auto-ingestion" as a transgressive, feminist gesture. He writes: "The cramming of arsenic directly from her hand into the mouth is not only a defiantly self-destructive act, it is also a regressive one. It has in itself the force of an anti-Freudian, radical feminist gesture. By that I mean that there is a return to an oral form of gratification which under the circumstances is the essence of perversity, in Freud's sense, since it is a return that occurs after the disappointing experience of three male lovers, of sexuality under the regime of the phallus. In other words, the mode as well as the choice of Emma's death constitute a bitter comment on male sexuality" ("*Madame Bovary* and the Question of Pleasure" 134).

19. Philippe Bonnefis made this observation in conversation with me.

20. See, for example, Nathaniel Wing, who writes: "Throughout the novel desire, narrative and writing in general produce corrosive effects. These are figured most directly and powerfully, perhaps, during Emma's agony, with the likening of the taste of poison to the taste of ink, and later in the same sequence when the narrator describes a certain black fluid oozing from Emma's mouth" (*The Limits of Narrative* 133).

21. See Schor's chapter "For a Restricted Thematics," in *Breaking the Chain*, and Beizer's chapter "Writing with a Vengeance," in *Ventriloquized Bodies*.

Chapter 5

1. Letter to Louise Colet, in Flaubert, *Correspondance*, 2:31.

2. My reading and understanding of "nothing" is not exactly the same as the articulations expressed by Jonathan Culler and Dominick LaCapra. Both Culler and LaCapra use Sartre as a point of departure for this question. Thus Culler glosses Sartre and adds his own revision as follows: "This nothingness cannot be articulated—not because it is so profound an experience but because it is defined precisely in those formal and dialectical terms: as the emptiness of any presence. But we can name some of the forms it takes. It is, for example, the *signifiant* without *signifié*: matter taken as a sign but which offers emptiness in the place of meaning" (*Flaubert* 73).

3. For an analysis of Flaubert's articulation of "style" according to a complex taxonomy of gendered body fluids and secretions, see Janet Beizer's superb chap-

ter "The Physiology of Style: Sex, Text, and the Gender of Writing" in *Ventrilo-quized Bodies*, 77–98.

4. It is significant that almost all critics are compelled, at one point or another, to use the words "perverse" or "fetish" when speaking about Flaubert—even when perversion and fetishism are not their explicit concern. Maurice Blanchot uses the word "perversion" in order to explain what "prose" means for Flaubert: "Mais qu'entend-il par la prose? Non pas seulement l'espace du roman ... , mais l'énigme du langage tel qu'il s'écrit, le paradoxe de la parole droite (*prosa oratia*), recourbée par le détour essentiel, *la perversion d'écrire*" [But what does he mean by prose? Not merely the space of the novel ... , but the enigma of language as it writes itself, the paradox of straight speech (*prosa oratia*), twisted by the essential detour, the *perversion of writing*] (*L'Entretien infini* 487). And Victor Brombert writes, for example: "C'est que Flaubert éprouve une satisfaction presque *perverse* toutes les fois qu'il peut écraser un personnage sous le poids de sa propre inanité" [The fact is that Flaubert feels an almost *perverse* satisfaction every time he can crush a character under the weight of his own inanity] (*The Novels of Flaubert* 57; italics mine). Among the many recent critics who have explicitly called attention to Flaubert's perverse tendencies are Kaplan, *Female Perversions*; Bernheimer, *Flaubert and Kafka*, 160–76; and Tanner, *Adultery in the Novel*, 284–91. For an extended meditation on the relationship between fetishism, history, and literature, see Redfield, *Phantom Formations*, 171–200.

5. I am borrowing the term "perverse strategy" from Louise J. Kaplan's definition of it in *Female Perversions*. I will be discussing Kaplan's articulation of the relationship between perverse strategy and *Madame Bovary* later on in this chapter.

6. For an analysis of the relationship among corpses, crypts, and the problem of the proper name, see Eugenio Donato's chapter "Who Signs Flaubert" in *The Script of Decadence*, 100–13.

7. By the end of the passage, Flaubert's language has absorbed some of the very forgetfulness enunciated by Berthe. The last sentence bears one of Flaubert's signatory unorthodox uses of the conjunction "et": "La gaieté de cette enfant navrait Bovary et il avait à subir les intolerables consolations du pharmacien" [The child's gaiety pained Bovary, and he had to endure the intolerable consolations of the pharmacist]. In the chapter "A propos du 'style' de Flaubert" in *Contre Sainte-Beuve*, Proust glosses Flaubert's idiosyncratic use of the conjunction "et" as follows:

> La conjonction "et" n'a nullement dans Flaubert l'objet que la grammaire lui assigne. Elle marque une pause dans une mesure rythmique et devise un tableau. En effet partout où on mettrait "et", Flaubert le supprime. . . . En revanche là où personne n'aurait l'idée d'en user, Flaubert l'emploie. . . . En un mot, chez Flaubert, "et" commence toujours une phrase secondaire et ne termine jamais une énumération. . . . Ces singularités grammaticales traduisent en effet une vision nouvelle, que d'application ne fallait-il pas

pour bien fixer cette vision, pour la faire passer de l'inconscient dans le conscient, pour l'incorporer enfin aux diverses parties du discours! (591–92). [The conjunction "and" has in no way in Flaubert the object assigned to it by grammar. It marks a pause in a rhythmic measure and sets up a scene. Indeed wherever one would put "and", Flaubert suppresses it. . . . On the other hand where no-one would think of using it, Flaubert does. . . . In a word, in Flaubert, "and" always begins a secondary clause and never finishes an enumeration. . . . These grammatical peculiarities do indeed translate a new vision. How much dedication was necessary really to fix this vision, to make it move from unconscious to conscious, and ultimately to embody it into the various parts of speech!]

8. For a compelling analysis of why this section of *Madame Bovary* is so rhetorically strange, see Jonathan Culler's close reading of a short passage from the opening section of part 2. Culler aptly observes: "It is not simply that each sentence appears to fritter itself away, as it runs down to the minute and trivial; that is almost a by-product of the spectacle mounted by a prose style determined to show how grammatical devices enable it to link together a set of disparate and trivial facts. If one reads the sentences deliberately, pausing on the numerous commas, one is tempted to laugh at the spectacle of this elegant prose straining to hold itself together—and to no obvious thematic purpose" (*Flaubert* 75–77).

9. For a subtle and persuasive treatment of the relationship between Flaubert's representation of the "Orient" and his interrogation of the problem of history, see Eugenio Donato's essay entitled "Flaubert and the Question of History: The Orient," in *The Script of Decadence*, 35–55.

10. For example, we find that a notable portion of the supporting cast of characters in Yonville bear names of Classical origin: Artémise, Hippolyte. We remember that "Nastasie" is replaced by "Félicité" in the final chapter of part 1.

11. For Walter Benjamin, the temporality of work that cannot be finished links the temporalities characteristic of modernity (gambling, factory work) to the time of hell (*CB* 177–79).

12. Avital Ronell is one of the few critics to mention Lestiboudois. Her suggestive remarks are limited to a few sentences: "The cemetery is linked to a manifest thematics of eating and vampirism through the agency of M. Lestiboudois, who exploits the land of the dead in order to grow potatoes. Potatoes—this dead vegetable, a somewhat organic inorganic fruit, dotted with eyes, blind like the seer of Emma's death—bloat the novel like the gastronomic fillers they are: morbid accompaniment to meat, they organize a kind of *objet petit a* on the plate of desire" (*Crack Wars* 118).

13. Levin, "*Madame Bovary*: Cathedral and Hospital," 425.

14. An interesting exception to this general rule is Janet Beizer's *Ventriloquized Bodies*. Although her book treats the relationship between *Madame Bovary* and the medical profession extensively, she makes no explicit mention of Dr. Larivière.

Given the feminist context of her critique of the collusion between Flaubert's literary authority and the authority of the medical profession that both produces Emma's "hysteria" and exploits it for its own ideological ends, one could conclude that Beizer makes a deliberate interpretive choice in refusing to recognize the "meaningfulness" of this paragon of paternal/medical authority.

15. In "Flaubert's Presuppositions," Michael Riffaterre provides an extremely subtle and complicated interrogation of the linguistic parameters of "adultery" in *Madame Bovary* (177–91). Although his reading is ingenious, it too represses an analysis of the perverse sex/death connection.

16. Once again, to his credit, Tanner's text ultimately defines adultery as a kind of amalgam of Marxist and Freudian notions of fetishism. In his final sentences on *Madame Bovary*, he writes: "In adultery Emma does not become another person, another role, another pose, etc., she becomes a *chose*, a thing devoid of indwelling determinants and thus *pliant* to the handling, shaping forces and figures around her. She enters the realm of interchangeable objects, which is the dehumanized, reified realm of the society and its prevailing currencies, financial and emotional" (*Adultery in the Novel* 367).

17. LaCapra, *Madame Bovary on Trial*, 27. All further in-text citations will refer to this text as *MBOT*.

18. Proust, *Contre Sainte-Beuve*, 586.

19. Ibid.

20. Apter and Pietz, *Fetishism as Cultural Discourse*.

21. As we have seen, Kaplan is not alone in reading the novel through Dr. Larivière. Indeed, her entire reading of *Madame Bovary* relies heavily on the trajectory marked out by Tony Tanner in *Adultery in the Novel*. Tanner credits Edward Said for making the connection between Flaubert and Bichat, and cites Foucault's discussion of Bichat in *The Birth of the Clinic*.

22. Robert, "Flaubert et Kafka," 27.

Bibliography

Addison, Claire. *Where Flaubert Lies: Chronology, Mythology and History*. Cambridge: Cambridge University Press, 1996.

Agamben, Giorgio. *Stanzas: Word and Phantasm in Western Culture*. Translated by Ronald L. Martinez. Minneapolis: University of Minnesota Press, 1993.

Apter, Emily. *Feminizing the Fetish: Psychoanalysis and Narrative Obsession in Turn-of-the-Century France*. Ithaca, N.Y.: Cornell University Press, 1991.

——. "Splitting Hairs: Female Fetishism and Postpartum Sentimentality in the Fin de Siècle." In *Eroticism and the Body Politic*, edited by Lynn Hunt. Baltimore, Md.: Johns Hopkins University Press, 1991.

Apter, Emily, and William Pietz, eds. *Fetishism as Cultural Discourse*. Ithaca, N.Y.: Cornell University Press, 1993.

Barnes, Julian. *Flaubert's Parrot*. New York: Knopf, 1984.

Barthes, Roland. "L'Effet de réel." *Communications* 11 (1968): 84–89.

——. *La Chambre claire*. Paris: Cahiers du Cinéma Gallimard Seuil, 1980.

——. *Camera Lucida: Reflections on Photography*. Translated by Richard Howard. New York: Noonday Press, 1981.

Bass, Alan. "The Problem of 'Concreteness.'" *Psychoanalytic Quarterly* 66 (1997): 642–82.

Bataille, Georges. *La Littérature et le mal*. Paris: Gallimard, 1957.

Baudelaire, Charles. *The Painter of Modern Life and Other Essays*. Translated and edited by Jonathan Mayne. New York: Da Capo Press, 1964.

——. *Oeuvres complètes*. 2 vols. Paris: Bibliothèque de la Pléiade, 1975.

Beizer, Janet. *Ventriloquized Bodies: Narratives of Hysteria in Nineteenth-Century France*. Ithaca, N.Y.: Cornell University Press, 1994.

Benjamin, Walter. *Gesammelte Schriften*. 7 vols. Edited by Rolf Tiedemann and Herman Schweppenhäuser. Frankfurt am Main: Surkamp Verlag, 1972–1983.

——. *Charles Baudelaire: A Lyric Poet in the Era of High Capitalism*. Translated by Harry Zohn. London: Verso, 1983.

——. "Central Park." *New German Critique* 34 (winter 1985): 32–58.

——. *The Origin of German Tragic Drama*. Translated by John Osborne. London: Verso, 1985.

——. *The Correspondence of Walter Benjamin: 1910–1940*. Edited by Gershom Sholem and Theodor Adorno. Translated by Manfred Jacobson and Evelyn Jacobson. Chicago: University of Chicago Press, 1994.

Berman, Marshall. "Baudelaire: Modernism in the Streets." In *All That Is Solid Melts into Air*. New York: Penguin, 1982.

Bernheimer, Charles. *Flaubert and Kafka: Studies in Psychopoetic Structure*. New Haven, Conn.: Yale University Press, 1982.

Bersani, Leo. *Baudelaire and Freud*. Berkeley: University of California Press, 1977.

——. "Emma Bovary and the Sense of Sex." In *A Future for Astyanax: Character and Desire in Literature*. New York: Columbia University Press, 1984.

——. *The Culture of Redemption*. Cambridge, Mass.: Harvard University Press, 1990.

Blanchard, Marc Eli. *In Search of the City: Engels, Baudelaire, Rimbaud*. Saratoga, Calif.: Anma Libri, 1985.

Blanchot, Maurice. *La Part du feu*. Paris: Gallimard, 1949.

——. *L'Entretien infini*. Paris: Gallimard, 1969.

Blin, Georges. *Le Sadisme de Baudelaire*. Paris: Corti, 1948.

Bloom, Harold, ed. *Emma Bovary*. New York and Philadelphia: Chelsea House Publishers, 1994.

Bonnefis, Philippe. "Exposition d'un perroquet." In *Mesures de l'ombre: Baudelaire, Flaubert, Laforgue, Verne*. Lille: Presses Universitaires de Lille, 1987.

Bonnefoy, Yves. "Les Fleurs du mal" et "L'Acte et le lieu de la poésie." In *L'Improbable et d'autres essais*. Paris: Gallimard, 1980.

Bourdieu, Pierre. *The Rules of Art*. Translated by Susan Emanuel. Stanford, Calif.: Stanford University Press, 1995.

Brombert, Victor. *The Novels of Flaubert*. Princeton, N.J.: Princeton University Press, 1966.

——. *Flaubert*. Paris: Seuil, 1971.

——. "Flaubert and the Status of the Subject." In *Flaubert and Postmodernism*, edited by Naomi Schor and Henry F. Majewski. Lincoln: University of Nebraska Press, 1984.

Brooks, Peter. *Body Work: Objects of Desire in Modern Narrative*. Cambridge, Mass.: Harvard University Press, 1993.

Buck-Morss, Susan. *The Dialectics of Seeing*. Cambridge, Mass.: MIT Press, 1989.

Burt, E. S. "'An Immoderate Taste for Truth': Censoring History in Baudelaire's 'Les bijoux.'" *Diacritics* 27, no. 2 (summer 1997): 19–43.

Burton, Richard D. E. *Baudelaire and the Second Republic: Writing and Revolution*. New York: Oxford University Press, 1991.

Cadava, Eduardo. *Words of Light: Theses on the Photography of History*. Princeton, N.J.: Princeton University Press, 1997.

Caruth, Cathy. Introduction to *Trauma: Explorations in Memory*. Baltimore, Md.: Johns Hopkins University Press, 1995.

———, ed. *Trauma: Explorations in Memory*. Baltimore, Md.: Johns Hopkins University Press, 1995.

Chambers, Ross. "The Storm in the Eye of the Poem: Baudelaire's 'A une passante.'" In *Textual Analysis: Some Readers Reading*, edited by Mary Ann Caws. New York: Modern Language Association, 1986.

———. *The Writing of Melancholy: Modes of Opposition in Early French Modernism*. Translated by Mary Seidman Trouille. Chicago: University of Chicago Press, 1993.

———. *Loiterature*. Lincoln: University of Nebraska Press, 1999.

Clark, T. J. *The Absolute Bourgeois: Artists and Politics in France, 1848–1851*. London: Thames and Hudson, 1973.

Clej, Alina. *A Genealogy of the Modern Self: Thomas De Quincey and the Intoxication of Writing*. Stanford, Calif.: Stanford University Press, 1995.

Cohen, Margaret. *Profane Illumination: Walter Benjamin and the Paris of Surrealist Revolution*. Berkeley: University of California Press, 1993.

———. "Reconfiguring Realism." Preface to *Spectacles of Realism*, edited by Margaret Cohen and Christopher Prendergast. Minneapolis: University of Minnesota Press, 1995.

Culler, Jonathan. *Flaubert: The Uses of Uncertainty*. Ithaca, N.Y.: Cornell University Press, 1974.

———. *The Pursuit of Signs: Semiotics, Literature, Deconstruction*. Ithaca, N.Y.: Cornell University Press, 1981.

———. "Reading Lyric." *Yale French Studies* 69 (1985): 98–106.

DalMolin, Eliane. "'Tout entière': A Mystifying Totality." In *Understanding Les Fleurs du mal: Critical Readings*, edited by William J. Thompson. Nashville, Tenn.: Vanderbilt University Press, 1997.

de Man, Paul. *The Rhetoric of Romanticism*. New York: Columbia University Press, 1984.

———. *The Resistance to Theory*. Minneapolis: University of Minnesota Press, 1986.

———, ed. and trans. *Madame Bovary*, by Gustave Flaubert. New York: Norton Critical Editions, 1965.

Demorest, D. L. *L'Expression figurée et symbolique dans l'oeuvre de Gustave Flaubert*. Geneva: Slatkine Reprints, 1967.

Depussé, Marie. "Les Innocents." *La Nouvelle Revue Française*, no. 317 (June 1979): 68–80.

Derrida, Jacques. *Memoires: For Paul de Man*. New York: Columbia University Press, 1986.

———. *Donner le temps: La Fausse Monnaie*. Paris: Galilée, 1991.

Donato, Eugenio. *The Script of Decadence: Essays on the Fictions of Flaubert and the Poetics of Romanticism*. New York: Oxford University Press, 1993.

Duchet, Claude. "Significance et in-significance: Le Discours italique dans *Madame Bovary*." In *La Production du sens chez Flaubert*, edited by Claudine Gothot-Mersch. Paris: Editions 10/18, 1975.

———. "Roman et objets: L'Exemple de *Madame Bovary*." In *Travail de Flaubert*, edited by Gérard Genette and Tzvetan Todorov. Paris: Editions du Seuil, 1983.

———, ed. *Modernité de Flaubert* (special issue). *Littérature*, vol. 15 (1974).

Felman, Shoshana. *La Folie et la chose littéraire*. Paris: Seuil, 1978.

Flaubert, Gustave. *Madame Bovary: Nouvelle version précédée des scénarios inédits*. Edited by Jean Pommier and Gabrielle Leleu. Paris: José Corti, 1949.

———. *Madame Bovary*. In *Oeuvres*, edited by A. Thibaudet and R. Dumesnil. Paris: Editions Gallimard, 1951.

———. *Madame Bovary*. Edited and translated by Paul de Man. New York: Norton, 1965.

———. *Correspondance*. 2 vols. Edited by Jean Bruneau. Paris: Editions Gallimard, 1980.

———. *L'Education sentimentale*. Edited by P. M. Wetherill. Paris: Classiques Garnier, 1984.

Freud, Sigmund. "Fetishism." In *The Standard Edition of the Complete Psychological Works of Sigmund Freud*, translated and edited by James Strachey. Vol. 21. London: Hogarth Press, 1961.

———. "Mourning and Melancholia." In *The Standard Edition of the Complete Psychological Works of Sigmund Freud*, translated and edited by James Strachey. Vol. 14. London: Hogarth Press, 1961.

Frey, Hans-Jost. "On Presentation in Benjamin." In *Walter Benjamin: Theoretical Questions*, edited by David Ferris. Stanford, Calif.: Stanford University Press, 1996.

Friedberg, Anne. *Window Shopping: Cinema and the Postmodern*. Berkeley: University of California Press, 1994.

Friedman, Geraldine. "Baudelaire's Theory of Practice: Ideology and Difference in 'Les Yeux des pauvres'." *PMLA* 104 (May 1989): 317–28.

Gaillard, Françoise. "L'En-signement du réel (ou la nécessaire écriture de la répétition)." In *La Production du sens chez Flaubert*, edited by Claudine Gothot-Mersch. Paris: Editions 10/18, 1975.

Genette, Gérard. "Silences de Flaubert." In *Figures I*. Paris: Editions du Seuil, 1966.

Ginsburg, Michal Peled. *Flaubert Writing: A Study in Narrative Strategies*. Stanford, Calif.: Stanford University Press, 1986.

Gothot-Mersch, Claudine. *La Genèse de Madame Bovary*. Geneva-Paris: Slatkine Reprints, 1980.

Green, André. *On Private Madness*. Madison, Conn.: International Universities Press, 1993.

Guerlac, Suzanne. "Baudelaire." In *The Impersonal Sublime: Hugo, Baudelaire, Lautréamont*. Stanford, Calif.: Stanford University Press, 1990.

Heath, Stephen. *Gustave Flaubert: Madame Bovary*. Cambridge: Cambridge University Press, 1992.

Hollier, Denis. *The Politics of Prose: Essay on Sartre*. Minneapolis: University of Minnesota Press, 1986.

Huss, Roger. "Flaubert and Realism: Paternity, Authority, and Sexual Difference." In *Spectacles of Realism: Gender, Body, Genre*, edited by Margaret Cohen and Christopher Prendergast. Minneapolis: University of Minnesota Press, 1995.

Jakobson, Roman, and Claude Lévi-Strauss. "Les Chats de Baudelaire." *L'Homme* 2, no. 1 (1962). Reprinted in *Introduction to Structuralism*, edited by Michael Lane (New York: Basic Books, 1970).

Jameson, Fredric. "The Ideology of the Text." In *The Ideologies of History: Essays, 1971–1986*. Vol. 1, *Situations of Theory*. Minneapolis: University of Minnesota Press, 1988.

———. *The Seeds of Time*. New York: Columbia University Press, 1994.

Jauss, Hans Robert. "Reflections on the Chapter 'Modernity' in Benjamin's Baudelaire Fragments." In *On Walter Benjamin: Critical Essays and Recollections*, edited by Gary Smith. Cambridge, Mass.: MIT Press, 1991.

Johnson, Barbara. *Défigurations du langage poétique: La seconde révolution baudelairienne*. Paris: Flammarion, 1979.

Kamuf, Peggy. "Baudelaire's Modern Woman." *Qui Parle* 4, no. 2 (1991): 1–7.

Kaplan, Louise J. *Female Perversions: The Temptations of Emma Bovary*. New York: Anchor Books, 1991.

Klein, Richard. "Baudelaire and Revolution: Some Notes." *Yale French Studies* 39 (1967): 85–97.

———. *Cigarettes Are Sublime*. Durham, N.C.: Duke University Press, 1993.

LaCapra, Dominick. *Madame Bovary on Trial*. Ithaca, N.Y.: Cornell University Press, 1982.

Laplanche, Jean. "Time and the Other." In *Essays on Otherness*. New York: Routledge Press, 1999.

Levin, Harry. "*Madame Bovary*: Cathedral and Hospital." In *Madame Bovary*, translated by Paul de Man. New York: Norton Critical Editions, 1965.

Lionnet, Françoise. "Reframing Baudelaire: Literary History, Biography, Postcolonial Theory, and Vernacular Languages." *Diacritics* 28, no. 3 (fall 1998): 63–85.

Lloyd, Rosemary. *Madame Bovary*. London: Unwin Hyman, 1990.

Loewald, Hans. *Papers on Psychoanalysis*. New Haven, Conn.: Yale University Press, 1980.

Lyotard, Jean-François. *The Inhuman*. Translated by Geoffrey Bennington and Rachel Bowlby. Stanford, Calif.: Stanford University Press, 1991.

Marder, Elissa. "Madame Bovary en Amérique." In *Emma Bovary*, edited by Alain Buisine. Paris: Editions Autrement, 1997.

Matlock, Jann. *Scenes of Seduction: Prostitution, Hysteria, and Reading Difference in Nineteenth-Century France*. New York: Columbia University Press, 1994.

McCallum, E. L. *Object Lessons: How to Do Things with Fetishism*. New York: The State University of New York Press, 1999.

Miller, Christopher. "Baudelaire in the Nineteenth Century: Black and White in

Color." In *Blank Darkness: Africanist Discourse in French*. Chicago: University of Chicago Press, 1985.

Miller, Hillis J. "The Geneva School: The Criticism of Marcel Raymond, Albert Béguin, Georges Poulet, Jean Rousset, Jean-Pierre Richard, and Jean Starobinski." In *Modern French Criticism*, edited by John K. Simon. Chicago: University of Chicago Press, 1972.

Nägele, Rainer. "The Poetic Ground Laid Bare (Benjamin Reading Baudelaire)." In *Walter Benjamin: Theoretical Questions*, edited by David S. Ferris. Stanford, Calif.: Stanford University Press, 1996.

Nancy, Jean-Luc. "Wild Laughter in the Throat of Death." *MLN* 102 (September 1987): 719–36.

Newmark, Kevin. "Paul de Man's History." In *Reading de Man Reading*, edited by Lindsay Waters and Wlad Godzich. Minneapolis: University of Minnesota Press, 1989.

———. "Traumatic Poetry: Charles Baudelaire and the Shock of Laughter." In *Trauma: Explorations in Memory*, edited by Cathy Caruth. Baltimore, Md.: Johns Hopkins University Press, 1995.

Nietzsche, Friedrich. *Untimely Meditations*. Translated by R. J. Hollingdale. Cambridge: Cambridge University Press, 1983.

Ovid. *The Metamorphoses*. Translated by Frank Justus Miller. Cambridge, Mass: Harvard University Press, 1916.

Phillips, Adam. *On Flirtation: Essays on the Uncommitted Life*. Cambridge, Mass.: Harvard University Press, 1994.

Pichois, Claude, and Jean Ziegler. *Baudelaire*. Paris: Julliard, 1987.

Pontalis, J.-B., ed. *Objets du fétichisme* (special issue). *Nouvelle Revue de Psychanalyse* 2 (autumn 1970).

Porter, Dennis. "*Madame Bovary* and the Question of Pleasure." In *Flaubert and Postmodernism*, edited by Naomi Schor and Henry F. Majewski. Lincoln: University of Nebraska Press, 1984.

Poulet, Georges. *Les Métamorphoses du cercle*. Paris: Plon, 1961.

———. *La Poésie éclatée: Baudelaire, Rimbaud*. Paris: PUF, 1980.

Proust, Marcel. *Contre Sainte-Beuve*. Paris: Bibliotheque de la Pléiade, 1971.

Rand, Nicolas. *Le Cryptage ou la vie des oeuvres: Étude du secret dans les textes de Flaubert, Stendhal, Benjamin, Baudelaire, Stefan George, Edgar Poe, Francis Ponge, Heidegger et Freud*. Paris: Aubier, 1989.

Redfield, Marc. *Phantom Formations*. Ithaca, N.Y.: Cornell University Press, 1996.

Richard, Jean-Pierre. *Littérature et sensation: Stendhal, Flaubert*. Paris: Editions du Seuil, 1954.

———. "Profondeur de Baudelaire." In *Poésie et profondeur*. Paris: Seuil, 1955.

Riffaterre, Michael. "Describing Poetic Structures: Two Approaches to Baudelaire's 'Les Chats.'" In *Structuralism*, edited by Jacques Ehrmann. New York: Anchor Books, 1970.

———. "Flaubert's Presuppositions." In *Flaubert and Post-Modernism*, edited by

Naomi Schor and Henry Majewski. Lincoln: University of Nebraska Press, 1984.

Robert, Marthe. *En Haine du roman: Étude sur Flaubert.* Paris: Balland, 1982.

———. "Flaubert et Kafka." *L'Arc,* no. 79 (1980).

Robert, Marthe, and Bernard Pingaud, eds. *L'Arc,* no. 79 (1980). Special issue on Flaubert.

Rochlitz, Rainer. *The Disenchantment of Art: The Philosophy of Walter Benjamin.* Translated by Jane Marie Todd. New York: Guilford Press, 1996.

Ronell, Avital. *Crack Wars: Literature, Addiction, Mania.* Lincoln: University of Nebraska Press, 1992.

Rousset, Jean. *Forme et signification: Essais sur les structures littéraires de Corneille à Claudel.* Paris: José Corti, 1984.

Sartre, Jean-Paul. *Baudelaire.* Paris: Gallimard, 1947.

———. *L'Idiot de la famille: Gustave Flaubert de 1821–1857.* 3 vols. Paris: Gallimard, 1971.

Schlossman, Beryl. "Benjamin's *Uber Einige Motive bei Baudelaire*: The Secret Architecture of 'Correspondances.'" *MLN* 107, no. 3 (April 1992): 548–79.

Schor, Naomi. Introduction to *Flaubert and Postmodernism,* edited by Naomi Schor and Henry F. Majewski. Lincoln: University of Nebraska Press, 1984.

———. *Breaking the Chain: Women, Theory, and French Realist Fiction.* New York: Columbia University Press, 1985.

———. "Fetishism and Its Ironies." In *Fetishism as Cultural Discourse,* edited by Emily Apter and William Pietz. Ithaca, N.Y.: Cornell University Press, 1993.

———. *Bad Objects: Essays Popular and Unpopular.* Durham, N.C.: Duke University Press, 1995.

Stamelman, Richard. "Under the Sign of Saturn: Allegories of Mourning and Melancholy in Charles Baudelaire." In *Lost Beyond Telling: Representations of Death and Absence in Modern French Poetry.* Ithaca, N.Y.: Cornell University Press, 1990.

Starobinski, Jean. "L'Echelle des températures: Lecture du corps dans *Madame Bovary.*" In *Travail de Flaubert,* edited by Gérard Genette and Tzvetan Todorov. Paris: Editions du Seuil, 1983.

Stoller, Robert. *Observing the Erotic Imagination.* New Haven, Conn.: Yale University Press, 1985.

———. *Perversion: The Erotic Form of Hatred.* New York: Karnac Books, 1986.

Tanner, Tony. *Adultery in the Novel: Contract and Transgression.* Baltimore, Md.: Johns Hopkins University Press, 1979.

Terdiman, Richard. *Discourse/Counter-Discourse: The Theory and Practice of Symbolic Resistance in Nineteenth-Century France.* Ithaca, N.Y.: Cornell University Press, 1985.

Valéry, Paul. "La Situation de Baudelaire." In *Variété, II.* Paris: Gallimard, 1930.

VanderWolk, William. "Memory and the Transformative Act in *Madame Bovary.*"

In *Emma Bovary*, edited by Harold Bloom. New York and Philadelphia: Chelsea House Publishers, 1994.

Virilio, Paul. *The Vision Machine*. Indianapolis: Indiana University Press, 1994.

Weber, Samuel. *Mass Mediauras: Form, Technics, Media*, edited by Alan Cholodenko. Sydney: Power Publications, 1996.

Wing, Nathaniel. *The Limits of Narrative*. Cambridge: Cambridge University Press, 1986.

Wolff, Janet. "The Invisible Flâneuse: Women and the Literature of Modernity." In *Feminine Sentences: Essays on Modernity and Culture*. Berkeley: University of California Press, 1990.

Yalisove, Daniel, ed. *The Essential Papers on Addiction*. New York: New York University Press, 1997.

Index

Cultural Memory | *in the Present*

Samuel C. Wheeler III, *Deconstruction as Analytic Philosophy*

David S. Ferris, *Silent Urns: Romanticism, Hellenism, Modernity*

Rodolphe Gasché, *Of Minimal Things: Studies on the Notion of Relation*

Sarah Winter, *Freud and the Institution of Psychoanalytic Knowledge*

Samuel Weber, *The Legend of Freud: Expanded Edition*

Aris Fioretos, ed., *The Solid Letter: Readings of Friedrich Hölderlin*

J. Hillis Miller / Manuel Asensi, *Black Holes / J. Hillis Miller; or, Boustrophedonic Reading*

Miryam Sas, *Fault Lines: Cultural Memory and Japanese Surrealism*

Peter Schwenger, *Fantasm and Fiction: On Textual Envisioning*

Didier Maleuvre, *Museum Memories: History, Technology, Art*

Jacques Derrida, *Monolingualism of the Other; or, The Prosthesis of Origin*

Andrew Baruch Wachtel, *Making a Nation, Breaking a Nation: Literature and Cultural Politics in Yugoslavia*

Niklas Luhmann, *Love as Passion: The Codification of Intimacy*

Mieke Bal, ed., *The Practice of Cultural Analysis: Exposing Interdisciplinary Interpretation*

Jacques Derrida and Gianni Vattimo, eds., *Religion*